Gender Politics in Turkey and Russia

Gender Politics in Turkey and Russia

From State Feminism to Authoritarian Rule

Huriye Gökten Doğangün

I.B.TAURIS

LONDON • NEW YORK • OXFORD • NEW DELHI • SYDNEY

I.B. TAURIS
Bloomsbury Publishing Plc
50 Bedford Square, London, WC1B 3DP, UK
1385 Broadway, New York, NY 10018, USA
29 Earlsfort Terrace, Dublin 2, Ireland

BLOOMSBURY, I.B. TAURIS and the I.B. TAURIS logo are trademarks of
Bloomsbury Publishing Plc

First published in Great Britain 2020
This paperback edition published in 2021

Cover image: *C.* 1931: Russian female worker using a plane while man
supervises her work at hammer & sickle factory. (Photo by Margaret
Bourke-White/The LIFE Picture Collection via Getty Images)

ISBN:	978-1-8386-0435-6
PB:	978-0-7556-4622-7
eISBN:	978-1-8386-0437-0
ePDF:	978-1-8386-0436-3

Series: Library of Modern Turkey

Typeset by Integra Software Services Pvt. Ltd.

To find out more about our authors and books visit www.bloomsbury.com
and sign up for our newsletters.

To Bahadır, my beloved brother

Contents

List of Abbreviations

AKP	Justice and Development Party
ANNA	National Centre of Domestic Violence
CEDAW	Convention of All Forms of Discrimination Against Women
CPSU	Communist Party of the Soviet Union
EGIDA	Society for Promoting the Social Protection of Citizens
EU	European Union
Ka-Der	Association for the Support and Training of Women Candidates
KSGM	General Directorate of Women's Status
KSSGM	General Directorate of Women's Status and Problems
NGO	Non-Governmental Organization
ŞÖNİM	Violence Prevention and Monitoring Centres
UN	United Nations
UNDP	United Nations Development Programme
UNESCO	United Nations Educational, Scientific and Cultural Organization
UNFPA	United Nations Population Fund
USSR	Union of Soviet Socialist Republic

Preface

My first encounter with the issue of gender equality in Russia took place when I went to Russia as an Erasmus exchange student to learn Russian. I was astonished to realize how Russian and Turkish women have similar problems despite these two countries having different cultural traditions and historical pasts. This experience drove me to think comparatively about the situation of gender equality in Russia and Turkey. In 2010, I had a chance to share and discuss my observations with significant scholars, whose fields of interest are gender in Russia and Russian politics at Michigan State University (MSU) in the United States, where I spent four months as a visiting scholar. Then, I decided to undertake comparative research on gender equality and examine the implications of the wider political context on women's equality, starting from the experience of state feminism in Russia and Turkey. At MSU, I carried out preliminary preparation, including a literature review and informal discussions with these scholars on developing my aim and arguments.

By the time I started my comparative research on gender equality in Russia and Turkey in 2010, there were gradual signs of authoritarianism and of a patriarchal revival (traditional values). The data pointing to the restoration of patriarchal gender order had not yet emerged. In the literature, the debate was gradually emerging but no one was quite sure. Something was changing but no one wanted to make strong claims. It was my observation/intuition that gradually emerging authoritarianism would have serious effects on gender equality. Unfortunately, I was not wrong and numerous data started to emerge while I was doing the literature review, collecting, analysing and writing empirical data, and even after finishing my research.

As the literature was already emerging, I decided to conduct expert interviews with the aim of acquiring an inside-out approach to examining the shift and its direction. Expert interviews have gained widespread acceptance in qualitative social research as a legitimate method of exploring and gathering information at the initial phase of research (see Bogner and Menz, 2009). As Meuser and Nagel propose, special knowledge, acquired through not only training and professional roles but also through privileged access to information granted by activity and possession of local knowledge embedded in the expert's milieu, is the subject matter of the expert interview (2009, p.24). Expert interviews help researchers obtain useful information and elucidation of the issues under investigation (Bogner and Menz, 2009, p.47). I deeply utilized in-depth expert interviews to acquire academic and personal insights and observations about a newly emerging social reality. This field research was conducted with the financial support of the Middle East Technical University. A year that I spent at the Centre for Middle Eastern Studies at Harvard University as a visiting scholar also provided me with particular opportunities, including participating in numerous seminars about my research topic, meeting important scholars in the same field, using library facilities and presenting my research at different academic venues and collecting feedback, to enlarge my research and convert it into a book manuscript.

Acknowledgements

I would like to express my deepest gratitude to my supervisor and chair Professor Dr Ayşe Ayata for her guidance, advice, criticism, encouragement and insight throughout the research.

I would like to show my gratitude to Sophie Rudland from I.B. Tauris, who supported me from the very beginning for this production and shared her valuable comments at every stage of writing this book. I would also like to express my sincere thanks to anonymous referees for their important and contributory suggestions and comments.

I am also deeply indebted to my family – Müjgan, Asım, and Bahadır – who have always believed in and unconditionally supported my efforts during the whole of my academic life. Without their patience and, most valuably, their never-ending care and encouragement, blended with their love, this study could hardly have been realized.

This book could not be written without the unconditional support and help of my KORAcans, Yelda, Zelal, Sezin and Gözde, and Asuman. Their academic contribution and emotional support made this long journey easier and tolerable. They did not deny their patience and encouragement at each step. I owe my deepest love to them. Dear Olga and Güzel lent me a hand with translation and with doing research in Russian. With their help, my research was enriched. Finally, I owe my thanks to all the interviewees, who kindly agreed to give me an interview and contributed to my research.

Introduction

In 1993, Huntington put forward a controversial thesis that the cultural and religious divisions between the different civilizations of the West and the rest of the world would be the new fault line for conflict in the post-Cold War period (Huntington, 1993). The clash of civilizations would be the main replacement of the ideological and economic sources of conflict that had constituted the core of the struggle between the two superpowers in the Cold War period. Huntington's predictions are only half right, because his work dealt extensively with Islam and the Muslim world as the prospective competitor of Western civilization. He was right in foreseeing that 'the efforts of the West to promote its values of democracy and liberalism as universal values, to maintain its military predominance and to advance its economic interests engender countering responses from other civilizations,' but he was mistaken in assuming that the reaction would come mainly from the Muslim world (p.29). It has recently been hybrid regimes, whether or not they are Muslim, which establish formal democratic institutions but fail to consolidate democratic norms and values, that compete with Western civilization. According to the latest Freedom House Survey (2018), in 2017 democracy was facing its most serious crisis in decades. The number of partly free countries had increased by 2017 from 33 to 63 while the number of unfree countries had risen from 42 in 1998 to 57 in 2017 (Freedom House Survey, 1998, 2018). These results show that the basic tenets of democracy, including the rule of law, free and fair elections, freedom of the press and of assembly, and the rights of minorities, are under serious attack in the world.

It is not inaccurate to say that the main characteristic of the increasing authoritarianism is the revival of patriarchal norms and values about gender, often framed by religion and tradition, in opposition to the Western norms and values about gender equality. As Inglehart and Norris put it, the new fault line between the Western and other civilizations is not democracy but gender equality and sexual liberalization (2009, p.4). They, unlike Huntington, suggest that the core clash between the Western and non-Western countries is not over political values in terms of understanding democracy as a form of rule. However, when it comes to attitudes towards abortion, contraception, sexual liberalization and LGBTI (lesbian, gay, bisexual, transgender and intersex) rights, the differences are striking. These issues, rather than capitalism, communism and fascism, have become the major axes of struggle and competition between Western and non-Western countries in the post-Cold War period.

From this perspective, Russia and Turkey constitute excellent cases to examine the ongoing confrontation with Western democracy on the grounds of gender values. Russia and Turkey have represented the avant-garde of competitive authoritarianism, in tandem with the revival of traditional patriarchy, in opposition to the West's moral authority. It is not inaccurate to depict them as the principal global supporters of patriarchal authoritarianism. Why have these countries drifted towards authoritarianism after a long decade of democratization? On what grounds have these regimes confronted the West? How have the changes affected the gender equality once claimed by the Soviet and early Republican regimes? These questions are interrelated and shed light on the reasons that these authoritarian regimes have sought the revival of traditional patriarchy. The current authoritarian drift in both countries has been accompanied by a reinvigoration of traditional gender norms in order to signify national and cultural authenticity in opposition to Western culture, and gain political legitimacy for the continuation of authoritarian regimes which, in contrast to fully authoritarian regimes, are dependent on electoral hegemony. These values have been mobilized for the purpose of restoring national power and pride against the West and invigorating social unity and homogeneity against foreign and domestic enemies that are associated with the West and/or pro-Western agencies in Russia and Turkey.

Whilst there are significant differences between Russia and Turkey, the Russian and Turkish cases show striking similarities in terms of the connections between the authoritarian regime and the revival of traditional patriarchy. First, Russia and Turkey constitute the most different cases with similar outcomes that are evident in the historical trajectory of the relationship between gender categories and the state. Just as the Soviet and early Republican regimes converged in embracing state feminism in the early twentieth century as a part of their modernization, so the concurrent revival of traditional gender discourse in Russia and Turkey has been accompanied by a drift towards authoritarianism. Second, the distinguishing characteristic of the authoritarian regimes in Russia and Turkey is that they base their rhetoric on the embracing of national authenticity, culture, tradition and religion, in opposition to the influence and moral superiority of Western culture. This rhetoric construes traditional gender order as the basis of national authenticity and superiority. Third, the focus on gender of these regimes is related to their strategic goals of survival. The propagation of traditional gender order helps perpetuate the strong connection between the charismatic leaders and the populace, leading them to sustain political legitimacy. The leaders are portrayed and supported as the genuine representatives and protectors not only of national power and pride but also of the moral order that is believed to be in decline in Russia and Turkey. Fourth, the performance of masculinity by both leaders in Russia and Turkey, President Vladimir Putin and President Recep Tayyip Erdoğan, is another contributing factor to masculinize Russian and Turkish national and cultural identity.

In both Russian and Turkish history, woman constitutes an important component of a variety of political debates (Engel, 2004; Zihnioğlu, 2003). Women's public visibility and participation occupied a central place in the debates over the course of modernization between Westernizers and Slavophiles in the Russian polity and between pro-Western secularists and Islamists in the Ottoman-Turkish polity as well as in the modernizing efforts of the Russian and Ottoman empires during the eighteenth and nineteenth centuries. Under the conditions of sociopolitical turmoil in the late nineteenth century, both Russian and Ottoman-Turkish women engaged in political struggle for equal rights as well as in movements dedicated to political liberation and social transformation.[1]

After the Bolshevik Revolution of 1917 and the Republican revolution of 1923, the newly established states embraced an official commitment to women's equality and linked its realization to broader social transformation, albeit via contrary routes. Due to their ideological roots in Marxism, the Bolshevik revolutionaries believed that the transition to a new socialist order, in which class structure and private property would disappear, would terminate the private subordination of women and guarantee their integration into society on equal terms through employment. For the Republican revolutionaries, women's equality would come about through education and its transformative capacity to replace the religious mindset and order with a modern society built on secularism and nationalism. In both cases, women were treated as a specific group in the newly established regimes' processes of building their hegemony; the new Soviet and Republican women were expected to take up the cause of the communist and/or secular nation-state, and thus raise future generations according to communist and secular-national premises.

However, revolutionary change in Soviet Russia and early Republican Turkey did not bring about a total rupture but a reintegration of pre-revolutionary traditions with communist/secular premises. The two post-revolutionary states adopted similar discourses of emancipating women and carried out progressive reforms, while still preserving many patriarchal norms and patterns. Traditional norms and values profoundly shaped the new image of Soviet and Republican women, the new understanding of family and the legal framework. Traditional family and roles were never treated disdainfully by the Soviet regime; the new Soviet woman was envisioned as educated and productive as well as responsible for the biological and cultural reproduction of the new Soviet generation (Kay, 2000). For the Republican regime, despite all the reforms encouraging women's public visibility, preserving morality in a desegregated public sphere remained a concern of the state (Durakbaşa, 1997, p.148). The Republican woman was identified as a patriotic citizen, who had the mission of 'educating the nation' in addition to her traditional roles (Sirman, 1989, p.9). Women's liberation was narrowly treated only as labour-force participation in Soviet Russia and patriotic citizenship in Republican Turkey.

In Russia and Turkey, where the state ideology and mechanisms are strong but different, political authorities use gender categories as an important strategy for governing and mobilizing society through certain symbols and premises. Despite the abundance of structural differences, the two countries have produced similar discourses and policy outcomes regarding women's rights, in accordance with the prevalent political context. The Russian and Turkish polities hosted significant experiences of state feminism as part of divergent but modernizing views. This ideology became an important tool that helped them break down the influence of the pre-revolutionary order and manage the social perceptions about the benevolence of the former, as well as being a symbol to show the achievement of as high a level of modernity as non-Western countries.

Until the late 1970s and 1980s, the idea that women's equality had been fully realized dominated the political discourse in Soviet Russia and Turkey. In the late-Soviet period, the political authorities revisited Soviet policies, due to economic stagnation and falling fertility rates from the 1970s onwards. They addressed the adverse effects of the working mother on family union and social order rather than women's emancipation, due to increasing rates of divorce, alcoholism, juvenile delinquency, drug addiction and sexual promiscuity. The disintegration of state socialism in the late 1980s and then the transition to capitalism in the early 1990s aggravated the continuing economic, social and demographic crisis. Against this backdrop, Soviet policies were criticized for destroying the natural harmony between the sexes and the authority of men in the home, leading to a crisis of masculinity. In this context, the political authorities in late- and post-Soviet Russia promoted a traditional discourse on gender that called women to return to the home. In post-Soviet Russia, traditional family values and roles have been presented by the state as ways to reverse the demographic crisis, socio-economic troubles and moral decline. The issue of reestablishing a traditionalist hierarchy of power between the sexes was strongly advocated under the guise of natural harmony, allegedly destroyed by Soviet policies, in political circles, media and public opinion. So, the democratic opening following the post-Soviet transition did not ensure a move in discourse and policy in a feminist direction and allowed the expression of a wide range of views, including highly traditional ones.

In Turkey, after the coup d'état in 1980, feminist women challenged the claim that legal gains would ensure women's emancipation and drew attention to the persistence of traditional norms and patterns preventing women from enjoying legal and de facto equality (Özbay 1990). The Islamist movement, emerging in the 1970s, challenged the official discourse, albeit with different motives than the feminist movement. Its proponents criticized secular modernization for destroying the natural balance between the sexes, leading to the disintegration of the family and moral decline. The Islamist feminist movement that emerged in the 1990s challenged male supremacy and religious dictates to develop a feminist framework. The harmonization of the legal framework with the EU acquis strengthened the leverage of the women's rights movement. In the early 2000s, various women's groups from feminist, secular, Kurdish and Islamist circles united to pressure the state to amend the civil and penal codes and domestic violence legislation. However, the politics of the body remains a controversial topic that prevents further alliance among these groups. In contrast to the 1980s when the feminist movement seemed to be harmless to the state, the women's rights movement has begun to be considered as a serious threat to the social order by Turkey's conservative government.

To sum up, the transition to democracy in the 1990s did not necessarily bring about feminist and emancipatory discourses on gender equality in either Russia or Turkey. On the one hand, gradual but considerable attempts towards gender equality were undertaken at the state level in both countries: the Beijing Action Plan and the Convention on the Elimination of all Forms of Discrimination Against Women (CEDAW) were ratified by both states; national gender equality mechanisms were established and national action plans for gender equality were prepared; feminist movements emerged, academic programmes on gender and women's studies were started at universities, and women's non-governmental organizations (NGOs) mushroomed and conducted thousands of nationwide projects. However, instead of a critical debate on patriarchy, a conservative approach has increasingly come to dominate women's issues, rights and liberties in the private and public realms.

In the early 2000s, after ascending to the presidency, Putin continued a similar trend of approaching women's interests and problems from the angle of the demographic crisis but with the difference of laying an emphasis on women's employment outside the home. The first significant incentive he introduced in 2006 was maternity capital legislation, which aimed to revitalize the type of the Soviet working-mother. Nevertheless, the orientation of Putin's gender equality agenda was not yet clear. By contrast, Turkey was still seeking accession to the EU and enacting legal amendments to establish gender equality. However, suspicion about the hidden agenda of the conservative government and its leader Erdoğan was already emerging, following his unexpected move about recriminalizing adultery in 2004.

A significant shift in the Russian and Turkish state discourse on gender equality has gradually become evident in tandem with the authoritarian drift. The authoritarian tendencies under the rule of Putin and Erdoğan have been consolidated on the basis of nationalism, religion and tradition. Both autocratic leaders are keen to ensure political stability, security and legitimacy by presenting their leadership and regime as the real representatives and protectors of national authenticity and shared values, often framed by religion and tradition, against both foreign and domestic threats. Russia under the leadership of Putin is positioning itself as the global defender of Orthodox values and state sovereignty against the security threats and moral attacks from the West, while Erdoğan's regime is presented as representing the genuine people of the country and their values as opposed to the Western-oriented secular elites.

Against this backdrop, these regimes invoke gender as one of the most important areas for reinforcing tradition and marking national authenticity against progressive and democratic achievements regarding gender equality. The state-led ideology of women's equality has been replaced with state-promoted family and motherhood, which is justified in reference to demographic, national and moral concerns. The importance of biological differences has increased and sexism, misogyny and hostility against feminism versus gender equality has found a wider place in political discourse, public policies, popular discourse and media in Russia and Turkey. This has had the result of restoring traditional patriarchy rather than going beyond the experience of state feminism to promote the establishment of more egalitarian relations between the sexes.

The two countries have converged in their recent efforts to promote traditional values and religion regarding gender norms and values, and have experienced a paradigm shift from being the trademark of women's equality to being the avant-gardes of global patriarchal revival. While acknowledging the differences, a comparative investigation of the Russian and Turkish cases shows that the tradition of a strong state accompanied by a patriarchal culture is a significant factor of gender (in)equality because these states do not tolerate variations from state discourse whether in defence of women's equality or traditional gender roles, and can therefore be very interventionist and restrictive regarding women's individual rights.

Gender, State, Legitimacy

The relationship between the state and gender is a complicated and controversial topic in feminist literature. Although there is no single widely accepted theory explaining this relationship, the idea that the state plays a central role in (re) formulating gender identities and relations is a well-known phenomenon. Economic and political movements, struggles and ideologies are all gendered processes. National security, demographic crisis, moral decline, labour-force participation, sexuality, reproduction, marriage and homosexuality are sites of political struggle over gender categories.

Pateman (1988) draws attention to the gender dynamic in social contract theories that regulate the relationship between the state and its citizens. As Pateman (1988) puts it, from its inception, the modern state has depended on an implicit agreement about the relations between the sexes – the patriarchal domination of men over women – while conceptualizing the notion of abstract citizenship. In a similar vein, Connell argues that the historical trajectory of the state reveals that 'the growth of the modern state depends on a change in patterns of gender relations' (1987, p.127). From the seventeenth century onwards, the state has been involved in the constitution and mediation of relations between men and women. The exclusion of women from social contract theories and from the rational bureaucratic mechanism, the women's suffrage movement in the eighteenth and nineteenth centuries, their participation in the labour market, their obligation to pay taxes as citizens, and their right to enjoy welfare services and benefits in the welfare-state period have continuously shaped the sexual division of labour (pp.130–2).

Connell (1987, 1990) addresses the gendered dynamics of the political process: the ways politics is reconstituted, contested and legitimated through the notions of femininity and masculinity. The state has a collective interest in biological categories and is therefore involved in the (re)construction of gender categories such as husband, wife, mother and homosexual, and circumscribes the range of possible relations between the sexes through legal and social arrangements. So, patriarchy is not an imperfection to be corrected or derivative of social relations to be erased by only legal changes. As Connell puts it:

> The patriarchal state can be seen, then, not as the manifestation of a patriarchal essence, but as the centre of a reverberating set of power relations and political processes in which patriarchy is both constructed and contested. If this perspective is sound, it makes the historical trajectory of the state vital to an understanding of its place and effects in sexual politics (1987, p.130).

Conversely, gender dynamics play a constructive role in the political process. Political actors benefit from cultural meanings and symbols deriving from society-wide notions of femininity and masculinity. This helps them establish strong ties and cultural resonance with the populace (Sperling, 2015, pp.6–9). Anthias and Yuval-Davis (1989) argue that the cultural meanings of femininity and masculinity influence the ways political, ethnic and/or religious communities are imagined, constituted and legitimated. In this articulation, the sexes are categorized in reference to biological differences and given biologically prescribed civic roles. Women are seen as biological producers of ethnic, religious, national and/or political collectivities; transmitters of their culture; signifiers and reproducers of boundaries between different groups; and participants in national, economic, political and military struggles. The interventions of the state in women's bodies and behaviours to identify the appropriate femininity are related to hegemonic discourses, which serve to culturally, politically and legally categorize 'other and us' within and beyond the national borders. Demographic crisis, national survival, socio-economic crisis, the burden of welfare policies (such as childcare) and low active labour force rates are some contextual examples to be utilized in articulating hegemonic discourses in terms of the biological and cultural reproduction of community, society and/or nation (Yuval-Davis, 1997, pp.66–8, 78).

Similarly, Kandiyoti (1991a), evaluating the role of women in nation-state building in Turkey in the 1920s, points out that the new Republican woman, educated and modern in outlook, became the most explicit symbol of the break with the past and of secular revolution. Women, as patriotic citizens, were assigned the national duty of educating their families, children and the nation to the end of establishing a civilized nation (see Durakbaşa, 1997; Sirman, 1989). Najmabadi's (2006) analysis of the debate in France over Muslim women's headscarves shows how women's outlook becomes an issue of state sovereignty and control over the modes of national belonging and identity in the postcolonial context.

Gal and Kligman (2000) underline the role that discourses and practices related to gender play in the nation-building process after the end of state socialism. The politics of gender, and particularly of reproduction, enables the newly established nation-state to (1) establish a connection with its populace and identify what makes an appropriate member (citizen, comrade, worker, subject, etc.); (2) (re)make the nation and its boundaries; (3) constitute women as a specific political group for the purpose of preserving and transmitting national and cultural values; and (4) gain political legitimacy by constructing itself as a good and moral actor. The politics of reproduction, which can be extended to gender, reveals the ways in which the state imposes ideological control in everyday lives and over women's bodies (21–33).

Therefore, rearticulating how 'good' women and men are to look, behave and live in accordance with specific sociopolitical ambitions is a salient field of political struggle that recalls the Gramscian struggle for hegemonic domination (see Buci-Glucksmann 1984). Gender gains significance as one of the important means of establishing and consolidating hegemony. As Rivkin-Fish remarks, in contemporary times the political discourses on gender and gender relations reflect 'the political struggles over reach of state power, the configuration of citizenship and the meanings of masculinity and femininity' (2010, p.703). The debates on family, reproduction, demography, morality and national unity can be 'a site of gender inequality as well as be productive of historically situated, contested meanings about gender' (703). The changing meanings of gender also show us the changing character of state–society relations (703).

Methodology

According to Connell, gender order is 'a historically constructed pattern of power relations between men and women and definitions of femininity and masculinity' (1987, p.99). Connell explains that the historically prevailing notions of femininity and masculinity are involved in the composition and constitution of gender order by hegemonic masculinity and emphasized femininity. The contemporary hegemonic masculinity is described as heterosexual and closely connected to the institution of marriage while emphasized femininity embodies the most appropriate form that is oriented to the former. Hegemonic masculinity subordinates not only women but also other forms of masculinities such as homosexuality, and emphasized femininity serves to prevent other modes of femininity from gaining cultural articulation. In this configuration, compliance with technical competence and rationality is attributed to men while women are considered more suitable for domestic work, gender-based employment, marriage and childcare (pp.183–8). This assessment could be applied to the humiliation of women who do not want to give birth, get married, comply with the legal restrictions on abortion, adultery, co-habitation, etc. in practice.

Kay (2000) contributes to Connell's framework with the concept of gender climate. In her understanding, gender order refers to the underlying norms and patterns regulating gender relations, while gender climate corresponds to the prevailing norms and patterns that regulate gender relations. In her terms, gender climate is 'the way in which the gender order is packaged and presented at a given time in a given society' (p.17). The gender climate does not fundamentally change the gender order, which, in Connell's understanding, relies on the subordination of women to male authority, but it does shape the attitudes and opinions about gender. However, it cannot be claimed that gender climate does not lead to any change in norms and patterns regulating gender relations and identities. It creates an environment that encourages people either to work to transform the gender order in the direction of more egalitarian gender relations – as happened in state feminism – or to protect it as vital for national power and survival. The state is integral to this process and determines the interaction between gender order and gender climate, manipulating the former in tandem with its sociopolitical and economic concerns and interests.

In this study, I draw on the conceptual tools of gender order and gender climate, offered respectively by R. W. Connell and Rebecca Kay, to examine rising gender inequality in connection with the rising authoritarian tendencies in the Russian and Turkish cases. Locating the intersectionality between regime type and the discourses and policies on the family, sexuality, reproduction and marriage increasingly rarely becomes a subject of inquiry in the literature. In her recent study on Russia, Chandler (2013) argues that Putin's discourses are aimed at legitimizing his own rule with fulfilling the role of a strong and paternal state in controlling morality, conformity, parenthood and sexual orientation. Kandiyoti (2016), similarly, remarks on the central role of conservative family values in Erdoğan's current discourse in marking what is authentically national or anti-national. With the help of these concepts, I discuss how the Russian and Turkish states have formulated a traditional and conservative approach to gender as they seek to legitimize their authoritarian tendencies with the help of a nationalist narrative. I examine this current shift from state feminism towards the restoration of patriarchal order in Russia and Turkey on the basis of historically shaped interaction between gender order and gender climate, influenced greatly by the wider political context. I argue that the state-led ideology of women's equality, treated as a matter of urgency and involving the requisition of the modernization paradigm, was an important factor in reinforcing the modernizing efforts of the early Soviet and Republican regimes. The current regimes under the leadership of Putin and Erdoğan revive the underlying traditional gender order, which was preserved to a considerable extent by the Soviet and early Republican regimes, and has surfaced since the 1990s with attacks on the previous egalitarian policies, on the basis of a conservative and nationalist narrative and with the purpose of establishing close ties with the majority via commonly shared values and acquiring their consent for authoritarian tendencies.

From the empirical findings that I obtained in my fieldwork, I identify the prevailing gender climates, which correspond to the restoration of traditional gender order – neo-traditional and neo-conservative in Russia and Turkey, respectively. State-promoted 'neo-traditionalism' and 'neo-conservatism' represent the autocratic leaders' ambitions to ensure political stability, security and legitimacy by promoting traditional values, which are understood as commonly held in the form of family values. These values are mobilized with the purpose of restoring national power and pride as well as invigorating social unity and homogeneity in the face of foreign and domestic enemies. In that mobilization, both leaders identify themselves and the regimes under their respective rules as the real leaders and the best choice for Russia and Turkey. Putin and Erdoğan aim not only to stake a claim for the moral and electoral representation of the people as an organic, unified whole but also to marginalize the demands for recognition of diversity, pluralism and gender equality, which recognition may eventually constitute a threat to regime survival. Traditional family structure as the supposed core of this organic unity would ensure the protection and future promotion of traditional values, perceived as representing society-wide norms and values regarding gender, thereby serving to restore the imagined greatness of the Russian and Turkish states and nations under the rule of these leaders. In this framing, biological sex differences, normalized in reference to religion, culture and traditional values, have become the rationale for gender inequality – rather than gender equality – in political discourse, law, public policy, popular discourse and the media in Russia and Turkey.

In addition to enabling me to contextualize the gender dimension of political legitimation, the concept of gender climate suggests three insights. First, gender climate functions as hegemonic discourse and praxis, as 'it affects the ways in which it is considered acceptable to speak about gender' (Kay, 2000, p.17). As a result, gender climate shapes the conditions for hegemonic domination by managing social perceptions of and attitudes towards gender, which tend to follow commonly accepted values. These values are meaningful to the majority of people, even though some of them may oppose or criticize the gender ideology of the incumbent political authority. Second, gender climate conceals the inconsistencies between ideology and praxis: not all women, even if they support the government as the representative and defender of certain values, can or do practise the prescribed roles imposed upon them by a specific gender ideology. Despite this, gender climate creates a general atmosphere of homogenous unity, thereby limiting the space for the expression of variations and unleashing traditional forces. Third, this concept allows for a gap between gender discourse and gender-related policies. This gap may emerge because of political concerns, social dissent, insufficient infrastructure, fiscal limitations and so on. Fourth, this concept enables us to observe the historical trajectory of state–gender interaction with the moments of continuity and discontinuity, and the implications of the past on the current situation.

Bringing gender into the wider sociopolitical framework helps us grasp the operation of authoritarianism at society level and its reflection over social perceptions and practices. Focusing on the interaction between state and gender without attributing an essence – such as patriarchal and capitalist – to the state proves to be a modest starting point. This effort requires us to address not only the patriarchal values and practices derived from tradition and culture, but also hegemonic praxis and discourse that serve to manage legal arrangements and social perceptions along certain normative codes. This outlined framework is an attempt to seek out how the society-wide notions of femininity and masculinity and the biological differences between the sexes are utilized by political power to shape political struggle and process, and how citizens feel and experience the state's ideological control in their everyday lives.

This study relies mainly on empirical data obtained through semi-structured in-depth interviews conducted in Russia during a two-month trip in 2011 and a two-week trip in 2013, and in Turkey during three months in 2013. In both Russia and Turkey, my fieldwork took place in urban areas including Ankara, Istanbul, Moscow and St Petersburg, and I did not visit relatively small cities. This is because the headquarters of most women's NGOs, women's shelters, public offices and highly ranked universities are located in these four provinces. In total, sixty expert interviews (thirty-one in Russia, twenty-nine in Turkey) were conducted with academics, representatives from international organizations and women's NGOs, feminist activists, and experts from women's shelters.

In both cases, I selected my sample from among academics known nationally and internationally for their academic production, engagement in feminist movements and pro-gender equality efforts; the leading representatives of long-term women's NGOs; country experts from international organizations; feminist activists and public officers. I did not experience difficulty in reaching possible interviewees or persuading them to be interviewed by a foreigner. On the contrary, particularly in Russia, all the interviewees were very welcoming with my request, appreciated my interest in gender equality concerns in Russia and found my research topic very interesting. I efficiently utilized the snowball effect in reaching out to the interviewees. However, I did struggle to arrange an interview with any representative from the parliament or government in Russia. Some of my colleagues and the officers from the Turkish Embassy in Moscow tried to help me arrange an interview but none of those approached agreed to give an interview. I could not visit any public shelter, again due to bureaucratic obstacles. In Turkey, I was able to conduct interviews with public officers from the General Directorate of Women's Problems of the Ministry of Family and Social Policies but they preferred not to have their names declared in my study. So, while presenting the empirical data, I specify the affiliation of the interviewees and the geographical location of the interview, but names and other identifying information are omitted for reasons of confidentiality. Apart from the UN representatives and one public officer based in Ankara, Turkey, no interviewee refused to be recorded. I conducted all of the interviews myself in Turkish, English and Russian. The interviews that I conducted in Russian were transcribed by a Russian translator.

The institutions that the interviewees were affiliated with include the Centre for Supporting Women's Initiatives, the Consortium of Women's Non-Governmental Associations, the Council for the Consolidation of Women's Movements, the Moscow Centre for Gender Studies, the National Centre for the Prevention of Violence (ANNA), the Society for Promoting the Social Protection of Citizens (Petersburg EGIDA), the Union of Russian Women, the UN Refugee Agency, the UN Women Regional Office for Eastern Europe and Central Asia, the Women's Crisis Centre, the Higher School of Economics, the Russian Academy of Sciences and the European University at St Petersburg in Russia, and the Capital Women's Platform, the Foundation for Women's Solidarity, the General Directorate of Women's Status, the Turkish Women's Union, the Association for the Support and Training of Women Candidates, the United Nations Population Fund, Purple Roof, the Middle East Technical University, Hacettepe University and Ankara University in Turkey.

My primary concern was to situate the shift in state discourse on gender (in) equality in its sociopolitical context and to identify the foundations upon which the neo-traditional and neo-conservative gender climates in Russia and Turkey, respectively, are being built. The interviewees were asked to evaluate whether there has been a shift in state discourse, policies and mechanisms on gender equality. To elicit information about the prevailing gender discourse, I asked them more specific questions, such as (1) What were the parameters of prevailing state discourses in Russia and Turkey? (2) What are the parameters of prevailing state discourses in Russia and Turkey? (3) Has there been a significant change compared to the previous period? (4) What are the reference points of the 'good' femininity mentioned by these states? (5) Does the existing legal framework provide sufficient gender equality? (6) What is the situation of women in the labour market and within the family? Do they encounter any discrimination? If so, why? The major themes emerged during the field research. After the interviews were transcribed, paraphrased and coded, the empirical data were elaborated, categorized and framed by drawing on the theoretical framework used in this article, as described by Meuser and Nagel (2009).

To provide background information, I also used the secondary literature on the history of women's equality and the current situation of gender (in)equality in Russia and Turkey, especially on the specific themes of female labour-force participation, pro-natal policies and domestic violence. To supplement the empirical data, the public speeches and statements of political leaders related to gender (in)equality were monitored through keyword searches in newspapers, magazines and broadcast media, including the BBC, BBC Turkish, *The Economist*, *The Guardian*, Reuters, *The Moscow Times* and mainstream Turkish newspapers. The official websites of the Russian Presidency, the Turkish Parliament and the Turkish Ministry of Family and Social Policies were also consulted. Reports prepared by the UN and UN-related bodies, and by international and national NGOs involved in promoting gender equality in Turkey and Russia were considered. The discussion is also based on statistical data and discourse analysis of official documents including text of laws, presidential decrees and official commentaries on the rationale of the legal amendments.

Structure of the Book

This book consists of seven chapters and is divided into two parts. Part 1 maps out the historical background and the current political situation regarding women's equality and gender equality in Russia and Turkey. In Part 2, neo-traditional and neo-conservative gender climates are sketched out on the basis of the empirical findings that were obtained during the fieldwork conducted in Russia and Turkey. The empirical findings are grouped into thematic units that represent the prevailing – neo-traditional and ne-conservative – gender climates in Russia and Turkey respectively. The findings show that the revival of traditional family and gender categories is embodied in the organization of three gender-related areas: pro-natalism, female labour-force participation and domestic violence.

Chapter 1 covers the emergence of state feminism or state-led ideology of women's equality in Soviet Russia and early Republican Turkey. An overview of the new legislation that ensured equality before the law between the sexes, the prescribed images of Soviet and Republican women, and the state-imposed restrictions on the feminist movement is given. The emphasis is on the interaction between the underlying gender order and the prevailing gender climate, which is embodied in the representation of traditional family and gender values in the Soviet and Republican notions of femininity and masculinity.

Chapter 2 outlines the gradually emerging shift in the state-led ideology of women's equality in the late-Soviet days and the period following transition to the civilian period in Turkey until the respective ascents of Putin and Erdoğan to power in the early 2000s. The implications of this shift over gender equality are examined on the basis of legal amendments, the appropriate notions of femininity and masculinity, the feminist movement and the institutional structure, including the establishment of national mechanisms to mainstream gender equality in both countries.

Chapter 3 deals with the rise of authoritarian politics in Russia and Turkey before its engagement of gender politics is discussed in the following chapter. I analyse the consolidation of the current regimes on four dimensions: the institutional and legal reforms, the understanding of state sovereignty and democracy, the relations with the West and the rise of social dissent against the current regimes. In this process, the reliance on nationalism, patriotism and religious values has increased in the political discourses of Putin and Erdoğan. I argue that all these dimensions gradually pave the way for the formulation of a conservative and nationalist discourse that predicates the restoration of patriarchal gender order.

Chapter 4 discusses the engagement of authoritarianism with gender politics around a conservative and nationalist narrative. It analyses the concurrent rise of sexism, misogyny and hostility towards feminism in relation to the political discourse and policies of Putin and Erdoğan's regimes, of which the previous chapter gave an overview. Rising sexism is related to the fact that traditional family and gender values gain significance in characterizing national authenticity, identity and unity via traditional values. It is also embodied in the political masculinity of Putin and Erdoğan, which enables the representation of the relationship between state and nation in terms of gendered hierarchies, and reinforces male authority as opposed to female subordination.

Chapter 5 focuses on the similarities that become evident in the imagined female traits and roles behind the incentives to help women reconcile work and family obligations in Russia and pro-employment initiatives in Turkey, without losing the sight of differences in the patterns of Russian and Turkish women's employment outside the home. In both cases, traditional family structure and biologically ascribed roles are used to explain gendered hierarchies and divisions in the regulation of the labour market. This chapter relies on empirical data obtained in expert interviews about the implications of extended maternity leave, the shortage of public kindergartens and the lack of compulsory parental leave over maintaining gender (in)equality.

Chapter 6 analyses the introduction of pro-natal incentives on the basis of demographic, national and moral concerns. Pro-natal incentives, formulated on the basis of promoting motherhood rather than egalitarian relations between the sexes, serve to reinforce the reformulation and representation of gender categories in a traditional and conservative way, with strong references to religion. Demographic crisis, maternity capital, abortion rules and the conceptualization of motherhood are comparatively presented and examined in this chapter.

Chapter 7 is concerned with the conceptualization of domestic violence and the discourses and policies to combat it. Although the Russian and Turkish cases diverge in terms of legislative framework, they converge in not seeing domestic violence as a violation of women's individual human rights. Domestic violence is treated as a characteristic of traditional family structure in Russia while the Turkish state tries to struggle with domestic violence with a pro-family approach that focuses on protecting family union and preventing divorce.

The concluding remarks draw together the main conclusions of the comparison between Russia and Turkey, and offer some reflections on maintaining gender equality.

Part 1

Discourses on Gender in Early Modernization, Transition and Authoritarian Eras in USSR/Russia and Turkey

1

Gender Climate in the Soviet and Republican Periods

It is over the Westernization and modernization period that dated back to the pre-revolutionary period in both Soviet Russia and Turkey that the woman question was integrated into different ideological frameworks for developing and westernizing the Tsarist Russian and Ottoman empires. Before the Bolshevik and Republican revolutions, the main transformative changes in terms of women's status and rights took place during the reigns of Peter the Great, Catherine the Great and Alexander II in Tsarist Russia, and during the Tanzimat era and Second Constitutional Period in the Ottoman Empire. In these periods, the woman question fluctuated between progressive efforts and retreats until a clear rupture took place with the proclamation of the Soviet and early Republican states' official commitment to women's equality in civic, social, economic and political life.

Tracing the Woman Question in the Russian/Soviet and Ottoman-Turkish Contexts

The changes in the social, political, legal and familial status of women date back to the first westernizing efforts, known as the Petrine reforms, initiated by Peter the Great (1689–1725) in the seventeenth century in Tsarist Russia. These reforms, which aimed to open a window to Europe and brought Russia into closer contact with Western European states, had a profound impact mainly on the lives of men and women of the imperial family and the court (Pushkareva, 1997, p.121). As part of his determination to modernize and secularize Russia, Peter issued a decree that ended the seclusion of women and ordered the sexes to mix socially (Atkinson, 1978, p.26). He defined women's most important duties as wifehood and motherhood, and assigned to them a new role of contributing to Russian society in the family and as the bearers of future subjects. The education of women as the mothers of future servitors gained significance as part and parcel of his westernizing reforms. Many of the projects intended to recast the Russian patriarchal order, including the education of women, did not succeed and the patriarchal order persisted in Peter's reign. His reforms took root only gradually and encountered some resistance outside the court and St Petersburg but had an irreversible impact on the lives of elite women. In the decades following Peter's death, it started to become a belief among the ruling elite and the nobility that greater public visibility and social participation of women were requirements of a refined society (Engel, 2004, pp.13–15).

Recognizing the significance of the education of women and its relation to the wider role of women for the reorganization of Russian society had its impact on the enlightening reforms of Catherine the Great (1762–96) during the second half of the eighteenth century. Catherine sought to extend the civilizing mission initiated by Peter. She realized the centrality of education for further westernization as well as the gap in terms of accessing education between the nobility and the rest of the population. During her reign, the state assumed public responsibility for women's education. In 1764, the first school for noble girls was established in St Petersburg for the daughters of the servitors from the elite as well as middle-level ranks of the military and civil service, especially those whose fathers had either died or lacked sufficient resources. For girls from humble origins, about twenty other institutions were founded in major cities and towns. In 1786, Catherine established free, public education for both boys and girls at primary and high school levels. However, the main purpose of women's education during Catherine's reign was restricted to the moral and spiritual instruction of family and children (Engel, 2004, pp.15–16, 23, 65).

A comprehensive discussion of the woman question arose in the aftermath of the Crimean War and the emergence of a new environment for initiating social reforms under the leadership of Alexander II (1855–81). The educated, socially conscious and reform-minded Russians sought the reduction of arbitrary authority and the increase of individual rights, and then they started to re-evaluate every traditional institution, including the patriarchal family. They linked the authoritarian family order to the lack of democratization and of individuality. Social backwardness was related to the traditional structure of gender relations, the traditional roles of women and the traditional family structure; and breaking these traditional structures was seen as a way to foster social progress (pp.68–9).

The progressive efforts concerning women's education, increasing public visibility and wider social participation proceeded in parallel with broad reformist attempts towards civilizing the country and remained limited in their ability to reach peasant women in Tsarist Russia. The pursuit of expanding the scope of education towards the larger segments of women repeatedly encountered backlashes during the periods of autocracy throughout the late eighteenth and nineteenth centuries (Lapidus, 1978a, p.30). These backlashes were often influenced by traditional and religious concerns that the Westernizing reforms would distort the moral health of women, family and, in consequence, the whole of society. The ups and downs terminated with the Bolshevik Revolution and its promise of a radical social transformation that would establish the full equality of women in economic, political and family life (Lapidus, 1978b, p.116).

In 1917, two revolutions fundamentally changed the political structures, the ruling elite and the ruling ideas in Russia. The February Revolution overthrew the imperial government and saw the establishment of the Provisional Government. Strikes by working-class women demanding peace and food over the winter played an important role in changing the political order. Educated women, female workers and peasant women, who had already been involved in protests against low pay and deteriorating working conditions since the war years, later became mobilized to claim citizenship rights in the new political order (McDermid and Hillyar, 1999, pp.144–88). The Provisional Government acquiesced in giving women the right to vote and to serve in the civil service on equal terms with men (Shnyrova, 2007, p.131). However, women continued to have grievances against the Provisional Government, whose policies did not bring about any improvement in their harsh working and living conditions. The disappointed female workers participated in demonstrations and strikes against the government and started to unite over the general demands for improvement in working conditions, an eight-hour day, a minimum wage and maternity benefits, with the significant help of leading Bolshevik activists such as Alexandra Kollontai. Between the two revolutions of 1917, the Bolsheviks began to recognize the importance of recruiting women as active participants and integrating them into the cause of the coming revolution by establishing a special bureau and publishing a journal, *Rabotnitsa*, to organize work among women. Hence, the female workers supported the revolution because the Bolshevik Party seemed to articulate their immediate concerns as women and workers (McDermid and Hillyar, 1999, pp.144–88).

The Bolshevik revolutionaries' devotion to women's issues was largely motivated by the widespread belief regarding the backwardness of women, and the rivalry with other political movements of the pre-revolutionary era. Early Bolshevik writings conveyed the concern that women needed to be integrated with the socialist revolution if the Bolsheviks were to achieve success. Russian women, who were portrayed as the most backward, illiterate and superstitious of the populace, were regarded as the potential constituency to resist the new social order and at the same time to help consolidate the revolution of the proletariat by joining the ranks of revolutionaries and raising the succeeding generations to defend and build socialism (Wood, 1997, p.3). Focusing on the backwardness of women provided the Bolsheviks with certain opportunities to integrate the distant regions, particularly Central Asia. The mobilization of Central Asian women gained prominence for the Soviet regime as part of its attempts to undermine the traditional social order and realize modernization in the region. For this task, the Bolshevik leaders relied on Muslim women, who benefited least from the established order based on tradition, custom and kinship, to create a surrogate proletariat (see Massell 2015). In addition, the Bolsheviks' fear between 1905 and 1917 that women workers might join the liberal feminist and Menshevik movements, with their respective bourgeois understanding of equality and offer of social democratic solutions to the problems of women's work, and might become distanced from the revolution of the proletariat had an impact on the Bolsheviks' increasing preoccupation with the woman question after 1913 (Wood, 1997, pp.30–3).

When the Bolsheviks seized power in the October Revolution and proclaimed the establishment of a new Soviet state, they had a specific agenda concerning the rights of women. The revolutionaries were determined to establish a new order, under which women's equality would be fully realized by going beyond the reformist attempts, such as female suffrage on the same terms with men. They envisioned a Soviet society, in which women's role in the economy, politics and the family would be ultimately changed and sexual oppression would disappear (Lapidus, 1978a, p.54). The Bolshevik approach to the woman question was influenced by socialist feminism and the theoretical works of Karl Marx, Friedrich Engels and August Bebel. Marxist writings constituted a legitimate resource for Soviet discourse, policy making and ideological commitment towards sexual equality. Despite Marx and Engels being concerned about the oppression of women and their sincere commitment to sexual equality, the greater part of their writings focused on elaborating the contradictory nature of the capitalist mode of production. Marx did not produce a systematic theory of gender relations but connected the oppression of women to the existence of capitalist relations of social production. Women's emancipation would accordingly be accomplished along with the entire abolition of capitalism and the transition to a new socialist order, when the class structure and private property would disappear (Buckley, 1989).

Further comments on women's oppression were made by Engels (2010) in *The Origin of the Family, Private Property and the State,* but the main Marxist feature of connecting the emancipation of women to an overall social and economic transformation did not change. Engels connected the emergence of various forms of family to different economic foundations that changed historically. In his framework, the modern – patriarchal and monogamous – family shows the mechanism and operation of bourgeois society at the basic level. In this form of family, the husband is obliged to earn a living and support his family and thus gains a position of supremacy, while the wife carries out domestic duties within the family and is excluded from participation in social production. The modern family is described as constituting the main source of all forms of social and economic oppression and a profound obstacle for women's participation in public industry. So, for Engels, to put an end to the domestic slavery of women and liberate them would primarily require the establishment of a legal and real social equality between the sexes and, more importantly, women being enabled to participate in public industry.

Like Engels, August Bebel treated the bourgeois family as a core unit of the state and society to be transformed. In *Women and Socialism*, Bebel (2005) described how the evolution from primitive communism to the rule of private property stemmed from the secondary position of women within the family. In bourgeois society, women suffer from restrictions and obstacles that are unknown to men, and men enjoy many social rights and privileges. Because of their dependent position, women regard marriage as a means of subsistence while men look upon it from a commercial point of view, considering its material advantages and disadvantages. So, a change in the capitalist mode of production would bring about the elimination of the social oppression of women. Despite the reservations of Marx and Engels concerning the women's suffrage movement, Bebel draws attention to its contribution. According to him, formal equality before the law should prioritize all attempts that enable women to participate in working life and become liberated. The connecting thread of the thoughts of Marx, Engels and Bebel is that women's oppression is connected to their economic dependence on men. They all overlooked other sources of oppression derived from ideology, culture, religion and so on.

Under the influence of these theoretical arguments, Bolshevism was fully committed to sexual equality and recognized equal civil, economic and political rights for women.

It differentiated itself from liberal feminism by accepting that political equality was not the ultimate goal but only a step toward full liberation that would take place through the transition to socialism (Lapidus, 1978a). The revolutionary attempts to transform the traditional family and abolish the private subordination of women were connected to women's integration into society through participation in social production. The Bolsheviks sought to erase the traditional patterns by liberating women from being socially and economically dependent on men, and the new state embraced the role of supporting working women's economic independence by providing public childcare (Kiblitskaya, 2000). A wide range of educational and occupational options was established for women; they were encouraged to acquire new skills, values, orientations and aspirations, surpassing their traditional roles. It was expected that the more educational and occupational attainments were enjoyed by women, the greater sexual equality and equal relations within the family would be (Lapidus 1982: xxxii).

In the Turkish context, the family system and the status and rights of women made an irreversible entry into political debate concerning the course of modernization via westernization or Islamism. The dilemma between the need for westernization and progress, and keeping Ottoman culture intact, influenced political debate on the woman question. While Islamists pointed to the corruption of Islam as the reason for moral decline and advocated a return to a purified application of Sharia, the westernizers suggested a radical break with Islam in the name of progress (Kandiyoti, 1997, p.124). In these ideological terrains, woman was approached as an important part of the modernization project but not as an individual or citizen so much as a mother and wife. For both westernizers and conservatives, women were defined as a social category that could contribute to the welfare and prosperity of society with their wisdom and intellect (Durakbaşa, 1998, p.36). This long period did not stand out as a period of substantial change and controversy regarding the position and rights of women. During the Tanzimat period (1839–76), which has been officially recorded as the kick-off of Ottoman modernization, the traditional Ottoman family structure, segregation, polygamy, arranged marriages and repudiation – that is, the unilateral divorce of the wife by the husband – were the main objects of criticism. However, even the most enlightened thinkers and reformists took care to remain in conformity with the religious dictates (Kandiyoti, 1989, pp.132–3). The issue of women's education was another subject of debate in this period: women started to attend the newly opened middle-level schools and a teachers' training college for girls in 1863, but a very basic education which was mainly religious in orientation was provided, with the aim of creating good Muslim mothers and wives (Kumari, 2016, p.27).

During the Second Constitutional Period, which started with the capitulation of power by the Union and Progress Party in 1908, the discursive limits in which the woman question could be discussed extended towards nationalism and created an interest in women as mothers and reproducers of the nation, going beyond the question of education. More high schools and teachers' colleges for women were opened, and the first university for women was established in 1915 (p.30). Women mobilized a little in educational facilities, social welfare activities and the labour force. The number of women's associations and periodicals increased, vocational schools for girls were opened, women were allowed to discard the veil during office hours and a tendency to participate in the women's struggle started to emerge among women in this period (Kandiyoti, 1989, pp.133–5; see Abadan-Unat, 1981, pp.7–8). Çakır (1994), in her study on the Ottoman women's movement, shows that Ottoman women expressed a right-demanding rhetoric in the women's journals that denied any difference between men and women on the basis of competency and opposed the formulation of feminine identity as subordinate. On the other hand, the judicial system failed to satisfy those who wanted to see fundamental changes in the family system. The Family Law of 1917 established marriage by mutual consent and made divorce more difficult by the introduction of a conciliation procedure but did not abolish polygamy (Kandiyoti, 1989, p.137). Moreover, the political authority continued to impose control over women's bodies and appearance in public: women were often forced by the police to return home if their skirts were shorter than officially allowed.

A clear rupture regarding the course of modernization and women's emancipation took place with the establishment of the new Republic in 1923. The new regime set the direction of modernization as westernization and secularization from a nationalist perspective. A series of legal, political, religious and cultural reforms were accomplished straightaway, in accordance with the changing priorities of the newly established state. The Caliphate was abolished in 1924. A secular Civil Code replacing Islamic law (Sharia) was accepted in 1926. Islam was ruled out as the official religion in 1928; religion was purported to be a matter of personal conscience, and its visibility and practice were restricted to the private sphere. In order to eliminate the symbolic power of the old regime and catch up with Western norms, the Republican regime started a cultural revolution that targeted the transformation of physical appearances and lifestyles of the populace, and the collective consciousness. A new Turkish alphabet modified from the Latin form was adopted (1928), the segregated education system and religious curriculum were annulled and free elementary education was made mandatory for both boys and girls (1924), there was a hat revolution (1925), a modern dress code for both men and women was encouraged, Western units of measurement and calendar were adopted (1925), and Sunday was set as the day of rest (1925).

This judicio-political rupture meant a completely new discursive shift for women's emancipation. In Turkey, it was assumed that the only way to modernize society was by deconstructing the religious law and order, including rules, customs and arrangements. The early Republican regime aimed to establish a civilized society on the grounds of secularism and nationalism. Kandiyoti (1991b) writes that in national projects the crises of post-imperial identity could be articulated as crises of the family system and women's status. The woman question in Turkey was politicized in this context of heightened Turkish national consciousness at the expense of a broad Islamic identification. The secularization of the legal system and the enfranchisement of women thus came about as part of a broader nationalist struggle to dismantle the religious basis of the Ottoman state and create a new state legitimizing ideology in the making of a national culture and history (p.4). As Durakbaşa (1997) states, Kemalist feminine identity provided a cultural solution for the socialization of citizens in accordance with new legal and institutional regulations and for the re-establishment of relations between men and women in conformity with the requirements of the nation-building project. Women's illiteracy, seclusion and subordination were denounced not only for restricting the individual rights of half the population but also for producing ignorant and uncivilized mothers and wasting half of the national resources (Kandiyoti, 1991b, p.10). Atatürk's own views on women's equality strike important parallels between a new family system and a civilized feminine identity for creating a progressive and productive nation. Speaking to the people in Kastamonu in 1925, he said:

> A society, a nation is comprised of two genders: male and female. Is it possible to lift a huge block up if you concentrate on one side of it and leave the other side completely unattended? Is it possible that a part of a society reaches the skies while the other part is tied to the ground with chains? Undoubtedly, the steps forward on the path to progress should be taken by both genders together (Ministry of Culture and Tourism, n.d.).

According to Atatürk, women's emancipation would come about of itself with the help of egalitarian legislation (Abadan-Unat, 1981, p.5). Against this backdrop, women's liberation was conditional on the establishment of a secular legal system that would guarantee equality before the law for both sexes, thereby emancipating women from repressive norms of Islamic law and tradition (p.178). The nomadic and egalitarian pre-Islamic Turkic past constituted the grounds of Turkish state feminism in this period. One of the principal theorists of the new Republic, Ziya Gökalp, suggested that the pre-Islamic Turkic civilization that dated back to the migration of tribal Turks into Anatolia in the eleventh century had relied on egalitarian, democratic and feminist premises, particularly in terms of family relations. The old Turkic family was described as including such norms as equality between husband and wife, monogamy as the form of marriage, communal property in land, women's ownership, parental family as opposed to patriarchal family, and parental rights regarding childrearing (Kandiyoti, 1989, p.141). He argued that Islam introduced a way of life that was not in conformity with egalitarian Turkic traditions. Therefore, Islam needed to be cleansed of misrepresentations in order to support the Turkish tradition of a democratic and egalitarian society (White, 2003, pp.147–8). The idea that Turkish women have historically been powerful can also be traced in Atatürk's own words:

> Our religion has never demanded women to be lower than men. What God commands to men and women is to acquire science and knowledge together. Men and women have to seek science and knowledge, and go wherever they could find them. A careful examination of Islamic and Turkish history would show that the rules we feel we have to obey actually do not exist. In Turkish social life, women have never been any less than men in science, knowledge or in any other field (Ministry of Culture and Tourism, n.d.).

Against this backdrop, family relations, the status and rights of women, and sexuality came to occupy a central place and role in the Soviet and Republican discourses of modernity. The revolutionary political elite in both Soviet Russia and early Republican Turkey altruistically realized the strategic and symbolic role of the woman question in dismantling the pre-revolutionary order and achieving a high level of modernity in accordance with communist and secular-national premises, respectively. In Russia, before the Revolution, the backwardness of the nation was interlinked with the backwardness and inferior status of women. In the Ottoman polity, despite the modernizing efforts which followed the Tanzimat era, the legal, political and social order continued to rely on religion and women constituted a social category that was one of the most oppressed and excluded from the non-egalitarian system. Thus, in both cases, women were expected to play a crucial role in the political, ideological and cultural struggle against the pre-revolutionary and religious order. In accordance with these motives, the newly established states embraced an official commitment to women's equality soon after the proclamation of the Soviet state and the Republic, and linked its realization to broader social transformation, albeit through opposing routes.

The official commitment to state-led equality by the revolutionary forces that emerged within the context of modernization shaped the gender climate in the Soviet and Republican regimes. However, whilst acknowledging the changes in the notions of femininity and masculinity, two common characteristics of the Soviet and Republican gender climates hindered a radical transformation in the underlying gender order. First, the revolutionary change in Soviet Russia and Republican Turkey did not bring about a total rupture but a reintegration of pre-revolutionary traditions with socialist and secular-national premises. In both Turkish and Russian cultures, the underlying gender order had been patriarchal for many centuries and this continued to influence new revolutionary efforts. The traditional notions of femininity and masculinity penetrated the content of socialist and secular legislation and policies regarding women's emancipation and shaped Soviet and Republican understandings of woman and family. Not unexpectedly, the Republican and Bolshevik revolutions, in terms of their cadres and culture, had their roots in the Ottoman past and Tsarist Russia, respectively. Second, the women's equality project was circumscribed by the requirement to remain true to the Soviet and Republican modernizing interests in both cases. The new economic and political context imposing 'more' urgent issues and restrictions to be dealt with by the new regimes led to an incomplete liberation for women along secular and socialist premises.

Early Legal Changes in the USSR and Early Republican Turkey

Although the gender climate during the Soviet and Republican decades reflected a pattern that oscillated between modernity and tradition, much of the radical legislation passed, especially in the early years of the Soviet and Republican regimes, did have a profoundly liberating effect on the lives of Soviet and Republican women. In Soviet Russia, the first attack was on the Tsarist Family Law with the aim of putting an end to the pre-revolutionary religious order, establishing formal equality before the law, and equal entitlement to civil and political rights for both sexes (Buckley, 1989, p.34). Under the old marital law, a woman was required to submit to her husband as the head of the family and master of the house with love, respect and unbounded obedience, while the husband was obliged to provide his wife with food and maintenance. Married women were dependent on the permission of their husbands to travel, work or study (Atkinson, 1978, p.33).

In October 1918, the code of laws concerning the Civil Registration of Deaths, Births and Marriages was introduced. In that code, marriage was defined as a civil rather than a religious union. The mutual consent of both parties was made obligatory for the union to take place. The choice or change of residence to be tied to the wishes of men was annulled. The automatic imposition of the husband's surname on his wife was also abolished; women were now allowed to use their own surname (Schlesinger cited in Buckley, 1989, p.35). Couples were not obliged to register their relationships, as these provisions covered any women in or out of wedlock. The illegitimacy of children born out of wedlock was resolved and they were entitled to the same rights as those born in registered marriages. But an unregistered wife was required to prove that a 'marriage', even in the form of a sexual relationship, did exist, which carried the possibility of opposition or deception on the part of the man (Attwood, 1999, p.41). These provisions were largely in conformity with Vladimir Ilyich Lenin's opinions on the realization of the equal rights of women, whatever their marriage status:

> Education, culture, civilisation, freedom – all these high-sounding words are accompanied in all the capitalist, bourgeois republics of the world by incredibly foul, disgustingly vile, bestially crude laws that make women unequal in marriage and divorce, that make the child born out of wedlock and the 'legally born' child unequal, and that give privileges to the male and humiliate and degrade womankind (2004, p.77).

However, only couples in registered marriages were entitled, in the event of divorce, to the right to alimony and even the distribution of property acquired by the spouses during the marriage. The 1918 Code promoted de facto marriages and making civil marriage unnecessary on the one hand, but left women who were not registered in civil marriage unprotected concerning alimony and the distribution of property in the event of a divorce, on the other. This disparity produced harsh social and economic problems particularly for women, who became massively unemployed because of the job cutbacks under the New Economic Policy (NEP) in the early 1920s (Farnsworth, 1978, pp.141–3). In November 1925, therefore, a new family code was drafted and, in 1926, it replaced the 1918 Code. The new legislation aimed to expand the rights of those in unregistered marriages to match the rights of those in registered ones. Concerning alimony, child maintenance and inheritance, registered and unregistered marriages were made legally identical by the new legislation (Attwood, 1999, p.46).

Due to this legal amendment, the family policy of the 1930s was strongly criticized for moving from being a radical piece of legislation to a conservative one. However, even the early Soviet Family Law was a partial restoration of pre-revolutionary attitudes and traditions and a partial restatement of Marxist principles (Berman, 1946, p.26). Early Bolshevism was not monolithic and there were conservatives against radicals on political, economic and social issues throughout the 1920s. The family was never regarded with disdain by the Soviet regime from the outset (Farnsworth, 1978, p.140). The 1918 Code failed to be 'truly communist' by including such provisions as male responsibility for women, parental responsibility for children's upbringing and the legal obligation of relatives for one another's economic well-being. As in a communist society, these tasks and responsibilities should be undertaken by the society instead of individuals. So, the marital stability-oriented legislation of the 1930s represented neither a reversal nor a betrayal of Marxist premises but the triumph of the traditionalist strains within Bolshevism (pp.140–1).

In 1917, the absolute right to appeal for divorce was granted to both sexes and the annulment of a marriage was made conditional on the request of at least one side rather than mutual consent (Schlesinger cited in Buckley, 1989, p.35). If both partners consented to divorce, an oral or written statement submitted to the local court or the marriage and divorce registry was sufficient to obtain a divorce (Attwood, 1999, p.42). The easy divorce procedure was regarded as an advanced step that recognized the rights of women in marriage in distinction to the restrictions of the Tsarist Law, which had denied women any rights, including divorce (Schlesinger cited in Buckley, 1989, p.36). As Lenin remarked, 'the decay, the corruption, the filth of bourgeois marriage, with its difficult divorce, its freedom for the man, its enslavement for the woman, the repulsive hypocrisy of sexual morality and relations fill the most active minded and best people with deep disgust' (quoted in Zetkin 2004).

The 1918 Labour Code stipulated the 'equal pay for equal work' principle, the obligation to work regardless of gender (between the ages of 16 and 50), an exemption from working for women on the point of childbirth, protective measures for women (regarding night work, overtime work, dangerous jobs) and maternity benefits (fully paid leave eight weeks before and eight weeks after birth, extra work breaks for nursing mothers and free access to social insurance) (Dodge, 1966, pp.57–8). November 1922 saw the ending of another law on inheritance that had excluded daughters from inheriting or granted them a smaller amount than sons; they were now guaranteed an equal share with their brothers (Schlesinger cited in Buckley, 1989, p.36).

In the modernizing Turkey, the legal reforms targeting women's emancipation primarily focused on guaranteeing the public visibility and civil rights of women, which had previously been restricted by the religious legislation. The institution of the family was taken as the first place in which to establish equality between the sexes. In 1926, the religious law was abolished and a slightly modified version of the Swiss Civil Code was adopted, for the reason that it was the most suited to the principle of secularism (Abadan-Unat, 1981, p.13). The code established equality between the sexes before the law and identified women as equal citizens with men. The new Civil Code abolished polygamy, which had previously been allowed by the religious law, and recognized women as the equals of men as witnesses in court, in the distribution of inheritance and in the ownership of property. Under the Islamic law, women's share of inheritance had been half that of men, and the testimony of two women had been treated as equal to that of one man. Women were now granted the right to choose their own spouses, to initiate divorce and to demand custody of children. A minimum age for marriage was identified for both sexes (18 for boys and 17 for girls) in order to prevent child marriages (Y. Arat, 1994, p.63). The new code stated that a religious ceremony could be held after the civil registration of marriage had been completed.

The Republican regime presented the new code as a victory for Turkish women and the Turkish family, which regained its 'authentic' roots (Kırkpınar, 1998, p.22). However, it was not only Islam but also a religion-tainted patriarchy that constituted the principal source of women's subordination and exclusion from the public domain in Ottoman society. The Republican elite failed to tackle the patriarchal culture that relied on male superiority as the principal source of oppression, focusing instead on the visibility of women in the public sphere. The new regime did not concern itself with gender hierarchies and inequalities in the private sphere. Some interviewees from academia pointed out that the failure of the new regime to consolidate the egalitarian premises was a result of their neglect of the inequalities in the private sphere:

> Since the early Republican period, the women's equality discourse remained superficial rather than substantial in Turkey. So, it remained at the formal level; it could not be transformative. There was almost no effort to transform the sphere of the family in accordance with the objectives of women's equality.

Thus, the traditional norms and patterns continued to have a considerable impact in the new legislation of Republican Turkey. Despite the legal principle of equality between the sexes, the new Civil Code was far from reflecting non-traditional values. According to Sirman, the equivalent of the Ottoman *mahrem* (secret, secluded) was the modern creation 'private', and men as heads rather than patriarchs continued to lead the private (1989, p.12). In the new code, male domination was preserved. There was no absolute equality; man was still defined as the head of the family and household, and as the primary breadwinner. The husband had the right to choose the domicile of his family, while the right of the wife to work outside the home was conditional on her husband's consent, despite the former's legal entitlement (Abadan-Unat, 1991, p.188). The traditional division of labour was reinforced as well: the wife was given the role of homemaking and her economic independence was reduced to contributing to the family budget (Arat, 1994a, p.64).

The Labour Code that came into force as late as 1936 firstly regulated women's participation in employment. The code guaranteed equal rights of workers regardless of gender but imposed certain restrictions on women's employment in order to protect the reproductive function of women and the family unit. Protective measures for women were introduced, including a prohibition from performing night shifts and dangerous or poisonous jobs in industry, mining and construction. These measures excluded women from seeking employment in these relatively high-paying jobs (Arat, 1994b, p.66). Women workers were entitled to maternity leave at half pay for three weeks before and three weeks after birth, provided that they had been employed in their job for at least three months in the previous six months. The status and rights of women in agriculture, which constituted the great majority of working women at that time, were not covered by this code (Kırkpınar, 1998, pp.24–5). This deficiency excluded these women from legal protection and kept intact the prevailing treatment that their contribution to the family economy was seen as a part of their domestic chores.

The traditional norms can also be found in the unequal treatment for men and women in the Penal Code. The regulation of adultery and abortion did not reflect equality and equal treatment. The reproductive rights of women were denied by banning abortion, and those who helped women gain access to abortion would be prosecuted. Adultery was regarded as a threat to public morality and a ground for divorce, and pronounced a criminal act. Both the definition of and penalty for adultery showed different treatment for men and women, at the expense of the latter. The grounds for a man to be charged with the crime of adultery was a continuous affair with another woman similar to the relationship of husband and wife, whereas for a woman one incident of sexual intercourse was sufficient. Moreover, the wife could charge her adulterous husband only if the accomplice was an unmarried woman. If the other woman was married, then a complaint from the adulterous wife's husband was required to bring the charge (Arat, 1994b, p.65).

Compared to Soviet legislation, the early Republican legislation can be identified as less liberal in terms of civil and labour rights. However, the gender climates converged at the point where traditional family and gender roles were never dismissed or belittled by either the Soviet or Republican regime. As modernizing countries, both Soviet Russia and Republican Turkey confronted the difficult task of maintaining a balance between the efforts to liberate women and the internalized patriarchal reactions.

The Image of Soviet and Republican Woman

In their pioneering work, Anthias and Yuval-Davis (1989) argue that the different treatment of the state towards women is motivated by the specific role prescribed for women because of the function of human reproduction. Women participate in the state-building process and related state practices as central participants in the ideological reproduction of the collectivity and as transmitters of culture to future generations. The prescription of these specific roles for women has an impact on state interventions in sexuality, family relations and gendered identities. The 'appropriate' feminine identity emerges as a discriminating representative of 'us' and 'them' that defines and reproduces the symbolic identity of the collectivity (Anthias and Yuval-Davis, 1989).

The arguments of Anthias and Yuval-Davis are relevant to both the Soviet and Republican cases. The endowment of equality between the sexes was promoted as a symbolic gain vis-à-vis the West as well as a specific marker of Soviet and Republican modernization. Men and women were defined as equal comrades and citizens, who were to share the same values, ideals and responsibilities to the end of establishing a communist state and a civilized, secular nation, respectively. However, women were treated as a specific group in the newly established regimes' processes of putting into practice their respective modernizing projects. In these new regimes, the Soviet and Republican identity of women was constructed differently than that of men: women were expected primarily to take up the cause of the socialist and/or secular nation-state, and to raise future generations along socialist and secular-national premises.

In Soviet Russia, the ideal Soviet woman was envisioned as a worker-mother, who needed to be educated, trained and an active participant in the labour force as well as the bearer of the next generations. In her work *The Woman Worker*, Nadezhda Krupskaia, Lenin's wife and one of the leaders of the Soviet Communist Party, addressed the multifaceted roles of women, as members of the working class who would engage in political work, as wives who would support their husbands' involvement in political work, and as mothers who would become educated and receive benefits from the state for their reproductive labour (cited in Wood, 1997, p.29). The statements of Lenin (1933) concerning family, women and work indicate that women's oppression was linked to economic and then social dependence in the bourgeois family and therefore women's emancipation was for their equal and full participation in social production:

> By destroying the patriarchal isolation of these categories of the population who formerly never emerged from the narrow circle of domestic, family relationships, by drawing them into direct participation in social production, large-scale machine industry stimulates their development and increases their independence, in other words, creates conditions of life that are incomparably superior to the patriarchal immobility of pre-capitalist relations.
>
> The status of women up to now has been compared to that of a slave: women have been tied to the home, and only socialism can save them from this (Lenin, 2004, p.62).

As Lapidus (1978b) puts it, the new roles that women were expected to perform were linked to a particular pattern of political, social and economic modernization, in which women not only remained as instruments and absorbers but were also beneficiaries of new rhetoric and institutional arrangements. The obligation to undertake paid employment regardless of gender accelerated the access of girls and women into education and training. Women constituted a substantial percentage of the professional class of physicians, lawyers, engineers and scientific workers. Their share in the labour force reached approximately 50 per cent as early as the late 1920s and 1930s (Dodge, 1966, p.43). However, reinforcing traditional female roles and responsibilities set certain limitations on women's participation in the labour force on equal terms, thereby leading to low levels of productivity and creativity (p.2). In both industry and agriculture, women were predominantly concentrated at the lower levels, in low-skilled, unprestigious and poorly paid positions. Their presence in managerial and supervisory positions did not automatically increase because of the glass-ceiling effect. The gender pay gap (approximately 30 per cent) characterized women's participation in paid employment during the whole of the Soviet period (Lapidus 1982).

The Bolsheviks promised to resolve the dilemma between work and family that capitalism created for women workers. Capitalism produced a population of double-burdened women who entered the labour force with the advent of industrialization but remained responsible for childrearing and managing domestic chores essential to the family. The Bolsheviks considered that the conflicted relationship between work and family obligations would confine women to the sphere of unproductive labour or constrain women's occupational commitments and achievements, and therefore this needed to be resolved with the transfer of domestic chores to the public sphere. Lenin repeatedly mentioned that this transfer would assure the de facto emancipation of women. 'It is the chief task of the working women's movement to fight for economic and social equality, and not only formal equality, for women. The chief thing is to get women to take part in socially productive labour, to liberate them from "domestic slavery", to free them from their stupefying and humiliating subjugation to the eternal drudgery of the kitchen and the nursery' (Lenin, 2004, p.82). 'In short, we are seriously carrying out the demand in our programme for the transference of the economic and educational functions of the separate household to society. That will mean freedom for the woman from the old household drudgery and dependence on man' (Lenin quoted in Zetkin, 2004).

Thus, the new Soviet state assumed public responsibility for childcare and domestic chores by setting up public cafeterias, laundries and childcare centres. Paid workers in communal facilities would undertake the tasks that had previously been performed by women on an unpaid basis at home, and the new Soviet women would be freed from the chains of unpaid labour, participate in social production and utilize the promises of the revolution on equal terms with men (Goldman, 1993, pp.2–3). The Soviet state did not succeed in establishing a sufficient communal system for childcare and housework, due to the scarcity of resources (Attwood, 1999). But, as an academic stated, '[gender politics] were strongly connected with the system of childcare in Soviet times'. Another interviewee from a national NGO expressed the view that the Soviet state assumed responsibility to enable women to fulfil productive and reproductive functions at the same time:

> At that time [in the Soviet period] both higher education and [primary and secondary] education, [along with] childcare, were taken care of. And women could work. Children [were] in [kindergarten]. [...] [So] the parents could have their own vacation with their own children and then for two months put them in summer vacation clubs. Many women could make very good careers [in their profession]. [Even so], at home they weren't as equal as at work because they [were also responsible for all of the housework].

Because of the hostility to liberal feminism, a more equal sharing of domestic and parental duties did not become a primary concern of the Soviet regime for realizing the emancipation of women. The unequal relationship between men and women in the private sphere and the double-burdened situation of working women remained intact throughout the whole of the Soviet era. An interviewee from the Women's Union based in Moscow stated that 'many women could make a very good career where they work. But at home [men and women] weren't as equal as in the workplace because [women] had to [assume the responsibility of performing] the whole [domestic] work at home.' So, the newly established Soviet state forced women to participate in the labour force but at the same time continued to treat women as primarily responsible for childcare and homemaking while men were identified as the main breadwinners (Kiblitskaya 2000).

The Soviet state staked a 'legitimate' claim on controlling maternity with the concern of guaranteeing the continuity of new generations. Motherhood was perceived not only as a natural right but also as a social duty of being a woman. Even Alexandra

Kollontai, the foremost theoretician of women's liberation, suggested that 'childbirth is a social obligation' for women (quoted in Goldman, 1993, p.257). As worker-mothers, Soviet women were treated as primarily responsible for the biological and cultural reproduction of the new Soviet generation. Against this backdrop, abortion remained the most controversial issue in the Soviet gender climate, in which women's rights could easily become a matter of concession when it came to more urgent economic, political and demographic concerns. Soviet Russia was the first country to legalize abortion in 1920. The decree explained the need to legalize abortion on the grounds of the moral survival and painful economic conditions of the present but it was never recognized as a right of women (p.256).

Although motivated by the protection of women's health and the prevention of abortions being carried out in non-hygienic conditions, the procedure was condemned in the decree as a serious evil. The new state accompanied the legalization with propaganda against this evil: posters were prepared, particularly for urban women, that represented female sexuality as linked to motherhood and children. Among the peasantry, women continued to regard abortion as a sin and rarely sought it but urban women, under difficult economic conditions and with limited state support, tended to see maternity and childrearing as a burden and sought abortion (Engel, 2004, p.161). By the late 1920s, the number of abortions surpassed the number of births in Briansk, Moscow, St Petersburg, and parts of Ukraine and North Caucasus. Although many other factors related to industrialization, collectivization and urbanization contributed to the fall in birth rates, the rise in abortion corresponded with the decline in births and stimulated the political authorities to outlaw abortion as a pro-natal measure. Eventually, in 1936, abortion was prohibited again with a prison sentence for the operators and large fines for the patients. The Soviet state, although confirming causality between rising numbers of abortions and harsh economic conditions, embraced the ban as a way of increasing the birth rate, along with the introduction of new incentives such as longer maternity leave, bonuses for mothers with many children, new clinics, nurseries and so on (Goldman, 1993, p.291).

The Bolsheviks had in view that the transformation of the traditional family would succeed under the transition to socialism in so far as economic fears did not constitute the basis of marital union. Kollontai suggested that the family as a bourgeois remnant would be transformed, like the state, under socialism and completely wither away under communism. Early Soviet legislation weakened the family by dissolving the differences between registered and unregistered marital unions, but many Bolsheviks, including Lenin and Joseph Stalin, did not intend to abolish the family and treated sexual freedom as a distraction from the cause of socialist revolution. In his correspondence with Clara Zetkin, Lenin wrote:

I ask you: Is now the time to amuse proletarian women with discussions on how one loves and is loved, how one marries and is married? Of course, in the past, present and future, and among different nations – what is proudly called historical materialism! Now all the thoughts of women comrades, of the women of the working people, must be directed towards the proletarian revolution. It creates the basis for a real renovation in marriage and sexual relations (quoted in Zetkin 2004).

According to Berman, Lenin was critical of the bourgeois family rather than of the family itself, which would transform into a union based on love rather than economic considerations under a socialist regime (1946, p.38). As Stites cites, from the very outset,

> Lenin explained to allow freedom from material considerations, religious, social, and parental prejudices, and narrow bourgeois surroundings in love; but not (among other things) 'from seriousness of in love'. ... The form of relations between sexes for the future predicted by most Marxists, then, was a 'marriage', or love union of some sort, rather than a series of love affairs (1991, p.261).

Another of Lenin's statements that 'one cannot be a democrat and socialist without demanding full freedom of divorce now, because the lack of such freedom is additional oppression of the oppressed sex – though it should not be difficult to realise that recognition of the freedom to leave one's husband is not an invitation to all wives to do so!' (Lenin, 2004, p.43) illustrates the limitations of early Bolshevism on sexual freedom and morality.

Under the harsh conditions of state-making and the industrialization drive under Stalin, accompanied by a declining birth rate and increasing family instability, myriad social problems including abuses over easy marriage and divorce, prostitution, homeless children, single mothers and male irresponsibility had a decisive impact on perpetuating traditional family and gender roles. The effort to promote the stabilization of the family, viewed as an important social institution performing vital functions for the new social order, was proclaimed in *Pravda*, the then official newspaper of the Communist Party of the Soviet Union as follows:

> So-called 'free love' and all disorderly sex life are bourgeois through and through, and have nothing to do with either socialist principles or the ethics and standards of conduct of the Soviet citizen. ... The elite of our country ... are as a rule also excellent family men who dearly love their children. And vice versa: the man who does not take marriage seriously ... is usually also a bad worker and a poor member of society (cited in Lapidus, 1978a, p.112).

In the rest of the Soviet period, preserving a stable partnership became a state concern and divorce became hard and expensive to obtain, despite remaining legal (Schwartz, 1979, p.68).

In Turkey, the agency of women in the public sphere was endorsed with certain duties related to national identity and moral codes. The ideal Republican woman was identified as a patriotic citizen who had the mission of 'educating the nation', in addition to her traditional role (Sirman, 1989, p.9). Due to the positivist origins of the Republican ideology, the emancipation of all citizens, particularly women, was conditional on education. Education was perceived as the most powerful tool and strategy to create ideal Turkish citizens (Abadan-Unat, 1991, p.183), as in many other nation-building projects. The transformative capacity of education to replace the traditional mindset with a modern and secular one was highly stressed (Arat, 1994b, p.61). Access to employment skills and opportunities was also linked to having access to modern education and training (Abadan-Unat, 1991, p.183). In one of his addresses to a public crowd, Atatürk stated:

> Our nation has to be a strong nation. Circumstances today require the advancement of our women in all respects. Therefore, our women, too, will be enlightened and learned and, like men, will go through all educational stages. Then, women and men, walking side by side, will be each other's help and support in social life (quoted in Arat, 1994b, p.60).

In this period, Turkish women enjoyed considerably the endowment of civil rights and became more visible in the public domain, education and professional employment. By 1932, the female enrolment in secondary education had achieved a six-fold increase compared to the number by 1923 (cited in Kabasakal-Arat, 2003, pp.57–8). The Republican reforms encouraged women to attend universities and become involved in professional life. In 1929, 26 per cent of all girls aged between 7 and 11 (compared to 51 per cent of boys) enrolled in primary schools nationwide. Women constituted 10 per cent of university graduates by 1938. In addition to teaching at girls' schools, young Republican women started to be ubiquitous in mixed-gender schools and to engage in professional careers in the fields of medicine, law, engineering, social sciences and natural sciences (White, 2003, p.150). Durakbaşa (1998), in her study on the oral history of the early generation of Republican women, reported that women working in sciences such as medicine and archaeology did not complain about any gender discrimination or gender-based hindrances in their educational and academic life. This satisfaction was mostly related to the enforcement of the egalitarian education policy of the Republic that did not view biological differences as an obstacle in the way of the intellectual capacity and development of women (p.33).

However, these rights were not evenly utilized by all segments of the female population across different regions and classes. Öncü (1981), in her very insightful study, draws attention to the class dimension of the recruitment of women into prestigious professions such as medicine and law. She suggests that university-educated women from upper-middle-class families were recruited not only because of their educational skills but also in order to constitute a suitable populace for the new cadres, which would otherwise be filled with men from manual-labour and peasant origins who might constitute a threat to the consolidation of new reforms. In contrast to urban women, rural women did not efficiently utilize their legal rights and educational facilities because of the weak integration of rural areas in the national economy and urban life. The prevalence of religious marriages, polygamy, underage marriages, the demand for bride price, the birth of children out of civil wedlock, and the uneven access of boys and girls after compulsory elementary-level education marked the lives of many rural women until the 1950s at the earliest.

Despite the egalitarian rhetoric of the Republic, Turkish modernity identified marriage and children as the national duty of Republican women (White, 2003, p.146). The ideal Republican woman was a citizen woman who should be a professional and a patriot but at the same time should not neglect her traditional role as a mother. Turkish women were encouraged to have a modern outlook and be visible in public life as well as a traditional role performing domestic roles and duties at home. Atatürk stressed the importance of motherhood, stating in 1923 that 'the most important duty of woman is motherhood. The importance of this duty is better understood, if one considers that the earliest education takes place on one's mother's lap' (Arat, 1994b, p.60). Women's domestic duties nevertheless gained a new form. As a requirement of being modern, women were expected to engage with modern science and technology and to reflect modern knowledge and skills while performing domestic duties such as housework, homemaking, cleaning, cooking, child-bearing, etc. (Durakbaşa, 1997, 141–4). In 1923 Atatürk declared himself in favour of children being raised scientifically by educated mothers:

> The education that mothers have to provide to their children today is not simple, as it had been in the past. Today's mothers have to attain several high qualities in order to bring up children with the necessary qualities and develop them into active members for life today. Therefore, our women are obliged to be more enlightened, more prosperous, and more knowledgeable than our men. If they really want to be mothers of this nation, this is the way (quoted in Arat, 1994b, p.60).

Despite all the reforms encouraging women's public visibility, preserving patriarchal morality in the desegregated public sphere as a condition of Republican women's emancipation characterized the gender climate of the Republican period (see Durakbaşa 1997; Sirman 1989). From the very outset, the woman question revolved primarily around the debate on morality in the Ottoman-Turkish context. Since the encounter of the Ottoman Empire with Western modernization in the nineteenth century, the intellectual debates focused on the compatibility of Islam with modernity, with a significant focus on the woman question, which constituted a significant cultural symbol (Coşar, 2007, p.115). In the Ottoman Empire, religious morality was preserved through a public sphere that was segregated and closed to women. The Republican gender climate represented a radical break with the Ottoman gender order for embracing women's public visibility, but the question of morality, as an indicator of the underlying gender order inherited from the Ottoman past, still dominated the debate on women's equality in the Republican period. Atatürk suggested the replacement of veiling with the internalization of moral codes as the guardian for preserving moral order:

> Friends ... our women, like us are intelligent and thoughtful people. Once we inject them with consecrated morality, explain them our national moral values and adorn their brains with enlightenment and purity, there is no need for selfishness. Let them show their faces to the world. And let them see the world with the careful attention of their own eyes. There is nothing to fear in this (quoted in Baydar, 2002, p.237).

The Republican regime never banned the veil but encouraged women to look modern when participating in the public realm, as a symbol of cutting the ties with the past. However, this did not change the domestic definition of women and their need to stay within the limits of sexual modesty and 'veil their sexuality in the male world of public affairs' (Durakbaşa, 1997, p.149). As Kandiyoti suggests, 'unlike the veil, which confirms her unquestionable femaleness, the severe suit and bare face of the woman civil servant can merit a powerful message of sexual unavailability by de-emphasizing femininity and projecting a "neuter" identity. Thus, the management of femininity and sexual modesty became part and parcel of the symbolic armour of the modern woman' (1997, p.126).

Thus, the legal and institutional changes emancipated Turkish women but did not necessarily liberate them from cultural controls over female sexuality that derived from the domestic definition of the female role and the double sexual standard (Kandiyoti, 1987). The Republican ideology valued a modern but modest image for Turkish women and presented them in direct contrast to their Western counterparts, who were criticized for low-cut dressing, overuse of make-up and sexual freedom (Kadıoğlu, 1998). Durakbaşa (1997) in her insightful analysis on the duality of modernity and chastity experienced by Republican women states,

> while a segregated Muslim society underwent secularisation and desegregation with a series of institutional reforms, Kemalist women emphasized their professional identities rather than their individuality and sexuality and viewed themselves as prestigious representatives of the government. Their ideological and institutional affiliations with the new Republic helped them to present a sexually modest and respectable picture that would not threaten the patriarchal morality. Thus, however modern an ideology it was, Kemalism could not alter the traditional norms of morality that guaranteed a biologically defined and socially constraining femininity for women. The notion of female modesty – that is, the traditional values of virginity before marriage, fidelity of the wife, and a particular public comportment and dress – was carried over with an even heavier emotional load to the new generations of Kemalist women and became the basic theme of the "new morality" for the Kemalist elite (p.148).

The issue of morality is linked to the projecting of the masculine dimension of the nationalist project, in the interviews it was noted that:

> There was a social conservatism in the early Republican period, as well. The society was already conservative and the Republic had [a sort of] conservatism. This conservatism could be clearly traced in the women's question. This conservatism was established on the basis of women's bodies and their existence in both public and private spheres. The masculine eye is its core. When we question conservatism, the masculine eye constitutes the existence of men in public and private spheres on the basis of the criterion of citizenship, specifically the criterion of ethics and virtue. On the other hand, the same conservatism mentions the public visibility of women and the existence of women in the private sphere with a focus on citizenship. However, at the same time, it pushes forward morality, chastity and motherhood. Here, we are talking about a sort of conservatism, which is embedded in masculinity [...] and maintained equality on the basis of citizenship along with the criteria of chastity, motherhood and honour.

In the *New Man* (*Yeni Adam*), the intellectual periodical which engaged in setting out the cultural parameters of the Republican regime during the 1930s and 1940s, sexual modesty and obscenity were primarily highlighted regarding the feminine identity. There, the ideal Republican woman was described as a woman-mother, who would educate her children in a secular orientation, provide companionship to her husband, be socially engaged and productive, and engage in a heterosexual relationship only with her husband and within the boundaries of marriage (Köksal, 1998). As Sirman (1989) suggests, Turkish women, in the early Republican era, were expected to marry and give birth to children as a duty to the nation. An interviewee from academia also mentioned the normative significance of family making for women:

> There was the employment of women but the employment of women is a very tragic policy in Turkey. I mention the general norm that the basic function of women is to start a family, to start modern families and to maintain them, which was the norm in the Republican modernization.

To the end of preserving patriarchal morality in the public sphere, the traditional notion of femininity was revisited in accordance with modernization and the nation-building process. In other words, the emancipation of women from the religious tradition was integrated into the reproduction of patriarchy as a part of a new national identity and values (cited in Coşar, 2007, p.117). Since the Republic's early days, the reformers were worried about the adverse effects of West-oriented modernization on women and society, such as moral decline, a rise in individualism and a decline in women's positive feelings towards family and motherhood (White, 2003, p.147). As an indicator of continuity with the view of the Ottoman modernization on family and women, the Republican regime promoted cultural controls over the sexuality of women as an indicator of the moral health of society. In doing so, a normative connection between morality and 'women' was established, thereby imposing the notion of an appropriate feminine identity for all women, holding them for the sake of society and considerably shaping the debate on women's rights in Turkish society.

Political Activism of Soviet and Republican Women: The *Zhenotdel* and the Turkish Women's Union

In the Soviet and Republican gender climates, feminism was not allowed to flourish: women's activism and autonomy were circumscribed by the need to remain committed to the state's modernizing project, which relied considerably on the underlying traditional norms of femininity (see Yaraman, 2001; Wood, 1997). The political rights of Soviet women, including the right to vote and to be a deputy of the soviets, were issued as early as 1918 (Buckley, 1989, p.35). However, women continued to be regarded as secondary figures in political life (Stites, 1991, p.326). In 1922, female membership in the party was only 8 per cent. Neither urban nor rural women utilized the new rights and opportunities to the full. To promote the integration and engagement of women with the new regime, a party department called *Zhenotdel* was established under the Central Committee Secretariat in 1919 (Lapidus, 1975, p.94). The *Zhenotdel* was assigned three main goals: to inform working and peasant women about their newly acquired rights and benefits, to train women for the political cadres, and to cooperate with other organizations in opening up public facilities (kindergartens, nurseries, communal dining rooms, laundries) (Buckley, 1989, p.66). In order to penetrate among the women and to increase political consciousness among them, the *Zhenotdel* invented delegates' assemblies for political education and recruitment, published regular journals and organized campaigns for female literacy, conferences and mass demonstrations (Lapidus, 1975, pp.94–6).

When the *Zhenotdel* began to make demands on women's behalf and to criticize the regime for its failings, the party leaders blamed the *Zhenotdel* women for provoking feminist deviations, and the organization was forced to take a more obedient and less independent stance (Wood, 1997, p.4). The *Zhenotdel* proved the potential for increasing the consciousness of women as women, encouraging them to take an active part in their own liberation and defending the distinctive needs of a female constituency (Lapidus, 1977, p.123). Throughout the 1920s, the resolutions at the party congresses drew attention to the danger of the rise of feminist tendencies in the *Zhenotdel*. They expressed the fear that separate organizations for improving women's way of life could lead to the isolation and disengagement of the female constituency from the common class struggle (cited in Lapidus, 1977). From the outset, feminism was treated as a bourgeois matter and most party members were suspicious of separate women's organizations. A special focus on women's needs and problems – or a more or less 'feminist' viewpoint on women's liberation – was not welcomed by the party leaders, with the excuse of the official claim of equality, the potential that gender would carry to mobilize and polarize the whole proletariat on the grounds of sex versus class, and the traditional attitudes that they held towards politically active women.

In Turkey, women sought to establish a political party in 1923 as part of their struggle for equal political rights. However, the political authorities did not authorize the establishment of a Women's Republican Party on the grounds of its being divisive and untimely but rather advised those involved in this political initiative to establish a union (Kandiyoti, 1991a, p.41). The Women's Union, with the mission of acquiring political rights, was established in 1924 (Yaraman, 2001, p.152; Toska, 1998, p.84). The Union declared its goals as improving the intellectual and social conditions of Republican women and helping to modernize them. To this end, the Union started to organize seminars and prepare publications to educate young women and girls as appropriate mothers, to carry out charitable activities for widows, orphans, the poor and the elderly, to encourage women to join in working life, and to be involved in the education and morality of the new Republican generation (Baykan and Ötüş-Baskett, 1999, p.149).

Eventually, political rights were endowed on women in 1930 and 1934 when they were respectively given the right to vote and to be elected to political office in local elections and full suffrage (White, 2003, p.151). Upon that, the Union was assumed in public opinion to have fulfilled its mission. After the International Women's Union Congress held in Istanbul in 1935, the Union dissolved itself. It was declared that, as women's equality with men was now held in all areas, the raison d'être for a sex-segregated organization had disappeared (Bozkır, 2000, p.25). As White remarks, 'state feminism, the state-led promotion of women's equality in the public sphere, monopolised women's activism and shaped it as a tool of the state's modernising project' (2003, p.155). The experience of the Women's Union revealed that the tolerance of the Republican modernization project for autonomous women's activism and the consequent development of female consciousness was limited, given that any organization carried the potential to threaten national unity on the basis of any category including sex.

As both organizations started to defend and voice the interests and needs of the female constituency from a feminist perspective, Soviet and Republican authorities felt uncomfortable with feminist deviations, which were believed to threaten the national cause (Wood, 1997, p.4; Lapidus, 1977, p.123). Then, the *Zhenotdel* was dissolved in 1930 and the Women's Union dissolved itself in 1935, declaring that the woman question had been solved and women's equality established. The liquidation showed that women's liberation was narrowly treated only as labour-force participation in Soviet Russia (Goldman, 1996, p.47) and as patriotic citizenship in Republican Turkey (Yaraman, 2001, p.152).

As a result of modernity, women's liberation was bounded to the prospective socialist transformation and the consolidation of a secular regime in Soviet Russia and Republican Turkey, respectively. Due to the sole focus of the Bolshevik and Republican revolutionaries on the capitalist and religious systems, they could not recognize traditional pre-revolutionary patterns and values as obstacles to women's liberation. So, the new regimes attempted to establish women's equality without attacking the root causes of women's subordination. The underlying gender order was undoubtedly contoured in the Soviet and Republican periods but could not be entirely transformed. In the new gender climates, patriarchal norms and patterns were to a great extent preserved, albeit in new forms and patterns.

Both the Soviet and Republican cases revealed that 'woman' would constitute a crucial social category in the process of hegemony constitution for the newly established regimes. In the Russian case, as Ashwin (2000) argues, what had been done in the name of women by the Bolshevik Revolution was significantly motivated by the aim of breaking the old social relations, and consolidating a new social structure and a new set of social relations. The transformation through women's roles and duties would symbolize the victory of the new regime and guarantee its legitimacy (p.1). In the Turkish case, Tekeli argues that women under Ottoman rule constituted the social category most deeply oppressed and subordinated in the religious order. The women's rights discourse served a strategic goal – that is, the struggle against religious hegemony (1981, pp. 296–7). That the revolution achieved women's liberation and equality with men would dominate the official discourse and served the purpose of providing a source of legitimacy for several decades in both countries.

2

Transition to Democracy, Market Economy and Gender (In)Equality?

The post-Soviet transition in Russia in the 1990s and the transition to civilian politics after the 1980 military intervention in Turkey paved the way for the emergence of new gender climates, which can be characterized by the critique of the modernizing efforts targeting women's equality and the consequent rupture from the state-led ideology of women's equality. As a result of the opening up to the world and initial democratization attempts, some feminist ideas were formulated and the women's rights movement started to spread out in academe and civil society, but this did not ensure a move in policy or a debate about gender equality in a feminist direction. At the same time, more conservative opinions about women's status and rights in liberal, anti-communist and nationalist circles in Russia, and liberal and Islamist circles in Turkey, surfaced in politics, the media and public opinion. In Russia, the post-Soviet transition, along with demographic problems and national concerns, had drastic implications for the debate on gender equality, while the liberalizing efforts of the women's rights movement in tandem with the rise of political Islam and the EU accession talks resulted in a contradictory picture in Turkey. However, the strengthening of the traditional family that was voiced without hesitation as a means of recovering from socio-economic crisis and moral decline at state level constituted a point of convergence between the Russian and Turkish cases in the 1980s and 1990s.

The Legacy of the Late Soviet Era

After a silence lasting for four decades, Leonid Brezhnev (1964–82) was the first Soviet leader to officially declare that the woman question had not been solved in the Soviet Union, despite women's emancipation having been achieved to some extent. This declaration reopened a new, serious and wide-ranging discussion on the woman question, although it was still restricted to economic growth, labour supply and population issues. The economic growth rates achieved during the Stalin years were falling; therefore, the rational use of labour supply, almost half of which was female labour, had become an urgent necessity. When economic stagnation was coupled with falling fertility rates, the contradiction between full-time paid employment and family roles (the double burden and over-exploitation) as well as the poor working conditions of women (low wages, low-skilled jobs, night shifts, hazardous jobs) began to be discussed by economists, sociologists, demographers, journalists and others (see Buckley, 1989, 161–7).

In the late 1970s, the over-burdening and over-mobilization of women emerged as a sound ground on which to criticize Soviet gender policies. A need to rehabilitate the definitions of femininity and masculinity started being mentioned by political leaders. In the media, debates revolved around the argument that Soviet policies had destroyed the natural balance between men and women, which had led to the elimination of 'the vital element in its citizens' personalities. In order to redress this imbalance, new discourses and rhetoric set out to remind women and men of their gendered identities and their allegiance to one of two fundamentally different, indeed opposite sexes' (Kay, 2000, p.28). The alarming social ills, including rising alcoholism, high rates of divorce, low rates of marriage and falling birth rates, that were observed in Soviet society in the early 1980s were consistently attributed to the damaging impact of full-time female paid employment on family life and relationships, thereby leading to disenchantment with the institution of the family itself (Lapidus, 1993, p.150). Therefore, the lively debate of the gender climate of the 1960s and 1970s over female roles was replaced by a new debate on low fertility rates in the early 1980s. The woman question came to be explicitly and directly linked to the reproduction of future generations and women's contribution to society was primarily defined as motherhood.

Nonetheless, women's withdrawal from the labour force did not constitute a topic of debate in the gender climate of the late 1970s and early 1980s. Instead, the Soviet state continued to address the long-lasting dilemma between production and reproduction by opting for incentives to relieve the double burden of women rather than promoting an equal division of domestic chores and care work between man and wife. Brezhnev's government tended towards strengthening the family with the introduction of a pro-natal campaign that aimed to encourage women to put the family at the centre of their lives and of an educational policy to ensure the adoption of more traditional gender roles by future generations (cited in Marsh, 1998, p.90). New incentives, including introducing a new family allowance programme, extending the scope and duration of maternity leave, liberalizing sick leave for parents with young children, diversifying part-time job opportunities for women, and improving the number and quality of childcare facilities, were introduced with the aim of helping women combine work and family obligations (Lapidus, 1993, pp.152–3). There were attempts to improve women's working conditions by reducing working hours, extending lunch breaks, providing care and food services, and improving health care (Vinokurova, 2007, p.74). In 1981, the need for wider and more effective measures to lessen the female double burden was officially declared in the 25th Party Congress (Buckley, 1989, pp.180–1). In 1981, maternity leave was extended again. In 1984, a new course entitled 'The Ethics and Psychology of Family Life' was introduced into the school curriculum, with the aim of teaching natural differences to boys and girls and thereby producing a gender-differentiated order consisting of real men and real women, which was defined as the main basis of stable families (Bridger, 1992, p.178). Brezhnev's concern to relieve women of their burden stemmed mainly from the desire to find a way to increase both productivity and fertility rather than from a wish to provide the conditions for female self-determination. Neither these supportive measures nor the arguments made during the Brezhnev period were more radical than those introduced by the Bolshevik Revolution (Buckley, 1989, pp.188–9).

Although Brezhnev had initiated a debate on the woman question, it was perestroika, launched under the leadership of Mikhail Gorbachev between 1985 and 1991, that created opportunities to open up a new and radical debate about women's silenced problems after long decades. Gorbachev introduced perestroika at the 27th Congress of the CPSU with the need to restructure the whole Soviet system and thereby accelerate economic development and democratization. The command-administrative system had reached deadlock and had paved the way to low growth rates, supply shortages, inefficient ministries, corruption and so on. Perestroika, described as a 'revolutionary process' by Gorbachev, was expected to establish a more efficient economy and a less bureaucratic system, thereby overcoming this deadlock (Buckley, 1993). One prominent issue that arose during perestroika was the woman problems. In 1987, Gorbachev declared that perestroika entailed discussing how women could be returned to a truly female destiny, which had been interrupted in pursuit of socialist development goals. In Gorbachev's own words:

> But during our difficult and heroic history, we failed to pay attention to women's specific rights and needs arising from their role as mother and homemaker, and their indispensable educational function as regards children. Engaged in scientific research, working on construction sites, in industry and the service sector, and involved in creative activities, women no longer have enough time to perform their everyday duties at home – housework, raising children and creation of a good family atmosphere. We have discovered that many of our problems – in children's and young people's behaviour, in our morals, culture and even industry – are partially caused by the weakening of family ties and a slack to family responsibilities (1987, p.117).

In contrast to the Brezhnev era, this idea, which was known by the popular motto of 'bringing women back home', dominated the gender climate of the late 1980s and early 1990s (see Bridger, Kay and Pinnick, 1996, pp.23–4; Waters, 1992, p.128). During those days, the crisis that the Soviet system had already been undergoing worsened, with high rates of unemployment and severe social problems such as drug addiction, alcoholism, juvenile delinquency, abandoned children, sexual promiscuity and anarchic young people. These economic and social problems were attributed to high rates of female employment, the broken family and the double burden of working women. The reassurance of traditional patterns and stereotypes, already on offer in the media and public opinion during the Brezhnev period, prepared the ground for handling this socio-economic crisis by reassessing the roles and identity of women in a traditional way (Kay, 2002, p.54). It was widely declared that women should leave the labour force in order to bring down unemployment and to focus solely on bringing up physically and mentally healthy children and restoring family relationships. The Soviet mass media launched a propaganda campaign in support of early marriage by portraying the lives of married women as peaceful and happy while single women were miserable and lonely because of their selfishness (Bridger, 1992, p.194). This campaign was supplemented by scrutinizing poor working conditions, wage disparity, unequal grading and promotions, and night shifts to which working women were subjected (Bridger, Kay and Pinnick, 1996, p.24).

Under the conditions of perestroika, it became possible to discuss previously taboo subjects such as sex education, contraception, discrimination and poor working conditions. Some feminist ideas were expressed and a sphere opened up for civic activism for women. Women's organizations mushroomed, ranging from nationalist organizations, professional associations, local groups and associations for mothers of soldiers and disabled children to lesbian groups and crisis centres as well as hotlines for women exposed to sexual and domestic violence and feminist organizations (Lipovskaya, 1997, pp.188–91). However, more conservative opinions regarding women's identity and rights at home, in the labour market and in wider society dominated the gender climate and continued to strengthen in public opinion. This tendency became evident in the legislative framework. During perestroika, only two documents – the USSR Supreme Soviet's Resolution 'On urgent measures to improve the position of women and to safeguard maternity and childhood' and the USSR Council of Ministers' Resolution 'On supplementary measures guaranteeing social protection of families in a regulated market economy' – that regulated the supplementary measures to protect family and motherhood were issued regarding women's rights. The State Programme for Improving the Position of Women and Childhood that was proposed in 1990 remained in draft (Posadskaya, 1994, p.177). In addition, political quotas and reserved seats for women were abolished in 1989 and 1990 respectively.

The Retreat of the Socialist State in Early Post-Soviet Russia

With the demise of the Soviet Union in 1991, the newly established Russian state was relieved from the historical dilemma of the Soviet state, which had been trapped between the ideological commitment to women's equality and its partial implementation in accordance with the changing socio-economic demands. Indeed, this dilemma, coupled with the underlying traditional values and patterns regarding gender, led to fluctuations and inconsistencies in state discourse and policies throughout the whole Soviet period. Nonetheless, an ideological commitment had never been abandoned and constituted a reference point for the Soviet state to justify its actions regarding women's equality. Despite his quite traditional message about bringing women back home, even Gorbachev had felt the pressure of the Soviet ideology of women's equality and tried to reconcile it with the provision of choice over whether or not to work, and with support for increasing the political involvement of women. However, the gender climate of the Yeltsin period represented a complete rupture with the state-led ideology of women's equality.

After the dissolution of the Soviet Union in 1991, the post-Soviet state started to implement neo-liberal economic policies. Macro-economic stabilization policies, including restrictive monetary and fiscal measures, tax-based income policies and privatization, considerably restricted the financial autonomy of the ex-Soviet state and reduced real wages, incomes and enterprise profits (Teplova, 2007, p.290). The fiscal crisis affected the daily lives of the whole population, with a severe reduction in quality of life, access to free education, health and other social services, employment and housing opportunities (Marsh, 1998, pp.88–9). Secondly, the multi-ethnic structure of the Soviet Union ceased to exist and a consequent need to identify Russia as a nation with national self-esteem, pride and confidence emerged among the Russian population. This led to searching for the historical origins of national identity in the pre-revolutionary Slavophile traditions and Russian Orthodoxy (Bykova, 2004). Finally, a severe problem of population decline emerged in the 1990s, with a national population decrease being officially recorded in 1992. Demographic decline and an imbalance between ethnic Russians and the non-ethnic Muslim population residing in rural areas led to the advocacy of ethno-nationalist concerns on the part of the new post-Soviet state in the interests of national survival and development (Kay, 2002, p.53). The transition problems had a dramatic impact on the status and rights of women, destroying the paternalistic contract between women and the state, as expressed by a leading gender expert from the Centre for Supporting Women's Initiatives in Moscow:

> During the Soviet times, we [women] had social security. The state supported us. When a woman had a problem, they could go to the administrative body and get help. There were some mechanisms to resolve their problems. [Since] the dissolution of the Soviet Union, women [have been] left alone to resolve their problems. Now, women have to count on themselves rather than state benefits.

However, the Russian state did not have a defined state agenda regarding gender during the transition period. Rather than gender equality per se, demographic decline, intersecting with the economic and political impact of the dissolution, occupied a substantive place in Yeltsin's discourse towards women's roles. A patriarchal nationalist discourse, in tandem with the rupture from the Soviet ideology of women's equality, was advocated and the institution of the family was ascribed significance in the claim to national identity and self-development (Marsh, 1998, p.94). Accompanied by the reinvention of the long-standing patriarchal system, the liberalized labour market reinforced women's vulnerability through the impact of increasing unemployment, discrimination and job insecurity. An academic from the Russian Academy of Sciences in Moscow commented on the absence of focus on the gender question as follows:

> For the first ten years of the post-Soviet state – of independent Russia – it was very difficult even to [talk about gender politics] at all because the gender question was not a focus at all. Even social questions [in general] were not as much in focus because [it was a period of] economic transition, and the [only] thing the state tried to take [into] account was [providing] social support to the [least privileged members] of the population. I think there [has never been any] special focus on gender or women [...] because that means other questions are more important [than gender].

First, paid employment ceased in 1991 to be an obligation for all citizens and became instead an option, especially for women. This had the impact of identifying women, particularly single parents and women with pre-school children, as social invalids in need of protection and encouraging working women to be concentrated in female ghettos rather than being part of the mainstream in the newly emerging job market (Khotkina, 1994, pp.98–9). The 1992 amended version of the Labour Code, not unlike Soviet legislation, prohibited women from working in numerous jobs and from undertaking night shifts, heavy work, overtime and business trips, especially in the case of pregnant women, under the guise of protecting women's reproductive health (Klinova, 1995, pp.50–1). In a new Labour Code enacted in 2001, women's employment was regulated in a more liberal way. In this code, the state drew up a list that limited employment areas for women; the prohibition on night shifts and overtime was made applicable only to pregnant women, not to women with toddlers; the provision that guaranteed the employment of pregnant women and mothers was invalidated, thereby leaving them much more 'vulnerable to discrimination' (Kozina and Zhidkova, 2006, pp.59–61). In addition, the code imposed no sanction on employers if gender was specified in job requirements or advertisements (Posadskaya, 1994, p.171). Second, motherhood was redefined as a private matter rather than a duty to the state, which shifted all responsibility from the state to the individual and imposed on men a traditional responsibility for running the household. The provision of childcare services, which had been formulated to support women's participation in paid employment, ceased to be a major concern and duty of the newly established Russian state (Issoupova, 2000, p.39).

During the transition period, the Russian state was seeking international acceptance, and therefore ratified certain international declarations and conventions, such as CEDAW, the Beijing Declaration, the Declaration and Platform of Action of the Fourth World UN Conference on Women, and UN, UNESCO and International Labour Organization (ILO) conventions (UNDP, 2005, p.59). While ostensibly this meant making a commitment to abolish violence and discrimination against women and to ensure equal opportunities for them in all spheres of social life, the legal framework was not harmonized in accordance with international gender equality norms as set out in these documents. The legal recognition of gender discrimination, one of the essential requirements of these documents, has not been accomplished by Russia (ABA/CEELI, 2006, pp.15–16). Nor has a national gender equality mechanism been established, which would directly make recommendations and influence the government on policy formation regarding women, attend the legislative process and be allocated a specific budget. Two National Plans in 1996–2000 and 2001–2005 were approved to improve women's status and roles in society, but they could not be effectively implemented due to budget constraints and have not as yet been developed at a federal level (UNDP, 2005, p.59).

Post-Soviet Notions of Femininity and Masculinity

Despite the multiplicity of male and female roles, the post-Soviet gender climate advocated a strict separation between these and devoted considerable attention to the issue of re-establishing 'correct' gender identities. The Soviet experience was criticized of destroying the natural harmony between men and women, and thereby, the natural balance of behaviours, characteristics and division of roles along 'correct' gender lines. The Soviet experience of emancipation was characterized as producing negative outcomes for women, their families and society (Kay, 2002, pp.58–9). The Soviet policies of equality were alleged to have damaged femininity as a result of the over-emancipation of women and oppressing masculinity as a result of the Soviet state's monopolizing the role of patriarch at home (see Ashwin, 2000). The image of Soviet woman was criticized as being overly masculine, with short haircuts, in trousers and with a sexless body language. Private life in general, and the kitchen in particular, emerged as a sphere of reaction to the old regime as well as a way of escaping from 'negative emancipation' (Lissyutkina, 1993, pp.276–8). The normalization of Russia was portrayed as reversing the alleged gender imbalance and restoring the traditional family structure, in which the man acted as the breadwinner and protector while the woman performed the role of wife and mother (Riabova and Riabov, 2002, p.31). In this portrayal, the underlying conviction that biological differences between men and women are fixed and normatively correct gained a new authority for nature or biology in defining issues of gender (Kay, 2002, pp.58–9).

Although various visions of the desirable forms of gender relations emerged in the early post-Soviet gender climate, the dominant issue regarding gender was identifying the essential features of the ideal man or ideal woman, rather than exploring differences, diversity or cultural richness and promoting the establishment of more egalitarian relations between the sexes. However, there was a widespread confusion about the proper male and female roles. The female population was extremely exhausted by the double burden and so tended to embrace the pre-revolutionary figure of the male as the main breadwinner of the family. At the same time, they had internalized working outside the home as a moral and national obligation for several decades of Soviet emancipation (Kiblitskaya, 2000, pp.64–5). Despite the increased airing of traditional views on gender roles, reaffirming women's destiny as mothers and homemakers and defining husbands as the breadwinners, the public recognition and economic independence enjoyed by the majority of Soviet women had an irreversible impact on the self-fulfilment of many women, and this rendered any efforts to return them to the home and remove them from the labour market highly implausible (Khotkina, 1994, p.91). Last but not least, alternative gender and sexual identities remained extremely limited in the early post-Soviet gender climate; homosexuality was still seen as a dangerous sign of individualism and described as anti-social behaviour (see Attwood, 1996).

Legal Framework and Gender Equality Mechanism

In the 1993 Constitution of the Russian Federation, the universal principle of equal rights and opportunities for men and women is set out (Article 19, paragraph 3). The Russian Federation also ratified certain international declarations and conventions, such as CEDAW, the Declaration and Platform of Action of the Fourth World UN Conference on Women, and UN, UNESCO and ILO conventions for abolishing violence and discrimination against women and ensuring equal opportunities for them in all spheres of social life (UNDP, 2005, p.59). Despite this, an essential requirement has not been accomplished by Russia – that is, the legal recognition of discrimination. The principle of equal rights for men and women is set forth in the Constitution; sex-based discrimination is prohibited in employment and political participation. However, there is a 'main defect' in Russian legislation: 'gender neutrality, the lack of any norms ensuring the equalization of men's and women's opportunities in the realization of their rights and freedoms (as) proclaimed by the (Russian) Constitution'. Gender neutrality reflects a lack of awareness and prevents the legislation of gender-specific laws, which would provide women with the legal right to realize equal opportunities (ABA/CEELI, 2006, pp.15–6). This has the effect of not recognizing specific forms of gender discrimination, as a representative from the Consortium of Women's Non-Governmental Associations in Moscow remarked:

> That's why you couldn't find any court decision where you can find statements about discrimination against women. Even if it is discrimination, the court says that it was a violation of labour law or something else, for instance. But our parliament says that we need to solve the problem of the family but we don't see [this happening].

The existing legal framework may not be completely inefficient but it is gender neutral rather than gender sensitive, which it should be. Equality before the law is a necessary but insufficient requirement to improve women's rights. For women to realize equal opportunities in all spheres of social life, gender discrimination needs to be legally defined and the necessary measures taken to eliminate the causes of discrimination. To this end, the state needs to have a gender equality strategy as well as a national mechanism. An academic from the Russian Academy of Sciences in Moscow drew attention to this need:

> There is, you know, a very paradoxical situation. On the one hand, we have the best articles in our Constitution, which say that women in Russia possess not only equal rights but also equal opportunities. This is the [positive element]. We have a lot of not very bad laws, which are proclaiming equal rights. But unfortunately, this is just lip service. We don't have a national mechanism of gender equality. Practically, we have only one facility in terms of women's mechanism in the State Duma, which is the Committee on Family, Women and Children's Affairs.

The Russian state has promulgated neither a legal definition of gender discrimination nor a specific law that directly points to mainstreaming gender equality and preventing gender discrimination. The Russian state depends on the fact that the Constitution of the Russian Federation proclaims equal rights for men and women at home, in the labour market, in politics and education. The impact of lacking a gender-sensitive legal framework on the prevention of gender discrimination was stated by a gender expert from the Consortium of Women's Non-Governmental Associations in Moscow:

In Russia, we don't have any law on gender equality and equal rights for women and men. We don't have a special law. We have this article in the Constitution and many in other laws. But we don't have any special law. One of the ideas of our organization is to promote a special law. Now, it is not adopted yet. First of all, it is a definition of gender discrimination. We don't have any definition in the existing laws in Russia. We just have statements about non-discrimination but we don't have any definition as in the CEDAW commission. We talk about harassment. We don't have a definition or law of harassment in Russia. It is a big law, political rights, labour rights of women. We talk about non-discrimination against women in the labour market. It is like equal work equal payment. And in political rights, we think about quotas.

In the context of realizing the basic provisions of the Beijing platform of action, a resolution signed in 1996 and approved in 2001, the government declared the state's commitment to the establishment of an independent national mechanism, which would directly recommend and influence the government on policy formation regarding women, attend the legislative process and have a budget. Several steps were taken in the development of such a national mechanism. In November 1993, a Commission on Women, Family and Demography, attached to the Office of the President of the Russian Federation, was established. An interdepartmental commission, which would act as a coordinating body for unifying the actions of the federal executive bodies and executive bodies of the component parts of the Russian Federation, was created in 1996. In January 1997, the interdepartmental commission was transformed into the commission on the questions of improving the status of women in the Russian Federation (under the leadership of the deputy president of the Government of the Russian Federation). The Committee on Women, the Family and Youth started to operate in the State Duma of the Federal Assembly of the Russian Federation in 1993, with the task of producing guidelines for future legislation to secure equal rights and equal opportunities for men and women. In 1999, in association with the Chairman of the Federation Council of the Federal Assembly of the Russian Federation, a Commission on Women was established and renamed in 2002 as the Social Commission attached to the Office of the Chairman of the Federation Council on Ensuring Equal Rights and Equal Opportunities for Men and Women in Russia. However, Russia has not yet succeeded in creating a national mechanism endowed with executive power and a budget and organized at a federal level.

Two National Plans, covering 1997–2000 and 2001–2005, were approved to improve women's status and roles in society. These Plans recommended specific measures to improve the status of women in the labour market, to protect women's health, to develop a system of social services for women, and to provide assistance to women faced with violence. Although the National Plans prove to be the most important tool of national mechanism, they could not be effectively implemented due to budget constraints and they have not as yet been developed at a federal level (UNDP, 2005, p.59).

Another tool by which gender equality is brought into the mainstream is gender statistics, which enable the authorities to monitor the status of men and women in all spheres of life, to make international comparisons, and to enable the efficiency of the implementation of government decisions and policies on mainstreaming gender equality to be assessed. There have been some, but still inadequate, improvements in collecting gender-segregated data. There are also concerns about a gradual decrease in the number of regional sub-divisions of Rosstat (the Government Statistics Agency) that produce regional statistical digests on gender issues. In 2009, only nine regions prepared regional statistical digests, as compared to eleven regions in 2008 and twenty-eight in 2007, although some indicators that show gender differentiation are presented in other statistical digests and bulletins (UNDP, 2010, pp.49–50). A gender expert from a United Nations Development Programme (UNDP) based in Moscow remarked that:

> Until I think 2004, not sure about years, we had a strategic plan that the government pursued in gender questions. There was also a group that pursued and a governmental mechanism to discuss the gender equality issue. Then the strategic plan was not pursued. There was a draft that was discussed before my arrival, not sure about the date, but it was the last strategic plan that was drafted but not pursued in 2006 or 2007. And then the follow-up hung in the air. The gender issues are being followed in the Ministry of Health, which is Health and Social Affairs. So, it has lost its prominence in the follow-up we had during the Soviet days. In Soviet days, there was quite a drive to have these women affairs at pretty senior levels in government and they stopped.

Women's Civic Activism and Feminism

Due to the ideological dominance of class identity in the Soviet Union, any kind of organization or activity based on gender was prohibited. After the abolition of *Zhenotdel* in 1930, with the claim that it had accomplished its mission, the Soviet Women's Committee was established in 1941, but with the aim of mobilizing the population alongside socialist goals rather than pioneering lively debates around women's concerns and interests and offering different resolutions from the official discourse (Buckley, 1997: 159; Sperling, 1999, p.18). Gorbachev, as a part of the perestroika reforms that aimed to encourage women's political participation, ordered the revival of the women's councils (*zhensovety*) under the administration of the Soviet Women's Committee. By 1987, approximately one million women's councils had been established throughout the USSR. But they remained ineffective in mobilizing women's support because of being state-directed organizations (Racioppi and O'Sullivan See, 1997, pp.55–6).

Under the conditions of the transition from socialism to democracy, a sphere was opened up for women's civic activism that was directed neither by the state nor by the party, but by the women themselves. Numerous women's organizations have mushroomed, ranging from nationalist organizations, professional associations and local groups to associations for mothers of soldiers and disabled children, lesbian groups and crisis centres as well as hotlines for women exposed to sexual and domestic violence, and feminist organizations (Lipovskaya, 1997, pp.188–191). Buckley (1992) makes a five-fold categorization of women's groups that emerged immediately after glasnost: women's sections within broader nationalist movements (especially in post-communist countries), women-only political groups or parties, professional women's groups, women-only consciousness-raising groups and women's self-help groups (pp.62–6). As mentioned by Racioppi and O'Sullivan See (1995), by 1994 there were three hundred registered women's organizations and many more unregistered ones, but only a few of them and a small group of activists and intellectuals employed feminism as a position and theoretical framework to explain the subordination of women in Russia.

This small group of feminists, who were familiar with Western feminist theory, expressed the need to create a new framework and new publications that were critical of the Soviet approach to women's equality came to be published. The Moscow Centre for Gender Studies, LOTUS (the League of Liberation from Stereotypes), the Centre for Women, Family and Gender Studies at the Moscow Institute of Youth, and the Moscow Assault Recovery Centre were established, with the involvement of leading feminist activists such as Olga Voronina, Zoya Pukhova, Anastasia Posadskaya, Natalya Rimashevskaya, Valentina Konstantinova, Yelena Yershova, Natalya Pushkareva, Natalya Rimashevskaya and Tatiana Zabelina. Voronina (1993) suggested the term patriarchy for a more useful examination of women's experience under the Soviet Union, breaking ground at the time. Similarly, Posasdkaya, Zakharova and Rimashevskaya, in their famous article 'How We Solve the Woman Question?' published in 1989, advocated a more egalitarian approach regarding the relations between men and women against a patriarchal understanding (Marsh, 1995, p.288). The feminist women's groups organized the First Independent Women's Forum, held in Dubna on 29–31 March 1991, and voiced their demands for political interest in women's rights with the slogan of 'Democracy without women is not real democracy.' Violence against women, the patriarchal culture, problems of the independent women's movement, political participation, transition to a market economy and lesbianism were among the main themes discussed in the Forum. The Forum was the first independent women's conference since the All-Russian Women's Congress of 1908, proving the success of women's organizations no longer being established by order from on high but on the initiative of women themselves (p.290).

In the early 1990s, Western aid to Russian women's organizations dramatically affected the development of NGOs in post-Soviet Russia, where civic activism was debilitated and civil society was domestically weak. With 450,000 civic groups in existence by 2001, Russia received the largest share of foreign funding, compared to other post-communist countries in receipt of foreign aid. The grants and assistance were channelled to supply organizational basics, including computer equipment, salaries for permanent staff, office space, the organization of domestic and international conferences on relevant issues, support for training and seminars for leaders, and funding for research and travel abroad. The idealistic expectation of foreign aid organizations was that financial and bureaucratic assistance for nascent voluntary organizations would build a vibrant civil society, which would in turn play an integral part in Russia's democratization. It is hard to deny that foreign aid dramatically contributed to the improvement of the organizational capacity, short-term financial viability and networking skills of the aid-receiving organizations. However, foreign aid had effects which were not always positive. The funded organizations started to imitate the centralized and bureaucratized structure of aid agencies, tended to reflect their agendas and priorities rather than domestic needs, and pursued short-term and individual goals instead of cooperating and engaging in activities with other NGOs. A group of civic elite within the domestic NGO community also emerged, creating a hierarchy among NGOs, centralizing funds in the hands of particular organizations and impeding the development of network building among foreign and domestically funded NGOs (Henderson, 2003, pp.6–11). Reliance on foreign funding was an important factor that impeded the institutionalization of the women's movement. The foreign-funded NGOs remained 'foreign' in the eyes of the domestic female audience, as they did not have the autonomy to put issues relevant to that audience, such as abortion and the double burden of women, on their agendas. They failed to mobilize the female population and build a domestic constituency, which is a crucial aspect of institutionalization (Sperling, 2006, pp.163–6).

The independent women's movement also encountered the challenge of widespread hostility to feminism, which dated back to the early Soviet era, in which feminism had been portrayed as alien and bourgeois. In the early transition period, the pattern persisted that described feminism as 'a social monster' or as 'an impermissible luxury' for a country under transition (Konstantinova, 1994, pp.61–2). In her insightful study on women's movement groups and activists, Sperling describes how a not insignificant number of activists reacted to feminism by equating it with 'total independence and concomitant rejection of men', while some adopted a more liberal account of feminism, 'advocating equal rights for women, but not entailing a radical restructuring of society, or a rejection of traditional gender roles and heterosexuality' (Sperling, 1999, pp.61, 63). Konstantinova (1994) points to the low level of feminist consciousness among women and women's groups that usually overlooked sexual discrimination when expressing their opinions about democracy, pluralism and the market economy (pp.58, 65). The tendency to connect insults towards and humiliation of women with the lack of democratization and of a strong civil society, an accountable state, the rule of law, justice and equality, and to connect the elimination of gender inequality and discrimination with broader socio-economic and political change towards the building of democracy was not weak in academic and public debates (Ferree et al., 1999).

The hostility to feminism is related to the negative resonance of equality, which for post-Soviet women meant working full-time both inside and outside the home. The concept of equality came under attack and a strong resistance to Western feminism emerged. As Sperling makes clear, the pursuit of femininity of which Soviet women had been deprived for seventy years counteracted feminism in the early transition period. '"Feminism" is understood to be a competitive ideology, which aims to sacrifice all that is "feminine" in women, in a mad pursuit of equal rights and opportunities with men; feminism is seen as an ideology which ignores the special responsibilities that women bear as mothers and disregards the bitter experience of women's "double (or triple) burden" in communist systems' (Edmondson, 1996, pp.95–6). As a reaction to the image of the masculine Soviet woman and physical uniformity in terms of dressing and hairstyle, post-Soviet women have tended to care much about their physical appearance, dress and make-up. While some feminist groups in the West react against consumerism and reject giving much attention to physical appearance, these carry the symbolic meaning of a return to individuality for post-Soviet women. Rituals such as chivalry, courtship and wedding ceremonies, rejected by most feminist groups for emphasizing innate differences between men and women, have become very popular for post-Soviet women, representing a contrast with Soviet culture (Lissyutkina 1993). The historical hostility towards feminism, combined with the lack institutionalization of the women's movement, has had a detrimental impact on the collective power and influence of the women's movement to unite and channel domestic needs and expectations to the political authorities.

The Experience of Women of Russia

The economic pressures and political reforms of the transition period dramatically reinforced the disadvantaged position of women, pushing them back into the domestic arena and away from political decision-making, with the abolition of quotas. But the establishment of 'Women of Russia' that accompanied the Russian Federation's first elections, held in 1993, as a bloc gave grounds for hope that the low status of women in politics could be overcome. Its members consisted of the representatives from the Union of Women of Russia (the former Soviet Women's Committee), the Association of Women Entrepreneurs of Russia and the Women of the Fleet. Women of Russia won 8.1 per cent of the vote on the party list and sent 21 female deputies out of 225 to the State Duma. Apart from Women of Russia, none of the five parties running in the elections put forward female candidates for higher positions (Buckley, 1997). In the State Duma, one of the leading members of the bloc, Alevtina Fedulova, occupied the post of Duma deputy chairperson. Other deputies from Women of Russia held positions in various committees in the State Duma but concentrated on social policy, which is globally acknowledged as the sphere of female responsibilities, including health protection, women, children, social protection and education (Slater, 1995, p.89).

One of the reasons behind the formation of 'Women of Russia' was that, as male politicians and other political parties neglected women's rights, there emerged a need for female politicians to represent and defend their issues (Buckley, 1997, p.159). However, once in the Duma, the bloc did not limit itself to the pursuit of women-centred politics and to tackling social problems specifically related to women, such as female unemployment, but claimed to be tackling general social problems related to the whole of society, including housing, access to consumer goods and wage differentials (Slater, 1995, p.90). The formation of Women of Russia represented a counter to the Marxist aversion towards separate politics according to gender and demonstrated women's increasing activism in post-communist politics. But their concentration on general social problems may have had the impact of strengthening the division of politics between the male and female spheres as well as the widespread belief that women are innately better suited to this area than men.

Before the 1995 elections, a lively debate was initiated on whether or not the faction would turn into a political party. However, in the 1995 elections, the bloc failed to exceed the election threshold and was left out of the Duma (Buckley, 1997, pp.158–9).

The Emergence of a Feminist Movement in Turkey

The military intervention in Turkey took place on 12 September 1980 and the military regime lasted until 1983. The declared aims of the intervention were to end the appalling violence stemming from the political and ideological struggle between the leftist and rightist groups during the 1970s, to correct the economy by changing its course from an import-oriented industrialization to an export-oriented growth model, and to restore stability and order. A military-led government, consisting of retired military men and non-party technocrats, was immediately established to carry out the administration of the country under the military regime (see Hale, 1993). The motives of the military regime were to depoliticize society with an attempt to end the social chaos of the pre-1980 period and to prevent the re-emergence of political and ideological fragmentation and polarization in the country. This had a dramatic impact on the political scene and the realization of political and civil rights. The National Security Council (NSC), chaired by the leader of the military intervention General Kenan Evren, dissolved the parliament and the government, and legislative power was transferred to the NSC. All political parties were shut down, their members taken into custody and all political activities banned. An extensive martial law that empowered the authorities to suppress the press and remove civil servants, mayors and the members of city councils from their office was introduced. Trade unions were abolished and strikes were declared illegal. Thousands of suspects, including trade unionists, journalists and political activists, were arrested for terrorism and illegal political activities (Dağı, 1996, pp.125–6).

After the national elections held in 1983, the process of transition to democracy started in Turkey. Under the conditions of a free market economy and globalization, the rhetoric of 'shrinking the state and expanding society' alongside the emergence of a consciousness of individualism and liberalism started to dominate the political discourse. As Keyman and Icduygu (2003) discuss, the legitimacy crisis of a strong state tradition that characterized Turkish modernization from the beginning, the emergence of alternative paradigms to Turkish modernization based on religious and ethnic identity, the increasing integration with Europe via the process of EU membership application and the impact of globalization all paved the way for the emergence of civil society as an important actor in Turkish politics. The number and activities of civil societal organizations, operating in the fields of human rights, environmental issues, peace building and so on, had increased in the 1990s.

Against this backdrop, an autonomous women's movement could find fertile ground in which to emerge. It contributed to the democratization of Turkey and the establishment of civil society by engaging more women in grassroots politics and enabling them to practise democracy. The feminist groups challenged the state discourse and policies that had preserved the patriarchal division of labour in society, and supported individualism and civil society against the strong state tradition (Y. Arat 1994) that had left little space for political opposition to the statist, corporatist and secular configuration. The feminist movement was particularly tolerated by the state, as, thanks to the heritage of the state-led ideology of women's equality, the feminist and anti-state rhetoric of the women's movement was probably not understood as a threat to the state (Tekeli, 1990). An academic from the Middle East Technical University in Ankara, who was involved in the feminist movement in the early 1980s, confirmed this statement:

> A feminist perspective to gender developed for the first time in Turkey, after 1980, originating not from the state but from civil society. Towards the end of the 1980s, this perspective penetrated into the state policies. To put it more accurately, in this period, the feminist perspective gradually influenced the state authorities to some degree. It is also a fact that in 1980, Turkey experienced a military coup followed by the rule of a military government in the post-1980 period. The military government perceived the 'woman issue' as a relatively benign matter. Thus, the feminist women's movement was given space to voice its complaints and raise its demands more freely than other civil society groups and movements. This proved to be a window of opportunity for the women's movement. Some progressive and liberal policy steps related to gender policies were, in fact, taken in this period.

The feminist women – young female academics who had completed graduate work abroad, become familiar with the second wave of feminism and were mainly involved in the leftist movements in the 1970s – voiced for the first time in Turkish history that the woman question had not been resolved. Behind this claim lay the fact that the legal gains of the early Republican era could not ensure women's emancipation, as the Republican reforms did not substantially change the patriarchal system prevailing in society, and these norms and values continued to prevent women from enjoying legal and de facto equality with men (Özbay, 1990). The motto 'the private is political' was advocated by feminist groups to challenge the limited impact of Republican egalitarian discourse and policies in the private sphere. The feminist women's movement challenged the identification of women as mothers, wives and sisters, identifying them instead as individuals who have the right and will to decide on their own life courses (Y. Arat, 1994, p.244). The feminist women brought up more individualistic subjects of sexual freedom, sexual harassment, violence against women, prostitution, gender relations in the family and the like (Toprak, 1994, p.299). The question of women's predicament and subordination in the labour force, politics and the private sphere, including domestic violence, sexual harassment, honour/custom killings and virginity tests, was explained through the persistence of the patriarchal system (Arat, 1993, pp.126–7). A researcher from the Middle East Technical University in Ankara contended that:

> In the post-1980s, the state had a positive attitude towards women's equality. It could be seen as the heritage of modernization. Probably for this reason, the emergence of a feminist movement was not perceived as a threat to the regime and the feminist demands were relatively fulfilled during the 1990s. The feminist

movement emerged as a grassroots movement in the 1980s. It demanded substantial changes to assure women's equality. The feminist women brought up public/private distinction and argued that many issues, which would be considered as private, were innately political.

Feminist women organized informal meetings at homes and conducted discussions in feminist journals and publications to raise awareness of feminist demands (Tekeli, 1986; Timisi and Ağduk-Gevrek, 2002). They organized public campaigns, street protests and sit-ins specifically to direct public attention towards violations of equality, such as domestic violence, virginity tests and sexual harassment, and to mobilize political action in support of necessary legal changes, primarily in the Civil and Penal Codes (Acar and Altunok, 2012, pp.37–8). The number of women's civil societal organizations increased from 10 in 1983 to 64 in 1992 and to more than 350 in 2004 (Diner and Toktaş, 2010, p.47).

The Early Legal Amendments

Despite the emergence of a feminist women's movement in Turkey, there was no evident change in the evolutionary legalistic approach of the Turkish state regarding women's equality in the gender climate of the 1970s and 1980s. In 1973, the state published a series of publications that praised the legal rights bestowed on women and their achievements for the 50th anniversary of the establishment of the Republic (Özbay, 1990, p.6). However, low rates of women's employment and introducing support mechanisms for working women to achieve a work and family balance did not occupy a place in the political texts prepared by the National Education Ministry in the 1970s (Ecevit, 2012). On 5 December 1984, after long decades, a special session was organized in the Turkish Grand National Assembly for the celebration of the 50th anniversary of Turkish women's political rights. In this session, women's equality was articulated as a social fact of Turkish society and the significance of the legal rights of women, as well as their role as the mothers of future generations, was emphasized. Women's low level of participation in employment and politics was touched upon in this session, but no concrete steps to overcome these deficiencies were mentioned. An expert from an international organization based in Ankara underlined the silence of the Turkish state regarding women's equality, which was assumed to have been resolved with the bestowal of legal equality after the early Republican period:

> Until the 1980s, the state did not do much [to ensure women's equality]. Until then, it [women's equality] was not seriously considered. The women's question was always perceived as having less importance than other issues. There were always some other issues having much priority. The women's question was on the to-do list but there were more important issues. Women's employment, participation in decision-making mechanisms, election to the parliament, active participation in social life, literacy was not regarded as [problems] by the state until the 1980s when the women's movement stimulated [these issues]. There was no awareness

about violence against women anyway. Frankly, women were not perceived as an important agent of social development. On the one hand, men and women were not differentiated on the basis of sex. For sure, the policies covered both men and women. The equality before the law was perceived to resolve any problem. How legal equality worked in practice was not considered.

In the late 1980s, the state had to become involved in women's issues in the face of feminist pressures and started to enact gradual legal amendments. In 1983 the military government legalized abortion during the first ten weeks of pregnancy, on the condition of the husband's consent in the case of married women. In 1990 the Constitutional Court abolished two discriminatory articles of the old Civil Code, which, respectively, deprived women of the right to choose their domicile and made a married woman's right to work outside the home conditional on the consent of her husband (Abadan-Unat, 1991, p.189). The Constitutional Court effectively decriminalized adultery, which had been classed as a criminal act in the 1926 Penal Code, for men and women in 1996 and 1998 respectively. Domestic violence eventually entered the state agenda in 1998, with the introduction of Law 4320 on the Protection of the Family (KSGM, 2008).

In the post-1980s, a more discernible political focus on the low rate of female labour force participation in Turkey was generated, in tandem with increased integration in the international community and its norms (İlkaracan Ajas, 2012, pp.201–2). In 2001 the government issued a new Civil Code and abolished the article that defined the man as the head of household (WWHR, 2005, pp.7–9). In the new code, the obligation of women to receive permission from their husbands for their choice of work was removed but a traditional clause prioritizing the family over the individual's right to work was retained, with a probable limiting impact on women's working outside the home. The new code still declares that 'the harmony and welfare of the marriage union should be borne in mind by spouses when choosing and performing a job or profession', which might be used as a ground to justify the violation of women's right to work (p.27) as well as to promote the housewifization of women.

The Establishment of a National Gender Equality Mechanism

The pursuit of international recognition following the military intervention was coupled with the pressures of the feminist movement and had the effect of forcing the Turkish state to enact the aforementioned legal amendments as well as to abide by the international obligations drafted in CEDAW, the Nairobi World Conference and the Beijing Action Plan. Women's human rights acquired a critical importance in the international community, mainly through the efforts of the United Nations. In 1975, the First World Conference on Women was held in Mexico City and 1975–1985 was proclaimed the United Nations Decade of Women. In 1979, the UN General Assembly adopted the Convention on the Elimination of All Kinds of Discrimination Against Women, described as an international bill of women's human rights. Turkey signed the Convention in 1985 and it came into force by 1986. Subsequent world conferences were organized in Nairobi in 1980 and in Beijing in 1985 to evaluate national efforts to eliminate gender inequality and discrimination during the decade. In 1985, many countries, including Turkey, adopted the Beijing Declaration and its requirement of the establishment of a national mechanism. Then, the Turkish state started to become a part of international conventions, put efforts into establishing a national mechanism, preparing national action plans and conducting various nationwide research projects and surveys, and subjected itself to international monitoring on the advancement in gender equality and women's human rights. An academic who was involved in the feminist movement in the early 1980s and has held senior posts in UN-related bodies, commented on the positive impact of the state's concern to gain international prestige on gender politics:

> Moreover, one of the most important factors, which revived 'the woman issue' and facilitated progressive steps in gender politics, was the pressure of international forces. There were already demands from civil society but there were also international bodies that supported these demands and helped their accumulation. The UN system was the significant international driving force of that period, namely the 1990s. At the time, women's rights and gender equality issues were rising topics within the UN itself; in fact, these were some of the most important human rights issues on the worldwide agenda of the United Nations.

In opposition to the attempts to establish a national mechanism to guarantee women's human rights and resolve gender inequalities, the neo-conservative wing of the then-government made a counter attack and established the Prime Ministry Family Research Institute in 1989. The founding aims of the Institute were declared as re-institutionalizing the traditional family structure and redefining the traditional role of women within that traditional family structure in the face of the allegedly damaging impacts of industrialization, internationalization, urbanization and mass migration (Acuner, 1999, pp.137, 144). The General Directorate on the Status and Problems of Women (KSSGM) affiliated to the Prime Ministry was established in 1990, following the Family Research Institute. This success is mainly attributable to the personal efforts of a female minister, Minister of Labour İmren Aykut, who personally persuaded and even manipulated her party members to hurriedly pass a draft law to establish the General Directorate of Women's Status and Problems as a national mechanism, and closely cooperated with the feminist movement (Acuner, 1999). An academic from Ankara mentioned how the inadequately funded and staffed General Directorate and ministers responsible for women were significantly supported in the 1990s by feminist activists and groups who provided them with academic background, expertise, consultancy and research. A public officer from the Ministry of the Family stated that:

> I understood that the establishment of KSSGM was not a deliberate and conscious decision. In other words, the state did not consider the women's issues as a problem. The state did not intend to establish a public policy as a result of women's demands and with an aim to meet them. Selma Hanım [Former General Director of KSSGM]

names it 'Infiltration Politics'. This is how it happened. There were [international] developments in the world; there were demands and several initiatives in Turkey. In this context, the General Directorate was hastily established; it did not have [qualified] human resource and an adequate budget. Its tasks were not clearly defined. I think that the issue of women was not [sincerely] embraced by the state organization. Rather, it [KSSGM] worked as an opposition inside the state and with the support of civil spirit.

However, the institution was established by legislative decree and continued its existence for eleven years without a law of establishment (Çitçi, 2011, p.426). At the beginning, there were just a few personnel and this limited the Directorate's capacity and activities to produce policies concerning women (Acuner, 2002, p.131). The establishment of a family institution could not hinder the establishment of a national gender equality mechanism. However, the whole process foreshadowed the fact that the strengthening feminist movement would have to confront the domination of family-oriented discourse in gender-related issues at the state level, particularly under the increasing religio-conservatism.

Since the 1990s, the Turkish state has aimed to be in alignment with international principles and directives, which are designed to ensure gender equality in all spheres of social life. The CEDAW, the European Social Charter, and the Convention on the Rights of the Child, the Millennium Development Goals 2015, conventions and recommendations of the ILO, the Organization for Economic Cooperation and Development (OECD), the Organization for Security and Cooperation in Europe (OSCE), the Cairo Conference on World Population and Development Action Plan, the 4th World Conference on Women Action Plan and the Beijing Declaration, and the EU directives on equality between women and men and, finally, the Istanbul Convention are among the international treaties and documents that the state has adopted (KSGM, 2008, p.14).

In 1985, Turkey signed and then became a party to CEDAW. The Convention is accepted as the declaration of women's human rights and is the only legally binding instrument at the international level concerning equality between women and men. Its main objective is to eliminate all forms and practices that are based on stereotypes regarding gender roles and identities, and that lead to discrimination between men and women. The Convention makes a clear definition of discrimination against women, intended to advise state parties in realizing legal amendments and taking measures to ensure gender equality and prevent gender discrimination. The Turkish state is obliged to prepare and submit reports to the Committee every four years (KSGM, 2008).

The decision to becoming a party to the Convention might be explained by the official state discourse, which was based on the Republican understanding of equality between men and women. However, the Turkish state placed some reservations on the Convention, due to the existence of discriminatory articles in the old Civil and Penal Codes at the time. Acar (2000) states that the hesitation on the state level to withdraw these reservations reflects the dilemma between traditional and progressive views on gender equality, identities and relations. However, eventually the reservations were removed in 1999 as a result of the promise given by the state in the 4th World

Conference held in Beijing in 1995 (p.207). The legally binding nature of CEDAW was further strengthened in two steps. First, Turkey signed the Optional Protocol in 2000 and ratified it in 2003. The Protocol enables the Committee to inquire in countries where there are serious and widespread violations of women's human rights. It also gives individuals the right to petition and complain to the Committee about violations of the Convention. Second, by adding a clause to Article 90 of the Constitution in 2004, Turkey accepted the superiority of international agreements in the fields of fundamental human rights, including CEDAW, in the case of conflict between international agreements and domestic law (KSGM, 2008).

In 1995, Turkey signed the Beijing Declaration and Action Plan, which were adopted at the UN 4th World Conference on Women, without any reservations (KSSGM, 2004). The Turkish state promised to withdraw its reservations to CEDAW by 2000, to decrease mother and infant deaths, and to increase women's literacy. In that regard, Turkey prepared the first National Action Plan on mainstreaming gender equality in 1996. The Plan was coordinated by KSSGM in a joint effort with relevant stakeholders from civil societal organizations, universities and government bodies. Women in education and health, violence, economic and political participation, and the leading role of a national mechanism are mentioned as critical areas of priority in the Plan (KSSGM, 2004).

The second National Action Plan for Gender Equality covering the period of 2008–2013 was prepared in the context of international documents on promoting gender equality such as CEDAW, EU *Acquis* and UN Millennium Development Goals. The Plan was an output of the project entitled 'Promoting Gender Equality Project – Strengthening Institutional Capacity Programme Twinning Project'. With the aim of enabling women to benefit from social opportunities on an equal basis with men and protecting women's human rights, the Turkey–European Union Pre-Accession Financial Assistance Programme of 2005 funded the project. The Plan addressed the current situation of women in the labour force, education, politics, health, media and the environment and provided a comprehensive agenda, including the definition of obstacles, objectives and strategies on the way to achieving gender equality (KSGM 2008).

The Islamist Movement and the European Union

In the gender climate of the 1990s, the rise of the Islamist movement and the prospective membership of the European Union must be underlined as the other dominating (f)actors in addition to the feminist women's movement.

The revival of Islam in post-1980s Turkey, according to the analysis of Arat (1998), was linked to various factors such as the deficiencies of the Republican modernization project, which excluded Islam from the public sphere not only as the religion but also as the culture of the rural constituency, the migration from rural to urban areas in the 1970s, the crisis of national identity and the rise of identity politics in the context of globalization, the extensive control of the state over religion and so on (p.123). The Islamist parties started to enter the electoral scene in the 1970s but were not able to become a major political force. The conditions of the transition to democracy, characterized by opposition to the modernist and secularist values of the state, the advocacy of liberal rights and values, and the expansion of civil society as an area of freedom of expression and organization, provided an opportunity for Islamic groups to defend their cause at the political level in the 1990s. The Welfare Party, which was the successor of earlier pro-Islamist parties, was established and became a nationwide political force with electoral victories in the 1994 local elections and 1995 national elections. These victories changed the image of the Islamist party, which had previously been treated as a peripheral political force confined to inner Anatolian roots (Onis, 1997). In addition, a conservative commercial bourgeoisie from the Anatolian rural side started to be born in competition with big business, the latter having a secular and modernist orientation. Islamist newspapers, magazines and journals started to circulate at unprecedented levels, and a group of Islamist writers and intellectuals started to find platforms in the media, civil society and academia from which to voice their Islamist ideology.

The Islamist movement, in its struggle to oppose the Western, modernist and secular political order and present an alternative based on an Islamist way of life, attached importance to the question of women and mobilized them at the forefront of the movement. According to Acar (1995), this was for two main reasons. First, Islam has from its inception addressed women's rights and functions because the configuration of an Islamic social order is related to the protection of the institution of the family and the establishment of the proper relations between men and women. Second, the woman question has been a major area of conflict between the conservatives and the apologists of the secular and modernist order since the Ottoman modernization. Therefore, the status and rights of women have gained a symbolic significance in the Islamist ideology, as in its Republican counterpart (pp.47–8).

The Welfare Party as a pro-Islamist party with Islamist women activists politicized women's issues on the basis of the advocacy of the public visibility of veiled women. The ban on wearing the headscarf in public institutions and educational institutions, including universities, enabled the party to hold a gender discourse and to mobilize women to join the party ranks. Islamist women strengthened party propaganda by visiting people at home and organizing social events, including charitable activities, praying days, fundraising events and so on. Islamist men and women frequently protested against the headscarf ban as discriminatory towards women in the streets and on university campuses. Their main demand was the abolition of the headscarf ban in public offices and universities. Turkey had never outlawed headscarves in daily life, and more than two-thirds of women habitually wear a headscarf, but university students and public employees were expected to wear Western styles of clothing. With the headscarf, the Islamist women challenged secular modernization and asked for public visibility without hiding their religious identity (Kadıoğlu, 2005, p.27). Interestingly, some secular feminist women supported the Islamist women on the grounds that the headscarf ban would prevent only Islamist women, not Islamist men, from receiving a university education and participating in professional life (Aksoy, 2015, pp.158–9).

Even though the headscarf ban was the main target of Islamist women's activism in the 1990s, some Islamist women brought various other issues into the discussion, including women's social status, women's roles in the family and motherhood, and women's education, careers and leadership (Aldıkaçtı Marshall, 2013, pp.79–80). Some Islamist feminist activists, scholars and organizations challenged the male domination in the Islamist movement that did not consider women's empowerment and circumscribed the Islamist women's activism with the headscarf struggle (Aksoy, 2015).

The Islamist movement, alongside women's activism, became involved in the debate that defined the proper male and female roles in intellectual circles, public opinion and the mass media. In addition to feminist literature, an Islamist literature that was critical of the Republican ideology of women's equality and advocated the moral value of the patriarchal family system as described in Islam was produced in the 1990s (Özbay, 1990, p.5). Since its emergence in the 1970s, the Islamist movement has been searching for a modest and traditional way of life with reference to Islam, as an alternative to the modern way established by the Republican reforms. For Islamists, not unlike Republican supporters of modernity, morality is of importance in society and is profoundly related to the status of women. In this portrayal, the Western norms introduced by the Republican reforms allegedly destroyed the natural order based on the traditional division of male and female roles and caused a degeneration of moral values. Women's working outside the home is considered to bring about confusion in family roles and a loss in the natural identity and duties of women – that is, as mothers and housewives. The institution of the family is portrayed as disintegrating, leading to disastrous consequences for social morality (Toprak, 1994, p.299). As Saktanber (1997) remarks, the Islamist emphasis on motherhood as the primary function of women for moral health is not so different from the Republican rhetoric regarding women's rights, but Muslim women are expected to teach their offspring to lead an Islamic way of life, while the Republican reformers forced women to educate the nation in the name of national progress.

By contrast, the Islamist movement has advocated preserving the natural order as prescribed by *fitrat* (nature) of the sexes, which refers to a difference as well as complementarity between men and women. *Fitrat* does not necessarily constitute a source of inequality between men and women; rather, women are expected to submit to their nature (*fitrat*) as the only possible form of existence. According to this, motherhood is regarded as the natural essence of being a woman, and family is sacred as the sphere to end women's subordination (Sirman, 1989, pp.23–6). This understanding – a patriarchal understanding of Islam – became evident in the statements of political figures from the Islamist movement. Necmettin Erbakan, the leader of the Welfare Party, explained once that he did not approve of women working outside the home and called it a threat to family union (Mengi, 2005). The state minister who was behind the establishment of the Family Research Institution expressed his attitude towards the family and women by declaring that 'there was no difference between a woman's flirting with a man and the practice of prostitution' (Diner and Toktaş, 2010, p.46) and 'feminism is perversion' (Bianet, 2018).

The EU, as another actor shaping the gender climate in Turkey, entered the political scene in the late 1990s. Turkey was officially declared a candidate country at the Helsinki summit of December 1999. The prospect of EU membership provided the appropriate conditions and incentives to induce a major transformation and democratization in the economic and political realms in Turkey (Öniş, 2003). The AKP, which is still governing the country, advocated full accession to the EU as a critical political priority and chose to abide by EU norms and requirements, including gender equality. The impetus of the accession talks with the EU also served the purposes of the women's rights movement that used the EU as an opportunity as well as leverage to enforce the AKP government to make necessary legal amendments from a gender-sensitive perspective. In line with harmonizing the Turkish legislation with the EU *Acquis*, the old Civil and Penal Codes were replaced with new ones that abolished gender discriminatory articles, and a number of progressive legal changes regarding women's employment and domestic violence were achieved. In 2003, the Turkish National Programme on the Adoption of the EU *Acquis* was accepted. The Turkish state agreed to harmonize its legal framework and align its policies regarding equality between men and women in the labour market with the *Acquis Communautaire*. Additionally, Turkey became a part of the Gender Equality Community Programme of the EU, which aims to guarantee equal treatment in employment, promotion, training and labour conditions, regardless of gender. As an academic from the Middle East Technical University based in Ankara remarked, the requirements imposed by the EU to establish gender equality in education, health, employment and political participation were principally accepted without significant reservations. A researcher from the Middle East Technical University underlined the impact of EU membership talks on the pursuit of legal amendments:

> In the 2000s, Turkey's candidacy for the EU membership was declared and the EU has a discourse on gender equality. This required an adaptation [and harmonization] process. In this process, pro-employment initiatives [were taken], legal amendments [were made], new Civil Code and Penal Code [were enacted]. The legal framework was restructured in accordance with the [EU's] understanding of gender equality.

In the EU membership process, the Islamist women's movement cooperated with the broader women's rights movement in Turkey. Some Islamist women's organizations, such as Capital Women's Platform, which identify themselves as both Muslim and feminist, participated in the Women's Platform for the Turkish Penal Code and cooperated with feminist and secular-Kemalist women to improve women's human rights in the legal framework. The Turkish Penal Code, which had been adopted in 1926, was amended in 2004 as a result of a three-year campaign, with the realization of thirty-five amendments towards the recognition of women's autonomy over their bodies and their sexuality. In the old penal code, women's bodies and sexuality were established as belonging to their families, husbands and society. The patriarchal construction of women's sexuality was evident in the old code in that honour crimes, rape and abduction were classified as crimes committed against the family honour and society, rather than against individuals. The old code reduced sentences in honour crimes if the victim was caught in the act of committing adultery or other illegitimate sexual relations, and dropped the case in cases of abduction and rape if the perpetrator eventually married the victim. In the new code, sexual crimes are classified under the section of 'crimes against individuals' instead of 'crimes against society' (Ilkkaracan 2007). The new code criminalizes marital rape and sexual harassment in the workplace, eliminates references to patriarchal and discriminatory expressions such as custom, chastity, honour, morality and shame, and removes the distinction between married and single women in the case of abduction and rape. During the campaign, in addition to pressure from the EU, the alliance among secular, feminist and Islamist women's rights organizations and groups was quite important in forcing the state to enact the legal amendments. This experience reveals how the demands from feminist, secular and Islamist women's groups overlapped on the grounds of recognizing some women's human rights. However, the differentiation of the women's rights movement still leads to crucial divergences on certain taboo issues, such as sexual orientation, pre-marital sexual intercourse, virginity and adultery, which are linked to the representation of the chastity of women and the morality of society in the traditional Turkish society, as an academic from Ankara University observed:

> There are some areas in which cooperation cannot be achieved because there are two important actors in gender politics today. One of them is Islamist women, the other one is feminist women. There are certain fault lines between Islamist women and feminist women. The main fault line is body politics, which refers to the sphere of individual rights, in which the body of woman belongs to the woman herself. So, there is a big difference [between them] regarding the women's fundamental, individual and humanitarian rights. There is no parallelism [between them] on issues such as abortion, virginity, marriage, sexual freedoms, pre-marital sexual intercourse and adultery. An agenda setting could not be achieved regarding these issues.

In addition to feminist and Islamist women, Kurdish women became active and organized actors of the women's movement. Both Islamist and Kurdish feminists criticized the feminist movement as ethnocentric and blind to other identities. The Kurdish women's movement has been organized against Republican nationalism and has become a part of the ethnic Kurdish movement. They have struggled against the male dominance in the Kurdish movement and against the discriminatory parts of their culture and tradition (Diner and Toktaş, 2010).

To sum up, the gender climate that emerged in the early transition period in Russia and the post-military intervention in Turkey paved the way for contrasting discourses with the state-led ideology of women's equality of the previous periods to be voiced as well as for the representation of feminist ideas that aimed at remedying the deficiencies of the early Soviet and Republican gender regimes. The dissolution of the Soviet Union prepared the ground for the rupture with the official Soviet commitment to women's equality. In parallel with demographic decline and moral-national concerns, highly traditional and conservative opinions, which placed an emphasis on biological differences between the sexes, dominated the gender climate and led to the suppression of feminist ideas. The critique of modernizing efforts and the promotion of traditional roles emerged from the state side in early post-Soviet Russia and Putin has reinforced this tendency. Differently, in Turkey, the critique of Republican egalitarian gender policies emerged in feminist and conservative circles within academia and civil society, and then moved to the state level in the following decade. In addition to the emergence of a women's movement from feminist, secular, Islamist and ethnic origins, significant legal and institutional advances to ensure gender equality in different fields were made during this period. Some of these advances encountered attacks or resistance from conservative media, civil society and even the early incarnation of Erdoğan's party and administration, but the political commitment to democratization and EU membership paved the way for the realization of certain goals regarding gender equality. However, the absorption of legal amendments has remained a controversial issue in Turkey, particularly after the AKP government adopted a more conservative stance regarding gender equality from 2007.

Rising Authoritarianism in Russia and Turkey

Despite significant differences in history, system, process and values, the current political regimes of Russia and Turkey show striking similarities. Attempts to classify and compare these regimes in the spectrum of democracy to autocracy have begun to emerge in a wide range of platforms from academic publications to analytical papers, newspapers, periodicals and blogs (see Ellis, 2015; Zizek, 2016). Competitive authoritarianism, electoral authoritarianism and/or hybrid regimes are used to capture the trajectory of regimes in these countries (see Gelman, 2014; Levitsky and Way, 2002). Generally, these definitions characterize civilian regimes, which are not full-scale authoritarian but in which formal rules coexist with informal ones. In these regimes, democratic institutions are viewed as the main tool by which to gain power, and the incumbent power relies on elections to maximize its votes and legitimize its rule, albeit on a highly uneven playing field.

A closer examination of the characteristics of the current political regimes in Russia and Turkey provides crucial insights for understanding the grounds on which the turn towards authoritarianism becomes possible and justified, in reference to the national idea and a set of national values. From the very beginning, the ideology and policies of Putin and Erdoğan have been guided by a set of core values and long-term goals. Their thinking contains a distinctive choice for national identity and global position for contemporary Russia and Turkey. It is possible to trace back their general outlines in the understanding of democracy, the conceptualization of the state and the definition of social unity as well as institutional reforms and policies motivated by the aim of tying the state apparatus to the president and avoiding checks and balances. This has helped to consolidate strong presidential rule in Russia and strong executive power in Turkey until the April 2017 referendum, in which the type of regime was changed from a parliamentary to a presidential system, and then the locus of power de jure moved to the office of president.

In the last few years, a wide range of incidents in domestic and foreign politics have accelerated the consolidation of the authoritarian regimes led by Putin and Erdoğan in Russia and Turkey respectively. With Putin's return to the presidency in 2012 and Erdoğan's third successive victory in the national elections of 2011, both leaders felt their position to be firmly consolidated. However, they also encountered rising dissent, exemplified by the Bolotnaya Square protests and the Gezi movement. In Russia and Turkey, the increasing tension with the West has paved the way for a drift towards authoritarianism in recent years.

The Characteristics of the Political Regime under the Rule of Putin and Erdoğan

In Russia and Turkey, the semi-presidential and presidential systems (after 2017) with free elections and a multi-party system continue to exist, but elections are marked by a lack of fair competition between the contesting parties. Bureaucratic abuses of power and resources, unequal access to financial and media resources and electoral fraud to maximize incumbent votes inhibit fair competition. The liberal features of a political system, including the rule of law, political rights, civil liberties and media freedom, are largely eroded in both countries (Cameron and Orenstein, 2012; Öniş, 2013; Sakwa, 2010; Soyarık, 2012). With the erosion of the separation of powers – the politicization of the judiciary, the increasing power of the executive and then of the presidency, the erosion of parliamentary power – the increasing personalization of rule under Putin and Erdoğan is achieved. Both leaders impose a firm tutelage over the party of power, the bureaucracy and the military through a set of administrative and legal measures. The institutional changes make possible the consolidation of the central authority of the president in Russia and previously of the executive and now of the president's office in Turkey. In Russia, Putin's administration has built up a political monopoly based on the hierarchical subordination of the state apparatus and of the dominant party, whereas the AKP's combination of increasing electoral authoritarianism and neo-patrimonial governance only began to be seriously institutionalized after 2010–2011 (White and Herzog, 2016).

At the time Putin came to power, Russia had been struggling with political, economic and social crises. Under nearly a decade of Yeltsin's leadership, the central power and efficiency of the state had been weakened, due to disorderliness, a power vacuum and undue foreign intervention. The Russian economy had suffered from growing inflation, deficits of consumer goods, lack of investment, foreign currency debt and fiscal crisis. The Russian people were terrified, with a sharp reduction in quality of life, severe poverty, unemployment, increasing criminality, demographic decline and problems in housing, health care and education (Putin, 2003). In this environment, Putin built up his claim for rule in ending political instability and economic crisis, and restoring the greatness of Russia, its territorial integrity and the unity of the Russian people (Putin, 2003). In his first major public statement, a strong state and strong executive power were presented as necessary in order to create the conditions for political stability and order, which were needed for implementing market reforms without leading to a deterioration in the living conditions of the Russian people (Putin, 1999). In addition to a strong state and an efficient economy, Putin promoted the Russian idea, which refers to the unity of Russian society around a set of shared traditional values, including patriotism, belief in the greatness of Russia, statism and social solidarity, and combining these values with universal principles of democracy as a key to Russia's recovery and growth (Putin, 1999). Putin has progressively consolidated an already strong presidential rule by increasing the power of the executive as opposed to the other branches of government under the guise of promoting political stability and economic growth (Hale, 2010; Sakwa, 1997). In his own words, this is 'the first time since the reforms have begun that such favourable conditions have been created for constructive cooperation between the executive and legislative branches of power' (Putin, 1999).

Shortly after his assumption of the presidency, Putin started to implement institutional changes for the centralization of power and to weaken alternative centres of power in politics and ensure that the other parties would pose no threat to the central political power. He initiated a set of institutional changes, with the aim of reducing the autonomy of the regional governors and tying them more tightly with the central power (Person, 2017). In 2000, an administrative restructuring reform, which created seven federal districts to be headed by presidential envoys to reassert central control over the federal agencies, was introduced (McFaul, 2007). The same year, regional governors lost their seats on the Federation Council – the upper house of the Russian parliament. In 2004, after the Beslan hostage crisis and massacre, the gubernatorial elections were abolished and replaced by a central appointment system (Person, 2015). In 2009, some amendments regarding the nomination procedures for governors that transferred nomination powers from the president to the regional parliament were issued by then-President Medvedev. In the wake of the Bolotnaya Square protests in 2011, Medvedev offered a significant concession by proposing the reintroduction of direct elections for governors, and his proposal passed the Duma in June 2012. However, the new proposal does not weaken the authority of the president, who is still able to dismiss governors for corruption, failure to perform their duties or other conflicts of interest (Person, 2015).

Another group of opponents over whom Putin imposed control were the oligarchs, particularly those controlling media outlets who constituted the most significant potential threats to Putin's strong presidential rule. In a famous meeting in July 2000, Putin announced to them that the Kremlin would not interfere in their business activities or renationalize state assets that they had acquired as a result of the questionable privatizations of the 1990s as long as they did not engage in politics or challenge and/or criticize the president (Goldman, 2004). When they did not comply with Putin's rules, he imprisoned several of the oligarchs (such as Mikhail Khodorkovsky and Boris Berezovsky) or drove them into exile and thus completed the establishment of his control over the economic administration.

Putin also moved to curb the power of the Duma, which had existed as a significant locus and centre of power outside the control of the Kremlin. A set of legal amendments and reforms were enacted with the aim of ensuring the Duma would be dominated by the party of power. In 2005, a law was passed that prohibited changing the political party of the Duma deputies and establishing electoral alliances. Under the reforms introduced in 2007, single-member districts were replaced by a system of proportional representation based on party lists. This change made it practically impossible to win a seat in the Duma as an independent deputy. The election threshold was raised from 5 to 7 per cent, and the conditions for political parties to be registered were hardened (Person, 2017, p.52). With the 2013 legal amendments, a mixed system for the Duma was reintroduced, the threshold was reduced to 5 per cent, independent candidates were allowed to be nominated for parliamentary elections, and the criteria for party formation were lowered. However, these amendments would not prevent the larger parties, including United Russia, winning a majority in the Duma through the single-member districts system (Clark, 2013).

Putin served in the office of prime minister from 2008 to 2012 because the 1993 Russian Constitution limits anyone serving in the office of president to two consecutive terms. He transferred the presidential post to Medvedev, who won the election with over 70 per cent of the vote in 2008, and Putin continued to exercise his considerable influence over Russian politics from the post of prime minister from 2008 to 2012. Shortly before the 2011 Duma elections, a very possibly prearranged hand-over of power seemed to happen between Putin and Medvedev, with the former announcing his return for the presidency and the latter nominated for the post of prime minister, if Putin were to win (Clark, 2013). Putin's announcement that he would run for the presidency for a third term and the widespread allegations of electoral fraud in the 2011 Duma elections provoked widespread social protest in Moscow, spreading into other large cities (Chaisty and Whitefield 2013). However, Putin conveniently won the elections with 63.6 per cent of the vote in 2018, albeit with seven million fewer votes than Medvedev in 2008, for the duration of six years, which was extended from four years with the constitutional amendment made in 2008 (Clark, 2013).

As Colton and Hale (2014) find in their analysis of the 2012 Russian Election Studies survey, Putin's regime continued to enjoy the broad support of the electorate in the 2011–12 elections. Despite a notable decrease in Putin's personal image and performance compared to his first and second terms, the 2012 elections showed that Putin's regime 'has survived for so long not only because of its institutional and repressive apparatus, but also because its leaders have managed to forge a set of important connections with its citizenry' (p.20). Putin has cultivated the sense of a lack of a viable political alternative with the necessary experience or knowledge to run the country. Besides, he has managed to establish durable connections with the electorate on the grounds of supporting the continuity of market reforms and relations with the West as an ally, rather than a friend or enemy (p.20). While the promises to provide political stability and achieve economic growth were the main reasons behind Putin's electoral success between 2000 and 2008 (McAllister and White, 2008), as Colton and Hale (2014) underline, the sense of Putin's irreplaceability, combined with his image, personality and performance, has helped him consolidate his personal rule and legitimacy, particularly after 2012.

Turkey faced a new political and economic rupture when the Justice and Development Party (Adalet ve Kalkınma Partisi, AKP), led by Erdoğan, won the national elections held in 2002. The Turkish state and society had gone through a severe decade during the 1990s, characterized by the political instability caused by the coalition governments and economic fluctuations. The rise of political Islam and the Kurdish movement triggered the long-standing security concerns of the Turkish state to protect the secular foundations of the regime and territorial integrity. In 2001, Turkey faced the most severe economic crisis that saw unemployment, poverty and social inequality reach a peak, which led to the introduction of a programme of restructuring state institutions in pursuit of efficiency, accountability and good governance. On the other hand, the European transformation process gained momentum after the declaration of Turkey's candidate status for full membership of the EU in the Helsinki

Summit of December 1999. This decision would lead to the initiation of an extensive democratic reform process and was therefore welcomed by those who were dissatisfied with the strong and politically influential central state for challenging the sociopolitical demands for the liberal principles of freedom, diversity and pluralism.

In this context, the victory of the AKP was welcomed by a large part of Turkish society in the hope that they might establish a strong majority government capable of actualizing political stability, economic growth, the alleviation of poverty, good governance and democratic consolidation (Çınar, 2006; Dağı, 2008; İnsel, 2003). The party accepted full accession to the EU as one of the most important priorities and initiated a series of political and legal reforms to remove the undemocratic features of the regime and prioritize society over the state. To this end, the state security courts were abolished. The government accepted the supremacy of the European Court of Human Rights over domestic jurisdiction in the case of a conflict between Turkish courts and the European Act of Human Rights. With the aim of expanding basic rights and freedoms, the AKP government took significant steps towards addressing the Kurdish question, including the partial extension of language and cultural rights to Kurdish citizens (Keyman and Gumuscu, 2014, pp.49–50). The procedures of banning political parties were hardened. The individual application mechanism to the Constitutional Court was recognized (Constitutional Court of Turkey, n.d.).

The EU's request that Turkish legislation be harmonized with the EU *Acquis* helped the AKP reduce the dominance of the military and judiciary, which had acted as the vanguards of the secular regime against the elected governments (see Cizre, 2004; Karakaya and Özhabeş, 2013; Müftüler-Baç, 2011). The civil-military relations were reordered, with the aim of reducing the institutional power of the military in the governmental decision-making process. In Turkish political history, the military has acted as the vanguard of the West-oriented and secular regime against religion and ethnic identity, which are treated as a threat to state power and unity. After the first military intervention of 1960, the National Security Council was established to keep the elected politicians in line with secularism and nationalism. The realm of authority of the council was expanded from security issues to education after the 1980 military intervention. With the Ergenekon and Balyoz trials, in which hundreds of retired and serving high-ranking military personnel, including the former chief of the general staff Ilker Başbuğ, were charged with planning a coup against the government, the AKP considerably undermined the political legitimacy of the military (Esen and Gumuscu, 2016, pp.1584–5).

With regard to the judiciary, the AKP redesigned the organization of the higher courts with the constitutional amendments of 2010. These amendments, consisting of twenty-five articles, were adopted by the parliament and then submitted to a constitutionally mandatory referendum. The package was passed with a 58 per cent majority in the referendum of 12 September 2010. The power and composition of the Constitutional Court, and of the High Council of Judges and Public Prosecutors (*Hakimler ve Savcılar Yüksek Kurulu*, HSYK), were changed to break the predominance of mostly secular judges and were made more autonomous and resistant to the encroachments of the executive (Özbudun, 2015).

However, the new structure of the high judiciary turned into a challenge for the AKP government when its alliance with the Gülen movement started to show signs of cracking (Özbudun, 2015). The Gülen movement is one of the most influential religious communities in Turkey. It is headed by a preacher, Fettullah Gülen, who has lived in the United States since 1999. The community has no official name but is usually referred to as the Service Movement (*Hizmet Hareketi*). The community conducts transnational religious, social and economic activities in the fields of education, media, publishing and other business sectors all over Turkey and in the world. The movement established close relations with the centre-right parties in the 1980s and 1990s. After 2002, the movement and the AKP joined forces to lead Turkey politically, populate its bureaucracy and subjugate the overactive military to civilian control. While the AKP has been governing the country, the Gülen supporters have increasingly entrenched themselves in the civil service, police force, prosecutors' offices, judiciary and even in the middle ranks of the military. In 2013, the Gülenist prosecutors opened an investigation against three members of the cabinet, their sons and some senior bureaucrats for corruption-related charges involving Erdoğan and his family as well (Özbudun 2014). Afterwards, new legislation was issued regarding the structure of the HSYK that would limit the powers of the Council and strengthen the role of the Ministry of Justice as its president in order to avoid any legal or criminal investigation being launched without Erdoğan's permission as well as whittling away the Gülenists' influence in the judiciary (Cizre, 2014; Özbudun, 2015).

Another challenge of the AKP is the presidency, a critical post in the balance of power between the secular establishment and the government. In 2007, Erdoğan made one of the AKP's founding leaders, Abdullah Gül, be elected as the president of the Republic, despite a serious crisis with the military and widespread social resentment. The widespread resentment in the secular segments of state and society became obvious with the announcement of Abdullah Gül as the AKP's candidate for presidency. The military released an official warning to the government via the internet, which later became known as the e-memorandum, to keep in line with secularism. The opposition groups organized large demonstrations, called Republican Meetings, against the anti-secularist tendencies of the AKP. In the same year, the election system regarding the presidency was changed in order that the president should be directly elected by popular vote rather than by parliament. In 2014, on his election as the first plebiscitarian president, Erdoğan empowered his political legitimacy and expanded the scope of presidential power de facto. In the previous system, the president of the Republic had been a more symbolic position with limited veto power over the legislative activities in the Turkish parliamentary system and had no executive power when Erdoğan was elected to the presidency in 2014. He developed a new position himself, in his own terms that of 'executive president', and relied in his violations of legal and constitutional terms on being the representative of the people (Selçuk 2016). Afterwards, Erdoğan initiated a regime change from a parliamentary to a presidential regime. With the presidential referendum held in 2017, executive authority was transferred to the president, while the sphere of authority of parliament was to shrink and the independence of the judiciary was to be seriously harmed (Esen and Gumuscu, 2017a; Öztürk and Gözaydın, 2017). In the national elections of 2018, Erdoğan achieved a decisive victory, winning the elections with 53 per cent of the vote and gaining vastly expanded authority over parliament and the executive.

While consolidating his party's power in the state apparatus, Erdoğan focused on the administration and ranks of the party in order to ensure his personal rule. At the beginning of its political venture, the AKP identified intra-party democracy, which is a feature lacking in political parties in Turkey, as a principle in the party programme. The decision-making mechanism, with significant leadership from the founding members of the party, had a pluralistic and collegial structure with the participation of other influential members who held the key ministries. Erdoğan, Abdullah Gül and Bülent Arınç left the Felicity Party (*Fazilet Partisi*) over their dissatisfaction with the party's pro-Islamist discourse and anti-globalization economic policies and established the AKP. All these figures wielded nearly equal influence, had their own followers within the ranks of the party and played a crucial role of balancing Erdoğan as the party leader. However, Erdoğan gradually sidelined them and their followers in the party administration, within the ranks of the party and in the cabinet before the 2011 national elections (Cornell, 2014). In the post-2011 period, Erdoğan established his one-man rule by cleansing the party and the cabinet of alternative or critical voices and replacing them with completely loyal figures, who do not transgress the boundaries of Erdoğan's vision (Taş, 2015).

In 2016, a group of mid-level military officers, allegedly from the Gülen movement, engaged in an armed coup against the Erdoğan government. But Erdoğan successfully defeated the coup attempt through the popular mobilization of his supporters, and with the support of the political opposition and media (Esen and Gumuscu, 2017b). After the failure of the coup, a state of emergency was declared that enabled the government to take anti-democratic measures. Erdoğan had governed the country with legislative decrees from 2016 till the end of the national elections of 2018, circumventing the checks and balances of parliament. Mass arrests and prosecutions of alleged Gülen supporters from the military, the judiciary, the bureaucracy, academia and the press began. The failed coup presented Erdoğan with a national cause – that the coup had targeted the president as the real representative of the nation – to legitimize anti-democratic measures, consolidating authoritarianism. This cause was also confirmed in a national public opinion survey conducted by KONDA in 2016, which reported that 43.6 per cent of the respondents thought the failed coup had been an attempt to overthrow the president (KONDA, 2016).

The Conceptualization of Democracy: Sovereign Democracy versus Conservative Democracy

Scrutinizing the conceptualization of democracy and state sovereignty in Putin and Erdoğan's discourse helps to determine (1) how they have aligned some values of liberal democracy with the consolidation of authoritarian tendencies and (2) how the conceptualization of democracy paves the way for basing authoritarian tendencies on national authenticity as a source of legitimacy. The distinctive feature of their conceptualization of democracy is the conformity with historical traditions. The focus placed on historical traditions and cultural authenticity in their conceptualization of democracy provides the ground for creating a nationalist narrative, upon which authoritarianism would rely by using the references of 'the will of the people', 'real representative of the people' and 'the majority of the people'. Authoritarian policies and interventions, which are justified by references to long-standing traditions, including paternalism, state sovereignty, social unity and a majoritarian understanding of democracy, would find their sources in the historical traditions of Russia and Turkey.

From the outset, both leaders have been against the imposition of the Western model of democracy, which it is claimed ignores the cultural authenticity of Russia and Turkey. They have proposed a synthesis between a market economy, historical traditions and cultural authenticity (including the religious traditions) of Russia and Turkey (see Trenin, 2007). In Russia, this synthesis is built upon the normative validity of state sovereignty as a long-standing tradition of Russia (state-dominant modernization) and Russian paternalism, while in Turkey it is based on challenging the Western-oriented secular elites (including the military, bureaucracy and judiciary), on the presumed dichotomy between Islam and modernity, and on the national will.

In the first two terms of his presidency (until 2008), Putin did not appeal to traditional values as a guide to ideology and policy-making in politics, economy, culture and foreign politics. His electoral success depended on the sustainable provision of political stability, economic growth and rising standards of living (McAllister and White 2008). However, Putin's ideology, from the very beginning, has contained a core of conservative traditionalism, which provides insights into the distinctive identity, position and trajectory that Putin casts for contemporary Russia. In his first major public statement, 'Russia at the Turn of the Millennium', he focused on the economic and political problems facing Russia on its way towards the transition to a market economy and democracy, while warning against importing 'abstract models and schemes taken from foreign textbooks' (Putin 1999). He argued that 'every country, Russia included, has to search for its own way of renewal. We have not been very successful in this respect thus far [...] We can pin hopes for a worthy future only if we prove capable of combining the universal principles of a market economy and democracy with Russian realities' (Putin, 1999). On several occasions, Putin has asserted that Russia has made a choice in favour of democracy and that the basic principles of democracy have universal validity, while consistently repeating that the development of democracy depends on the historical specificities of any given country and democratic rules and institutions must be adapted to Russian conditions, values and traditions (Putin, 2005a, b, c).

In Putin's discourse, a strong state and the centralization of power constitute important features of Russian reality and tradition (Putin, 2003). State sovereignty constitutes the backbone of the Russian way of developing and strengthening democracy. According to Putin, 'from the very beginning, Russia was created as a super-centralized state. That's practically laid down in its genetic code, its traditions, and the mentality of its people' (Putin quoted in Evans, 2008, p.904).

> We believe, and I personally believe, that the implementation and the strengthening of democracy on Russian soil should not compromise the concept of democracy. It

should strengthen statehood and it should improve people's lives […] democracy is not anarchy. It is not a licence to do as you please or to rob the people of any country. Democracy is, among other things, and first and foremost, the possibility to democratically make democratic laws and the capability of the state to enforce those laws (Putin 2005c).

In Putin's view, Russia should undertake a unique path of development because it is a Eurasian civilization, neither European nor Asian but superior to the West (Kuzio, 2015). Russia is framed as a unique Eurasian civilization, which draws its national strength from the Russian people, language and culture, religion and traditional values as opposed to Western ones (Nechemias, 2016). In his understanding, the model of democracy which would suit Russia well has to arise from the national traditions and moral values of the country (Anderson, 2007). In order to restore the national strength and pride of Russia, which is claimed to have been eroded in the previous decade, Putin made a feature of the idea of national authenticity and relied on the Orthodox Church as a major ally to bolster social cohesion, morality and citizenship (see Papkova, 2011). To this end, he promoted an articulation based on patriotism, tradition and moral values in pursuit of the spiritual and moral restoration of Russia, and fostered this with the help of Orthodox teachings about traditional values, morality, nationalism and anti-Westernism (Anderson, 2007; Verhovsky, 2002).

An attempt was made to formulate Putin's ideas as an ideology by Vladimir Surkov, a prominent member of Putin's administration, and this was presented under the concept of sovereign democracy in February 2006.[1] Putin and Medvedev carefully distanced themselves from the concept but there is a considerable convergence between the ideas comprising sovereign democracy and Putin's ideas (Robinson, 2017, n1). Sovereign democracy has become a code to represent Russia's challenging the export of the Western model and demanding international recognition for its own form of rule (Surkov, 2007). As Okara (2007) states, sovereign democracy carries two messages from the United Russia party to Russian society. On the one hand, it says that the party in power commands state power and sovereignty, and derives its sources of legitimacy from Russian traditions and culture, unlike the pro-Western 'guided democracy' of the Yeltsin era. On the other hand, it says that sovereign democracy and the party in power, as its real representative, will guarantee the sovereignty and survival of Russia against the threats of globalization and external enemies. This understanding is quite consistent with Putin's general view of modernization and democracy, which prescribes for the state a greater role and control in managing the destructive impact of globalization on historical traditions and culture (see Wallander cited in Evans, 2008, p.902). The preservation of traditional values is also stressed as protecting the uniqueness of Russia's state-dominant civilization as opposed to the damaging effects of cultural globalization (Robinson, 2017, pp.13–14).

The concept of sovereign democracy presents illiberal features and authoritarian tendencies as part of the longstanding Russian political culture: a sovereign, unifying national idea, the will of the people, and collectivity versus individuality. In this model of democracy, which is characterized by Kazantsev (2007) as a form of collective democracy, people, nation and state constitute an organic unity and presidential power is assigned as the real representative of the will of the people. In this framework, any kind of opposition can be stigmatized under the slogan of 'respect the will of the people', which allows presidential power to leave no room for pluralism and to justify its interventions in the daily lives of the people. The advocacy of a specific model of democracy should be considered against the backdrop of the contemporary Russian debate. Because of the difficult experiences of the 1990s, good governance and democracy generally carry the same meaning as disorder and instability for the populace (Hutcheson and Petersson, 2016, p.1110).

Choosing Russia's 'own' way of implementing democracy consistent with Russian specificities has popular support. According to many public surveys conducted by VTsIOM, one of the leading public survey companies, Yeltsin's term is mainly identified with crisis, instability and disorder, while Putin's term is seen as having ended the turbulent years, increased economic welfare and established order, prosperity and greatness (VTsIOM, 2016; 2015). Even in a recent Levada Centre survey of 2015 almost half of respondents said that Russia needs a special kind of democracy consistent with Russia's national traditions, when asked 'what kind of democracy Russia needs' (cited in Willerton, 2017). In another survey conducted by the Levada Centre in 2012, the respondents identified economic and political stability and strengthening order as more important than democracy, freedom of speech, religion, movement and association, and reform (Levada Centre 2012).

In Turkey, the AKP emerged from the ranks of political Islam but, despite its pro-Islamist origins and National Outlook Action legacy, the party leaders rejected the idea that the AKP relied on Islam for its political ideology and that it is a religious party. Rather, the AKP claimed itself to be the new heir of a centre-right identity and positioned itself on the centre right of the political spectrum (see Coşar and Özman, 2004; Hale, 2006; Öniş and Keyman, 2003). The AKP identified itself as an economically liberal and socially conservative centre-right party that supported state reform, anti-corruption measures, democratization, social justice and membership of the European Union. This identity claim was based on a synthesis between the liberal market and community/tradition-based norms (Keyman and Gumuscu, 2014).

During the early years of power, the leading members of the AKP rejected any attribution of Muslim democrat and identified the party as conservative democrat (Hürriyet, 2005b). The party's core values were formulated under the concept of conservative democracy by Yalçın Akdoğan, the advisor to then-Prime Minister Erdoğan (see Akdoğan, 2004). According to Özbudun (2006), this concept was created more as an image than as a political ideology. Yavuz (2009) stated that this concept is formulated to create new imagined political roots with the centre-right political parties and to distance the AKP itself from earlier pro-Islamist parties. It was suggested that the AKP, with this concept, was hoping to gain support from the United States and the EU as well as to overcome any criticism or suspicion about the party's alleged/hidden anti-secularism among secular state elites (pp.88–9).

It would not be incorrect to say that, by means of conservative democracy, the AKP was seeking to reconcile universally accepted liberal values with the cultural and religious roots of the Turkish identity and value system. As Erdoğan (2006) himself stated, we are bringing about a new concept [conservative democracy] not in an abstract manner, but also in a concrete manner. ... A significant part of Turkish society desires to adopt a concept of modernity that does not reject tradition, a belief in universalism that accepts localism, an understanding of rationalism that does not disregard the spiritual meaning of life, and a choice for change that is not fundamentalist. Conservative democracy is an answer to the desires of Turkish people.

With the democratic aspect, the party indicated the significance of liberal values, such as democracy, the rule of law, popular sovereignty, fundamental rights and freedoms, limited government, pluralism and tolerance of diversity (Akdoğan, 2006, pp.50–1). In the Development and Democratization Programme of the AKP, democracy is conceptualized as the manifestation of popular sovereignty via elections, the *sine qua non* of individual rights and liberties, and a regime of tolerance (AKP Kalkınma ve Demokratikleşme Programı, 2002). As Dağı (2005) stated, under the strong opposition of the secular state elites to the Islamists, the party realized that the 'legitimising power and the virtue of democracy ... turned out to be a means to highlight people power vis-à-vis state power' (p.31). The emphasis on the common values of Turkish society versus the Turkish state's ideology is reflected in Erdoğan's remarks as follows: 'the ideal is not to have a mechanical democracy that is reduced to elections and certain institutions, but an organic democracy that pervades the administrative, social, and political fields. We refer to this – we coined a new term for it – we refer to this as "deep democracy"' (Erdoğan 2006). The AKP believed that the national will can be sovereign only if a pluralist and participatory democracy is established, in which political rights including freedom of expression and the right to live according to one's beliefs can be freely exercised (Hale and Özbudun, 2010, p.20).

The AKP's conservatism is expressed in the references to family values, the Ottoman past and Islam as a moral system in the definition of national identity and public good.[2] The party relies on a particular understanding of the Turkish nation – that it is a Sunni, ethnic-Turk homogenous entity, bounded by religio-communal values and a glorified Ottoman past. This organic understanding of society excludes cultural, ethnic, religious and class differences, and envisages the state as the guardian of religio-national values in the face of the challenges of globalization (Yavuz, 2009, p.100). The conservative discourse of the party challenges the Kemalist-secular modernization paradigm. It advocates in its place further political and economic integration with the EU while empowering the traditional and religious norms and values (Keyman and Gumuscu, 2014, p.42). On the other hand, the conservative aspect touches on the preservation and reproduction of the values that are assumed to form the identity of Turkish society (Coşar and Özman, 2004, p.63). In Erdoğan's vision, 'a religiously-imbued nationalism' (Coşar, 2012, p.80), which takes religion as a moral value system, is capable of representing all segments of Turkish society, regardless of ethnic, class and gender differences. This line of thinking also includes a perception of the West as an imperial power, devoid of justice and modesty (see Tuğal, 2009), which carries the possibility of confrontation with the norms and values represented by the EU.

The commonly held national identity and national values (*milli değerler*), framed by tradition and religious values, are presumed to be constructive to social peace and a pluralistic environment (Akdoğan, 2004, pp.70–1). This understanding presumes an organic unity between state and society (Turkish nation), and therefore defines political activity as the revelation of the national will and a consensual platform that excludes any conflict (Coşar and Özman, 2004, p.63). As Erdoğan claimed, the AKP replaced the notion of politics based on conflict with a new one based on reconciliation and compromise (Hale and Özbudun, 2010, p.25). However, the conflict mentioned here refers not to those related to ethnic, religious, regional and class divisions within society, but to the gap that emerged between state and nation (society) because of imposing a top-down Kemalist ideology over the people without considering their values (Tepe, 2005). In the AKP's discourse, the national will (*milli irade*) is placed above all else and the AKP is its genuine representative. Erdoğan and the other leading members of the party have always appealed to the national will by broadly stating that 'the national will shall be manifested', 'there is no will superior to that of the nation', or 'respect the national will' (BBC Türkçe, 2015; Birgün, 2015). By doing so, the AKP promotes conservative democracy as the method of filling this alleged gap, and uniting state and nation in both political and cultural terms.

This sort of understanding of democracy has in turn been confined to a narrow vision of democracy, based on an extreme understanding of majoritarianism and harmonious unity, and implies a decisive failure of the liberal democratic values of individualism, freedom and recognition of difference (see Coşar and Yeğenoğlu, 2011; Öniş, 2015; Yavuz, 2009). This controversy has paved the way to justifying authoritarian tendencies in recent years when the party has consolidated its majority in the parliament and electoral hegemony. This kind of rule has created excessive polarization and a deepening mistrust between those who form the majority, and therefore benefit excessively from the policies of the ruling party, and the others who feel increasingly excluded, unfairly treated and marginalized by the discourse and policies of the AKP (Öniş, 2015).

The Changing Course of Relations with the West

In both Russia and Turkey, the way that the West is treated and the changing course of relations with Western countries constitute another fault line in the drift of the regimes towards authoritarianism around a nationalist narrative. Both Putin and Erdoğan have relied on their conceptualization of democracy in justifying their counter-conduct against the West and stressing of nationalist sentiments, which has combined with their determination to stay in power. However, we should recall that Erdoğan's motives for establishing relations with the West in his early years in power were different from those of Putin. Erdoğan identified full accession to the EU as a priority and continued the process of reform, which had already begun under the previous government, to meet the requirements for accession. Despite the nationalist reactions to EU membership, Erdoğan embraced the goal of political and economic integration with the West while preserving cultural authenticity and adopting conservative democracy at a discursive level. As a result of a loss of motivation concerning democratization efforts and the uneven relations (ups-and-downs) with the West, the government has tended to establish much closer relations with Middle Eastern and African countries, on the basis of Ottoman heritage and religious identity. In contrast, Putin has been circumspect in approaching and establishing ties with the West from the very beginning. His approach to the West is motivated by a desire to insulate domestic politics from Western influence and is characterized by a lack of hesitation to confront the West at the cost of international sanctions.

Putin has diverted Russia from the Western course followed by Gorbachev and Yeltsin. Instead, he has advocated following a more suitable path that should come from the unique cultural traditions and historical trajectory of Russia. Yeltsin and Gorbachev, notwithstanding their many differences, had similar conceptions of Western Europe and Western experience of social democracy as providing a model for normalizing the political and economic system in Russia. Gorbachev attempted to westernize Soviet institutions and to urge the party to become a medium for the transition to social democracy. Yeltsin's conception attached greater weight to democracy than socialism and started a programme of change to bring the features of Western democracy and capitalism to Russia (Zimmerman, 2014).

Putin has never refrained from repeating that Russia is historically a European country that shared common values and experiences with the other European countries and 'passed through the same stages of establishing democratic, legal, and civic institutions' (Putin quoted in Evans, 2008, p.901). He preserved this attitude during his presidential rally in 2012 by saying 'Russia is an inalienable and organic part of greater Europe and European civilisation. Our citizens feel European. We are not indifferent to developments in United Europe' (Putin, 2012b). In Putin's view, establishing closer links with the West is essential for preserving Russia's economic, political and military strength in a highly competitive global era. However, his intentions are limited to economic integration and are not motivated by sharing the political values of Western democracies (see Trenin, 2007). A dual dynamic, as summarized by Tsygankov (2015), shaped the course of Russia's relations with Western countries: developing strong ties with them but at the same time aspiring for recognition for their own values, which are culturally distinct from Western ones and not acceptable for the modern world in Western eyes.

In his first term, Putin did not oppose the United States over the expansion of NATO, although he saw it as threatening Russia's national security, and sought for collaboration with Western countries on the common goals of counter-terrorism (Tsygankov, 2015). After 2004, Russia's stance towards the West started to turn into a challenge to the influence of Western leadership, which assumes its values to be universal but combines them with its own power ambitions in international affairs and its status as the 'moral authority', as Trenin (2007) states. Various reasons can be given for this. Under Putin, Russia has challenged the unipolar international order and staked a claim to equal status with the United States and the European Union in international affairs. In addition, it has sought to restore its position of power in the former Soviet space against the aspirations of, in particular, Georgia, Moldova and Ukraine to establish closer relations with Europe (Averre, 2007; Flenley, 2008; Gretskiy et al., 2014; Haukkala, 2008). Within this broader context, the expansion of the EU and NATO towards the western borders of Russia stimulated the perception that the Western countries had hostile intentions towards Russia. These attempts were seen as constraining Russia and targeting its national security (Putin 2008). Also, the growing European criticism of the Russian political regime for its deficiencies of democracy and liberal values stimulated the Cold War perception of the West as a hostile power (Shlapentokh 2007). At the G8 Summit in St Petersburg in 2006, Putin admitted that Russian democracy was still evolving but rejected any kind of external interference in the domestic affairs of the country. He criticized the Western countries for treating Russia as a country 'to be led' and trying to play a civilizing role towards Russia under the name of democratization and democracy (Putin, 2006b, c). Another factor initiating the tension, as Kramer argues, was Russia's obsession with the colour revolutions taking place in Georgia, Ukraine and Kyrgyzstan. From then on, Russian attitudes and foreign policies towards the West were considerably motivated to counter the spillover of Western-supported revolutionary demands over the whole region, which would undermine Russia's role and status (Kramer, 2014). The Western countries were also accused of encouraging the liberal opposition in Russia under the guise of spreading democracy in order to change the regime, as seen in Ukraine and Georgia (Shlapentokh, 2007).

Russia shifted from having a defensive position vis-à-vis Western countries, which was formulated as sovereign democracy during the first Putin era, to an aggressive position with Russia staking a historical claim in post-Soviet regions. Against this backdrop, Russia's internal values, particularly sovereignty, combined with its security interests, started to influence its foreign policy priorities in establishing relations with its neighbours and Western countries. The concept of sovereignty has been used as a response to Western criticism of the regime in Russia as well as a reference point for establishing legitimacy for Russia's assertive foreign policy choices (Putin, 2008, 2012b, 2013b, 2014a). As Riabova and Riabov summarize, 'sovereignty is seen as an opportunity for Russia to decide its own fate, [...] to make it a subject rather than an object in world politics, to lay claim to a measure of self-sufficiency' (p.27). Within this framework, Russia defended its support for the separatist movements of South Ossetia and Abkhazia and then recognizing them as independent states on the grounds of sovereignty and self-determination (Allison, 2009). The annexation of Crimea was also framed as national defence against the alliance of hostile powers to restore control in its historical territories (Rogov, 2015, p.102). The pro-European orientation of Ukraine and social demands for democratization, inspired by Western values and funded by Western money, was seen by the Kremlin as bringing about instability and a loss in Russia's sovereignty in its sphere of influence (Laruelle, 2015).

In Turkey, during the AKP rule, the global, regional and intercultural role that Turkey would play because of its historical legacies and geopolitical position has been largely emphasized (Öniş and Yılmaz, 2009). The party has followed a pro-active foreign policy and diversified the strict pro-Western Kemalist/Republican orientation by enhancing regional and global engagements with the Middle East, Africa, Central and Far Asia and Caucasus (Altunişik and Martin, 2011). Based on the formula of 'zero problems with the neighbours', Turkey aimed to remove all sources of tensions with its immediate neighbours, including Armenia, Greece, Syria, Iraq and Iran (Gultekin-Punsmann, 2010). The changes in Turkey's foreign policy have become visible in increased multilateralism in policy formulations and increased reliance on diplomatic tools and economic measures, such as trade and capital flows, instead of the use of force motivated by security concerns (Müftüler-Baç, 2011).

During its early years of government, prospective membership of the EU was the main engine of democratization as well as a path of deeper integration with global markets by the AKP. For Erdoğan, in conformity with the concept of conservative democracy, Turkey was aiming for 'a local-oriented stance in a globalising world' under the rule of the AKP. Turkey would set a good example that demonstrated the possibility of synthesizing universal values of participatory democracy, the rule of law, freedom and pluralism with the local features of a predominantly Muslim country (Erdoğan cited in Alpan, 2016, p.18).

The indications of a shift from a firm to a loose commitment to Europeanization started to emerge towards the mid-point of the first AKP government (Aydın-Düzgit, 2016; Müftüler-Baç, 2011). This loosening in connection with fulfilling accession to the EU had several reasons of domestic and EU origin. On the EU side, some of the EU's key decisions had led to disappointment within the government and among the public. In 2004, the European Court of Human Rights (ECHR) had not decided to overturn the headscarf ban at universities and public offices.[3] The EU had failed to keep its promises to Northern Cyprus in return for playing a positive role towards a peaceful resolution of the Cyprus conflict and in 2004 accepted South Cyprus as an EU member under the name of the Republic of Cyprus. In addition, the negotiations with Turkey were partially stopped, as Turkey did not accept opening its ports to the Republic of Cyprus (Öniş, 2009). Another factor was related to EU conditionality. After the last wave of enlargement in 2007, the EU has been undergoing a European identity and economic crisis. The EU's tendency towards self-withdrawal combined with rising Islamophobia and nationalist populism has resulted in the prevailing feeling of otherization and exclusion in Turkey (Scott and Houtum, 2009).

Against this backdrop, combined with the electoral hegemony of Erdoğan, Turkey's increasing economic strength and Erdoğan's increasing international prestige, the EU as a normative political context and an indispensable goal has lost its soft power over Turkey while continuing to be a significant narrative (Alpan, 2016, pp.21–4; Aydın-Düzgit and Kaliber, 2016). Particularly after the 2011 electoral victory, Erdoğan and the AKP governments have counteracted the EU's criticisms about their authoritarian tendencies and violations of fundamental rights and freedoms on the basis of non-interference in the domestic affairs of Turkey, European hypocrisy, external forces, Islamophobia and national security (Al Jazeera Turk, 2014; T24, 2013; Yeni Şafak, 2016).

The problems with the EU, combined with the pro-active and multilateral strategy of the AKP, have led to the increasing diversification of Turkish foreign policy, particularly towards the Middle East (Öniş, 2012). The ambitions for regional leadership and a mediating role in Middle Eastern affairs have been apparent in the deterioration of Turkish–Israeli relations after the Gaza War (2008–9), the favourable treatment of Iran in nuclear disarmament negotiations, open contacts with Hamas, increasingly close relations with Syria, and active involvement in the Arab Spring and the Syrian civil war (Aktürk, 2017; Altunişik and Martin, 2011). The increasing emphasis on developing relations with the Middle East has not signified a complete change of objectives and a reorientation from the West, as Turkey's attraction to the Arab world is largely related to its EU membership, democratization process and economic dynamism (Öniş, 2012). Conversely, the historical, cultural and economic assets that Turkey seems to possess regarding the region have been emphasized in the EU's further engagement with the Middle East (Öniş, 2011). Yet, the increasing emphasis on developing relations with the Middle East still represents an important transformation, showing that Turkey has become more independent of its Western allies in foreign policy (Altunişik and Martin, 2011) and has opted to place more emphasis on Islamic and Eastern aspects of Turkish national identity as well as on the Ottoman legacy (Oğuzlu, 2008). The commonly held belief within the high ranks of the party after 2011 is that Turkey, as the inheritor of the Ottoman Empire, holds a particular responsibility for the normalization of the Middle East history by strengthening democracy and economic restoration and restoring regional integration on the basis of Ottoman identity (Başkan, 2017).

Confronting the cultural and moral superiority of the West prompts national pride and self-confidence in both Russia and Turkey. Both countries have been trying to be a part of Europe for centuries but are not recognized as necessarily European. In the eyes of the public, the international status of Russia has been largely characterized as a country that lost the Cold War and became dependent on foreign aid in the 1990s (Riabova and Riabov, 2014, p.27). Turkey has been seen as a country waiting at the gate of Europe for decades. In Turkey, public opinion surveys conducted by Kadir Has University in 2016 and 2017 point to the increasing tiredness and despair of the Turkish public regarding the prospect of EU membership. The support for EU membership decreased from 66.7 per cent in 2016 to 48.4 per cent in 2017 (Kadir Has Üniversitesi, 2016). Those who think that Turkey will never become an EU member state increased from 47.6 per cent in 2015 to 81.3 per cent in 2017 (Kadir Has Üniversitesi, 2017). The confrontation with the West has the effect of restoring the feeling of exclusion widespread in both Russian and Turkish society and inspiring a feeling of self-sufficiency and in favour of self-determination.

Social Dissent: The Bolotnaya Protests and Pussy Riot, and the Gezi Movement

The furthest fault line of authoritarian consolidation in recent years has been the deepening disconnect between the regime and civil society following the rise in social dissent in both Russia and Turkey (Rogov, 2015). Protest movements have broken out in both countries, despite the considerable popularity and electoral support of Putin and Erdoğan. In Russia, after the disputed elections of 2011, large-scale street protests, known as the Bolotnaya Square protests, broke out in Moscow with demands for fair elections and honest government, which Putin and his administration were accused of ruining. The government counteracted the protestors with a repressive strategy, police brutality and mass arrests (Luhn, 2014; Smyth, Sobolev and Soboleva, 2013). A few months later, a feminist rock group known as Pussy Riot protested against Putin's regime and its alliance with the Orthodox Patriarch in the Cathedral of Christ the Saviour in February 2012. The band members were arrested for religious hatred and hooliganism (Johnson and Novitskaya, 2016, p.224; Rutland, 2014). But Pussy Riot was a feminist reaction to the increasing misogyny and masculinity in Putin's politics that had emboldened the Orthodox Church to stand for anti-feminism, and produced sexist and homophobic policies (Johnson, 2014). In Turkey, the Gezi movement began as a civil environmental protest in 2013 but soon spread across the country and turned into an anti-regime protest, in response to the use of extensive police violence against the protestors.

In both cases, the protestors were accused of having been mobilized by the Western powers and were demonized as unpatriotic, targetting not the leaders themselves but the Russian and Turkish states' sovereignty and power (Göçer-Akder and Özdemir, 2015; Smyth and Soboleva, 2014; White, 2014). In his speech at the rally on the eve of presidential elections, Putin (2012d) said: 'we showed that no one can impose their will on us. Not anyone, and not in any form. We showed that our people know how to distinguish between the desire for change and renewal, and political provocations that pursue the sole objective of undermining Russia's statehood and usurping power.' In a similar vein, Erdoğan blamed an international conspiracy for the Gezi protests by inventing fictitious enemies called the 'interest rate lobby' and using a vague notion of 'outside forces' (Al Monitor, 2013). He used the compelling argument of an international plot against Turkey when an investigation into some ministers and senior bureaucrats for alleged corruption was initiated in December 2013. In his own words, 'there are extremely dirty alliances in this set-up, dark alliances that can't tolerate the new Turkey, the big Turkey' (Reuters, 2013).

Both leaders felt for the first time the legitimacy of their regimes being under threat, with increasing social unrest, mobilization and resistance. These crises led to the consolidation of authoritarianism as the governments tightened state control over the media, social media and civil society activism, and took coercive measures against the protestors. Under the guise of state security, anti-terrorism, social psychology and child protection, tight state control by legal regulations was imposed over social media (YouTube, Twitter, VKontakte) and civil society organizations. In Russia, the most notable legal development is a law, issued in 2013, forcing NGOs that receive foreign funds to register as foreign agents. Other regulations include the Dima Yakovlev Act, enacted in response to the Magnitsky Act in the United States, the anti-extremism legislation that gives law enforcement agencies additional powers and mechanisms to suppress social dissent, the Liberal Act, the Official Secrets Act, the Internet Restriction Bill (On Protecting Children from Information Harmful to Their Health and Development) and the recent legal amendments that tighten internet restrictions by prohibiting the use of internet proxy services, which provided internet users with access to blocked content (Radio Free Europe/Radio Liberty, 2017).

Similarly, in Turkey, two important bills that securitize dissent were passed following the Gezi protests. In February 2014, legal amendments were issued to the

Internet Law No 5651 that expand the jurisdiction of the government-controlled Telecommunications Authority (TIB) over websites and decrease judicial oversight over its decisions. In March 2015, the Internal Security Package that increases police authority during protests and limits the need for court approval of police searches, detention and phone-tapping was passed in the Turkish parliament. In the same year, a document that defines acts of civil disobedience, protest and social media activism encouraging dissent as threats to national security was adopted by the National Security Council.

In both cases, the government controls have been supplemented with expanding surveillance over the media via mass firings, media blackouts, disciplining the mainstream media, buying off media moguls, imprisonment of journalists and securitization of journalism by legal regulations. The owners and/or editorial teams of major media groups have been replaced by individuals who are more loyal and acquiescent towards the leaders and regimes in both countries. In social media, paid bloggers, known as trolls, have taken to performing aggressive campaigns to discredit any criticism of the regime as betraying and/or being harmful to the country. In the state-aligned media, the framing of Russia as a united, Orthodox and conservative nation, and the opponents as a minority that sow discord among the nation, has increased (Yablokov, 2014).

Within this context, both leaders have started to depend on a narrative based on national authenticity, traditional values and religion to justify an assertive foreign policy and to restrict media independence and civil society activism. In Putin's and Erdoğan's discourses, all opposition figures are dehumanized, demonized and excluded from the Russian or Turkish nation respectively. The conception of the Russian and Turkish nations ostracizes anti-government groups. Authoritarian measures restricting fundamental rights are presented as protecting national authenticity, traditional values and religion from the 'others' within and beyond state borders. Their nationalist and conservative narrative leaves no legitimate room for political opposition and social dissent and helps consolidate the legitimacy of the authoritarian regimes by showing that the leaders have the support of the majority.

4

The Rise of Sexism in Political Discourse

In the last few years, there has been a declining trend for gender equality in Russia and Turkey. According to the Global Gender Gap Reports (2007, 2012, 2017), published annually by the World Economic Forum, Russia was ranked 45 out of 128 countries included in the index in 2007 and dropped to 59 out of 135 in 2012 and 71 out of 144 in 2017, while Turkey dropped from 121 out of 128 in 2007 to 124 out of 135 in 2012 and 131 out of 144 in 2017. According to the report, there is a degree of gender equality in Russia apart from political empowerment, while Turkey is in a considerably lower position than Russia in economic empowerment, educational attainment and health. The evident disappointment with gender equality in both Russia and Turkey is not unrelated to the consolidation of authoritarian politics around a nationalist and conservative political discourse. Despite the abundance of differences, the regimes in Russia and Turkey show striking parallels in drifting towards authoritarianism, accompanied by the concurrent revival of traditional gender discourse and the related decline in the pursuit of progressive policies for gender equality.

In Russia and Turkey, where state ideology and mechanisms are strong but different, political authorities use gender categories as an important strategy for governing and mobilizing society through certain symbols and premises. Despite their structural differences and divergent views, the two countries produce similar discourses and policy outcomes regarding women's rights and gender (in)equality in accordance with the prevalent political context. After the Soviet and Republican revolutions, the newly established regimes embraced a state-led ideology of women's equality as part of divergent but modernizing views. This ideology became an important tool that helped the new regimes break down the influence of the pre-revolutionary order and manage social perceptions about the benevolence of that order as well as a symbol to show the achievement of as high a level of modernity as Western countries. Almost a century later, the two countries have come to show similarities in their recent efforts to promote traditional values and religion regarding gender norms, accompanying the authoritarian drift. In both countries, the authoritarian tendencies that intertwine with the nationalist narratives have implications for gender equality. The current authoritarian drift is accompanied by a reinvigoration of traditional gender norms as signifying national and cultural authenticity and as vital for national security and survival against progressive and democratic achievements regarding gender equality.

Gender as a Marker of National Authenticity, Identity and Unity

Under this rising authoritarianism, Putin and Erdoğan have extensively used the politicization of gender to define the boundaries of the Russian and Turkish nations, establish control over the modes of national identity, and distinguish the national authenticity and superiority of the Russian and Turkish cultures versus Western values (see Rivkin-Fish, 2010; Sperling, 2015; Yazıcı, 2012). The nationalist and conservative narratives include an aspiration for traditional family values and traditional gender order, which are believed to contain the core values and relationships vital for national unity, power and survival. Traditional values gaining ground started not with the Putin- and Erdoğan-led regimes but in the early post-Soviet period and the post-1980 period in Turkey. However, referring to these values as a way of distinguishing the existing regimes and justifying restrictive political measures has become central to politics in recent years.

As discussed in Chapter 2, after the dissolution of the Soviet Union, the demographic crisis that Russia has been dealing with since the late 1970s paved the way for revisiting and reframing the traditional gender order. Similar to the late Soviet times, if the demographic decline was approached as a matter of national security and survival, promoting the traditional family was understood as the remedy to this crisis and hence the state gradually started to create a neo-traditional gender climate that prescribed state intervention in the realm of family and sexuality with pro-natal policies. Following this trend, Putin also laid emphasis on traditional values in his domestic political discourse, blaming the supposed crisis of the family on the erosion of these values and holding the family and women responsible for the protection and future promotion of these values. He identified demography as one of the building blocks of 'the national' and maintained the prevalent discourse that conceptualizes the demographic crisis as a national and moral issue.

Unlike in the 1990s, however, the traditional values are not only framed as a matter of survival for the Russian nation to reverse demographic decline but as the distinguishing feature of Russian national authenticity, unity and even superiority vis-à-vis the West. Traditional family values have been reiterated as the main mechanism through which the Russian nation can revive in the face of the negative effects of dissolution and globalization over Russian cultural values and morality. In the 1990s, Russia, once a superpower in the Cold War era, came to be portrayed as associated with sex trafficking and prostitution. This resulted in the collective de-masculinization of Russia, so that Russian men felt incapable of protecting either their family or their nation. The networks of human trafficking fallen into by many Russian women, who had been lured abroad with promises of high prices, aggravated the process of de-masculinization at individual and social levels. Moreover, the de-masculinization had an impact at foreign policy level, in that Russia in the 1990s was often internationally portrayed as the country of origin for prostitution rather than as a mother (Riabova and Riabov, 2014, p.23). In his study on the connection between prostitution and the metaphors of nationalism in Russia in the early 1990s, Bornstein comments that prostitution was associated with a weakening Russian state and nation. This image represents the anxieties of post-Soviet times, when the demise of the Union, the onslaught of the market and the opening of Russian natural and spiritual resources to Western competition were construed as male sexual humiliation and national humiliation (Bornstein, 2006). The propagation of traditional gender order under Putin's rule and his focus on masculine politics might be seen as a reaction to the weakening image of Russia in the 1990s – a feminized Russia versus a masculine Russia that would restore the feelings of national power and pride among the populace.

As discussed in Chapter 2, in Turkey the spread of religious conservatism under the guidance of pro-Islamist political parties prepared the ground to reframe the religiously patriarchal features of the underlying gender order with attacking Republican modernization in the 1990s. The rise of political Islam as a counter-ideology to Republican modernity revolved around the debate on non-Western modernization that prescribed a traditional and conservative rather than secularly oriented lifestyle (Göle, 1997, p.54). As Republican modernizers, Islamists tackled modernization on the grounds of morality but a religiously imbued one, which made the emancipation of women conditional on the embracing of traditional gender roles – obedient wives and good mothers who only work outside the home in the case of economic need (see Acar, 1991, 1995). Unlike the previous pro-Islamist parties, the AKP under the leadership of Erdoğan engaged in ideological moderation in the economy and foreign politics but not in respect of issues regarding women (Çavdar, 2010). In tandem with the same trend, the AKP's discourse and policies have created a neo-conservative gender climate, particularly towards the end of the 2000s, which has reinvigorated notions of the traditional family, modesty and chastity of women for the sake of societal morality as well as the distinguishing features of national culture in opposition not only to the West but also to the Western-oriented, secular-minded groups in Turkish society.

The recent development of traditional values, including family and gender roles, as a political concept related to national sovereignty and unity, broadly parallels Russia's increasing confrontation with the Euro-Atlantic block and the emergent divergence between Turkey and the EU in recent years. Challenging the West has overturned the widespread perception of inferiority in the Russian and Turkish societies and corresponded to the expectation of self-sufficiency and self-determination. Both countries have been trying to be a part of Europe for centuries but are not recognized as necessarily European. In the eyes of the public, Russia has been largely characterized internationally as a country that lost the Cold War and became dependent on foreign aid in the 1990s (Riabova and Riabov, 2014, p.27). Similarly, the prevalent public view in Turkey is that we have been waiting at the gate of Europe for decades. The image of a strong and assertive country has been flattering for national pride in both Russia and Turkey, and has increased the political and personal prestige of Putin and Erdoğan as strong leaders.

This shift in geopolitical direction of Russia and Turkey has a symbolic resonance and brings with it a challenge to the cultural and moral superiority of the West. The turn to traditional family and gender roles as an indicator of Russian and Turkish national authenticity comes to be explained by conspiracy theories and the thesis of cultural sovereignty. In Russia, Western countries are suspected of utilizing family planning measures as tactical weapons to weaken Russia and wipe out the Russian nation. In Turkey, similarly, Erdoğan implied that family planning measures were being driven by supposed secular elites that remained under the influence of Western values and who harboured impulses of extinction against the traditionally and religiously minded but 'real' people of Turkey. Within this narrative, Western culture has been portrayed as the antithesis of Russian and Turkish morally upright civilizations with Orthodox Christian and Islamic roots, respectively. Westerners are fictionalized as living in a selfish, egotistic and promiscuous way and as anti-family individuals, while the Russian and Turkish people embrace family, children and the elderly.

The appeal to traditional values as a framework to identify the boundaries of national identity and a symbolic ground for consolidating national unity comes with the rise of domestic opposition that emerged in the period 2011–12 before Putin's return to the presidency and during the Gezi movement in Turkey in 2013. In the face of rising opposition, both leaders started to rely more on nationalist and conservative narratives (Putin, 2013a, b). They have endorsed these not only to rally support against the West but also to contain the opposition and forge consensus. As Laurelle (2017) remarks, Putin's promotion of conservatism aims to present the status quo of his regime as the best possible choice for the country's stability and security, delegitimize the liberal opposition and Western influences, and achieve the passive engagement of the public with the regime.

Against this backdrop, combined with the declining economic performance, cementing the ties with their core constituency became more of an issue for the continuity of Putin and Erdoğan's regimes. They explicitly tackled identifying the values of the majority, which are supposed to be embedded in the Russian and Turkish cultures, traditions and religions – Christianity and Islam. Their nationalist narratives that include the visible use of religious values and traditional norms serve to reinforce the dichotomy between 'us' and 'the other' as well as envisioning the Russian and Turkish nations as homogenous communities that share commonly held values without any significant variety or conflict. These values that define the core constituency of Putin and Erdoğan – loyal Russians and Turks – are then deployed against the regime's opponents, who may be accused of being mobilized, supposedly by foreign powers and enemies, with the aim of destroying the Russian and Turkish states and nations (see Yablokov, 2014).

These conservative and nationalist narratives are predicated on the aspiration for a traditional gender order, which is assumed to contain the core of traditional values. The discourse of traditional family values is extended to invigorate social unity on the grounds of a set of 'commonly held' values. This has the impact on the gender climate of restoring traditional patriarchy rather than promoting egalitarian relations between the sexes. Moreover, in embracing traditional family values and gender norms, these authoritarian regimes construct the autocratic leader as the real and moral representative and protector of the people, including of their true values and interests, as well as identify the modes of being real/ideal citizens and not against the 'others' (see Muller, 2016). In the Pussy Riot and Gezi movement, for example, both leaders promoted an approach to social dissent from a moralizing angle that brings female dignity, motherhood, religious hatred and hooliganism to the fore in order to demonize the protestors. Putin criticized the band members for behaving disrespectfully in a religious venue. During the trials of Pussy Riot, leading figures from the Church and the prosecutors did their best to equate feminism with terrorism, thereby configuring the supposed act of religious hatred as a matter of national security (Bitten and Kerimzade, 2013). Erdoğan accused the protestors on religio-moral grounds for attacking a veiled woman and drinking alcohol in a mosque. The protestors were presented as mounting an attack against traditional values associated with the people and family rather than acknowledging their dissatisfaction with increasing authoritarian tendencies. Previously, in 2011, Erdoğan used morally humiliating language in saying that 'I don't know if she is a girl or woman' when reacting to a female protestor being vocal against his policies (CNNTürk, 2011). He connected the legal right to protest with being morally deviant and delegitimized the protest, as this phrase implies that she might have had premarital sexual intercourse, which still equates for the majority with the loss of female dignity.

Putin and Erdoğan's conservative and nationalist discourses describe the West as a significant threat to the underlying gender order that the Putin and Erdoğan regimes are trying to reinvigorate on their way to engineering new Russian and Turkish societies. The Russian Orthodox Church equates anti-feminism with resistance to protect Russia against the devastating effects of cultural globalization (Nechemias, 2016). The head of the Russian Orthodox Church, a vocal supporter and close ally of Putin in spearheading Russia's conservative turn, claims to have found feminism very dangerous because it leads women to look beyond the traditional family for fulfilment and to stay outside of marriage, which for him implies a pseudo-freedom for women (*The Guardian*, 2013). Putin identifies homosexuality and same-sex relationships as gender deviation, a consequence of Western countries having rejected their religio-moral roots, accompanied with the development of liberal values (Nechemias, 2016). In tandem with this discourse, Putin issued a law in 2013 that recriminalizes the promotion of non-heterosexuality in the public sphere, on the basis of protecting minors from gender variations.

In a similar vein, Erdoğan blamed feminists, who are supposedly from secular circles with Western-oriented life aspirations, for rejecting the idea of motherhood, which Islam prescribes for women (*The Guardian*, 2014). As early as 2004, during the parliamentary debates on changing the Penal Code, Erdoğan confronted feminists. When he very unexpectedly expressed his desire to recriminalize adultery, which is regarded as a threat to public morality, feminists fiercely protested against this attempt and Erdoğan reacted by insulting these groups as 'vociferous marginal women' who 'cannot fit to the moral norms of society'.[1] Erdoğan brought up recriminalizing adultery again in 2018, expressing regret that he had previously stepped back because of the EU. He stated that 'our society is in a different position with regard to moral values' now, which implies the increasing power of his regime against secular elites as well as a loss of momentum over EU accession (*The Guardian*, 2018). In tandem with this religio-moral discourse, sexuality and LGBT issues serve as indicators of Turkey's genuine national identity, which is supposedly denied under the imposition of Western and Kemalist discourse in Erdoğan's conservatism (Birdal, 2013).

Moreover, this framing relies on the authenticity and superiority of Russian and Turkish thinking, living and culture, distinguished by the preservation of traditional family values and gender roles, and the otherization of Western culture. The West is imagined to be in moral and demographic decline and lacking the benefits of strong family ties. This has the impact of refusing the import/imposition of Western culture and signifies an authentic way of modernity for Turkey. Putin stated, 'Russian democracy is the power of the Russian people with their own traditions of self-rule, and not the fulfilment of standards imposed on us from outside' (Putin, 2012a). As repeatedly declared by Erdoğan, 'we [the Turkish nation] have to combine our national values and Western science' (Hürriyet, 2008; Sabah, 2008).

So, Putin and Erdoğan's nationalist and conservative discourses led to the reformulation of gender categories in reference to religious values and traditional norms as the signifiers of national authenticity and the cement of national unity. This has had the impact of creating neo-traditional and neo-conservative gender climates in Russia and Turkey, respectively. In the direction of a conservative and nationalist discourse, an open backlash against gender equality is predicated on the repression of women under the family and denies the legitimacy of gender equality concerns and feminist struggle and even configures feminists as a threat to the nation, state and family. However, whilst in both leaders' discourses nationalism and conservatism are expressed in reference to family values, the glorified past and religious values as the source of morality, a significant difference should be noted. Erdoğan promotes a 'religiously-imbued nationalism', in the words of Coşar (2012), as opposed to the secular modernization paradigm. In contrast, Putin's discourse rests on a civic identity as the basis of Russian civilization and a set of shared values mainly comprising state sovereignty, paternalism and patriotism without losing the connection with religious roots (Putin, 2012a).

Promotion of Family at the Intersection of Patriarchy, Tradition and Religion

The propagation of the traditional family marks the neo-traditional/conservative gender climates in Russia and Turkey. The protection and promotion of the family plays a key role in Putin and Erdoğan's political strategy, as the regimes led by them have replaced a state-led ideology of women's equality with the idea of state-promoted family and motherhood. In Putin's speeches, the family is identified as the main pillar for developing, strengthening and supporting Russia and guaranteeing the moral health of Russian society (Kremlin.ru, 2014, 2016). Strengthening the family and creating the necessary conditions for giving birth, raising children and affirming family values is mentioned as one of the top priorities to be considered in national development and plans and projects (Kremlin.ru, 2014). In Erdoğan's understanding, the family is both the main pillar of society and a bulwark to protect society in the case of socio-economic crisis, which should be strengthened with the help of religio-conservative values.[2] In this narrative, strong family ties are identified as what makes us 'us' and the strong family is emphasized as leading to a strong society, economic development and demographic trends (Yazıcı, 2012, pp.108–17).

In Russian and Turkish culture, the traditional family is usually imagined as a heterosexual family with father, mother and children, ruled by love, mutual understanding, respect for elders and a sexual division of labour. In a similar vein, multi-child and/or extended families are set as the normative form of family at the official discursive level. The traditional Russian family that is officially depicted represents a hybrid form of de facto Soviet family and pre-revolutionary features, such as the extended family (Murvayeva, 2014). Putin stated that families, particularly those with more than three children, embody the finest Russian traditions and constitute one of the main pillars for strengthening Russia and guaranteeing a moral and healthy way of life for Russian society (Kremlin.ru, 2016). In 2008, the Order of Parental Glory was established by a presidential Executive Order, which is awarded to parents (including adoptive parents) raising seven or more children and ensuring due care for their health, education, and physical, spiritual and moral development (Kremlin.ru, 2016). Erdoğan identifies the ideal family as one with 'at least three children' and living with elderly relatives. He frequently appears at wedding ceremonies and repeats his clichéd phrase, calling on married couples to have at least three children: 'One or two (children) is not enough. To make our nation stronger, we need a more dynamic and younger population. ... One (child) means loneliness, two means rivalry, three means balance and four means abundance, and God takes care of the rest' (Taylor, 2014).

In using an idealized notion of family that refers to heterosexual couples with children and excludes many other family forms that exist in Russia and Turkey, both leaders lean on religion, rather than on communist ideology or secularism, as a cementing tool to reinvent the traditional and conservative (see Murvayeva, 2014). In Russian culture, religion is seen as a traditional and conservative force per se (Murvayeva, 2014). Orthodoxy is understood as the main source of traditional norms and values, and the Russian Orthodox Church and traditional family as their main institutions (Wilkinson, 2014, p.368; see Bilinov, 2014). According to the Orthodox Church, there has been a moral decline in Russian society stemming from the expansion of unlimited freedom and individual autonomy, ignoring the public good and traditional values (Anderson, 2007, p.190; see Bilinov, 2014).

On the basis of shared concerns about the traditional family, the demographic crisis, moral decline and homosexuality, Putin sides with the Orthodox Church as the preeminent moral authority in enforcing traditional gender roles, opposing feminism and LGBT equality (Riabova and Riabov, 2014; Vasilyeva, 2016). In one of his speeches, Putin mentioned the involvement of the Orthodox Church in resolving the demographic and moral crisis and summoned it 'to revive family values and change people's attitudes towards the family' (Nechemias, 2009, p.24). The Church and its leaders are encouraged to play a moral guidance and supportive role for Russian society in general (Anderson, 2007). The Church with its emphasis on traditional family values has gained influence in public debates and legal regulations related to gender equality. *Domostroi*, which is guidance from the sixteenth century prescribing traditional household rules and relations, is often referred to by the Orthodox Church and conservative groups when any legal regulation incompatible with gender equality is being enacted (i.e. criminalizing gay propaganda and decriminalizing domestic violence).

In the case of Turkey, the traditional family is depicted as having strong connections to religious culture and values and consequently serving as the moral foundation of Turkish society (Yeğenoğlu and Coşar, 2012, pp.199–200). In tandem with this tendency, Erdoğan adheres to the religious notion of *fıtrat* in defining normative femininity and masculinity. *Fıtrat* means 'nature' and refers to biological differences as well as complementarity between men and women. In a meeting with the representatives of women's NGOs in 2010, when he was the prime minister, he declared that he did not believe in equality between men and women but rather in equality of opportunity. When expressing his ideas on women's contribution to social development, their employment and domestic violence, he underlines the necessity of considering their *fıtrat*. At the Women and Justice Summit, hosted by the Women and Democracy Association in November 2014, he once more voiced his objection to gender equality and mentioned 'equivalency' rather than 'equality'. He stated, 'Sometimes, here they say "equality between men and women". But "equality among women" and "equality among men" is more correct. However, what is particularly essential is women's equality before justice' (*Hürriyet Daily News*, 2014).

Although both leaders converge in their approach to religious values as the main source of traditional norms and values regarding family and gender, Putin underscores these values as being of national importance in Russian civilization whereas for Erdoğan they symbolize social discontent with the secular modernization paradigm. In one of the articles published during his presidential rally in 2012, Putin identified Russia as a civilization determined by a common culture, shared values, patriotism and commitment to Russian identity, which is prioritized against religious diversities (Putin, 2012c). Indeed, according to a recent Levada Centre survey (2016), the degree of religiosity shows little relationship to the involvement of religion in politics for Russian society. For Erdoğan, Islam, a set of religiously imbued national values constitutes the core of Turkish national identity (see Coşar, 2012). As 'a religiously-imbued nationalism' constitutes the core of Turkish identity for the AKP (Coşar, 2012), the AKP's self-identification of common values, to be shared by all regardless of ethnic, religious or class differences, is extensively based on Islam as the main, if not the only, source of an authentic national moral order. However, in both cases, promoting religion has the impact of trivializing gender equality concerns as understood by Western culture and international feminist politics.

Institutional Shifts

One indication of a neo-traditional/conservative gender climate at the political-institutional level is that gender equality has been marginalized. This is evident in the reorganization of the executive bodies responsible for implementing gender equality policies. The reorganization reflects the transformation of the policy of the Russian and Turkish states towards gender: women's issues come to be integrated into bodies responsible for the family, youth, demographics, poverty, social services, etc.

In Russia, under the guise of administrative reform, the core elements of the national mechanism for ensuring women's equality were dissolved in 2004. In the executive branch, the subdivisions of departments responsible for policy implementation to secure women's empowerment were reorganized, which meant in practice the equivalent of being abolished. For example, the Department on Medical and Social Problems of the Family, affiliated to the Ministry of Health and Social Development, was reorganized. The Department of Social Welfare remained under the ministry but its mandate to achieve gender equality was redefined as optional. As a gender expert from an international organization based in Moscow remarked, 'it has met only twice or three times [so far]'. In 2005, the Commission on the Status of Women of the Russian Federation was replaced by the Inter-departmental Commission for Gender Equality, which was subsequently dissolved in 2007 (UNDP, 2010, pp.49–50). A gender expert from UN Women based in Moscow remarked that:

> It has been twenty years [since] the dissolution [of the Soviet Union]. In the 1990s, the women's movement was quite active. There were civil society organizations and commissions established, and they worked efficiently. A national mechanism [for gender equality] was established. Commissions were established under the Presidency and Prime Ministry. There was the Coordination Council under the Ministry of Labour and activities carried out in the Duma. But by 2004, when Putin came to power, an administrative reorganization took place. Some changes happened in the ministries. Previously, there were many ministries but now some are united and put under the same roof. Now there are ten or eleven ministries. Then, the national mechanism was abolished. I mean, all the commissions were dissolved. [The government] tried to re-establish but it was really difficult. Now, there is the Coordination Council under the Ministry of Health and the Counselling Council [the Committee on Family, Women, and Children's Affairs] in the Duma. That is all. There are no more institutions, which worked in cooperation before.

Today, there are two advisory bodies to the executive related to gender equality policy. The Coordinating Council on Gender Equality is under the Ministry of Health and Social Development and chaired by a deputy minister. The government has declared this council to be the national mechanism of policy planning, but it does not have the authority or resources to function as the national gender equality mechanism across all government agencies (UN, n.d.). The other institution is the Committee on Family, Women and Children's Affairs of the State Duma. This Committee does not have the power, budget or ambition to promote government-wide gender mainstreaming in all ministries and policy areas. It has not supported anti-discrimination legislation; for example, it did not promote a draft law on domestic violence. It did, however, propose legislation limiting access to abortion and prohibiting gay propaganda (Temkina and Zdravomyslova, 2014). Experts from ANNA and the Women's Union, which are based in Moscow, commented on the inefficiency of the existing institutions, respectively, as follows:

> There is an inter-agency commission [which is like the national mechanism and is called the Gender Equality Committee] under the Ministry of Health and Social Development. It is not an agency commission but a council. Basically, this council's role is to oversee and make sure that the Russian Federation fulfils

the recommendations of the CEDAW Committee. The representatives of all the ministries are members of this council. There are some members from NGOs. We come together quarterly at least. We talk and discuss the situation of pregnant women, the situation of women in the North Caucasus, women's labour rights, trafficking [...] This council is what [the members of the council] refer to as the national mechanism.

Now we have also nothing [at the national level] to promote women. No ministry for example. We don't have a government commission. There was one but it was dissolved. The committee headed by Mizulina is the only one but it isn't a national mechanism and has no executive power. They propose laws but nobody is interested in implementing them in the ministries. We have nothing in the administrative bodies. The commission under the government was dissolved. They said that they don't need it.

The absence of a national mechanism prevents the generation and promotion of a comprehensive gender equality approach on the state level. The legal and institutional measures for mainstreaming gender equality and empowerment could not be designed, coordinated or monitored at central level. As a representative from the Consortium of Women's Non-Governmental Associations in Moscow remarked:

We don't have any national mechanism, which was suggested by CEDAW. Last summer, in 2010, we talked about it in the CEDAW Committee. The committee has suggested to our government [that they should] have a national mechanism for gender promotion with executive power. But our government says that 'we have the Committee on the Family in the Duma; what is the problem?' And family [means] woman. We don't have women's problems but those of childhood and the family.

Russia still has no gender equality law to ensure equality of opportunity for men and women in education and work. The first draft of the law was prepared by the Parliamentary Committee on Women and Family and first submitted to the Duma in 2003. The attempts to issue a federal law on 'state guarantees of equal rights and freedoms and equal opportunities for men and women in the Russian Federation', which would promote gender equality and women's rights, encountered strong conservative attacks inside and outside the Duma in January 2012 and then ceased. An expert from the Women's Union based in Moscow summarized the long but failed process as follows:

We have fought for some years for the adoption of a gender [equality] law. We started in 1994 and, in a few years, we had a model law, which includes all the points of gender mainstreaming. We wanted Parliament to adopt this law, but our fight was unsuccessful because the men in the majority in the Duma didn't want to adopt this law. They said all the points you [propose] are included in different laws, which already exist. We said that in the courts the judge should have all these [in one place], where he could find [a particular] point. If the law is compact, including all these different points, it will be much easier for them to judge and decide. But we were not successful. Then we wanted to adopt the so-called "anti-discrimination" law, [including all aspects of discrimination]. We didn't succeed. Two attempts were unsuccessful.

In March 2017, the government initiated a new gender equality programme, called the National Strategy of Actions in the Interests of Women in 2017–2022. According to this document, the mechanism of implementing this strategy was to be developed in the period 2017–18. The measures targetting the low representation of women in politics, the gender pay gap, discrimination in the labour market, gendered stereotypes and violence against women are to be implemented between 2019 and 2022 (Pravitel'stvo Rossiiskoi Federatsiyi, 2017). A gender expert from UNDP based in Moscow underlined that 'one of the main issues that we raised at that point was the need for a strategic approach again at the very senior level in government to have coordination, a committee or body of follow-up on all the good advances and suggestions that have been made over the time on gender issues'. It is too premature to measure the implementation and results of the programme, whether or not it offers a restructuring of gender relations, but even the promotion of gender equality becoming a concern of the Russian state is an advance, considering its increasing indifference to gender equality in the last decade. S/he continued by saying that:

> Unfortunately, we would say it has not been created at the Prime Minister's level as an umbrella [mechanism] over different ministries that have these sectors that should have this mainstream agenda. But it has again been created under the Ministry of Health. It is chaired by the deputy minister. But it is a consultative committee and brings the governmental bodies and civil society organizations together. It is still working. But it has not been terribly active and [not] meeting often enough for that. But there are discussions on the draft laws.

In Turkey, the previously mentioned General Directorate of Women's Status and Problems (KSSGM) was established in 1995 as a result of the individual efforts of a group of dedicated feminists and was directly linked to the Prime Minister's office. In 2004, the name of KSSGM was changed to the General Directorate on the Status of Women (KSGM). A law of establishment was enacted and the General Directorate was affiliated to the state ministry in charge of Family and Women's Affairs under the Prime Ministry. 'KSGM was restructured as a national mechanism to "carry out activities aiming at the protection and development of women's human rights, strengthen women in social, economic, cultural and political life, and ensure women enjoy equal rights, opportunities and possibilities". Thus, through this legal status, the General Directorate was provided with the opportunity to perform all its duties more efficiently' (UNECE, n.d.).

In 2011, Erdoğan's government initiated an administrative reorganization that established the Ministry of the Family and Social Policies and moved the General Directorate of the Family under the ministry. A former senior officer from the General Directorate interpreted the move as a downgrade in the hierarchical position of the

General Directorate and in its power to influence public policies from a women-oriented point of view. The strong demand from feminist circles to put women or equality into the name of the ministry was rejected by the government because the ministry's vision is clarified as creating an affluent society consisting of happy individuals and strong families that supposedly perform social welfare functions.[3] A feminist activist from Ankara and a public officer from the Ministry of the Family respectively suggested:

> After 2008, the winds of reform got silenced. KSGM was restructured under the Ministry of the Family [and Social Policies]. As a result, family has replaced 'women' in policy formulations and practices. Women have come to be identified within family. This has been reinforced by the legal framework and by [newly] established mechanisms.

> There was more emphasis on [women as] individuals [in the 1990s]. The starting point was human rights and women's human rights. In Turkey, the sake of society and of the family is prioritized [over women's rights]. In the 1990s, the focus was on women, human, women's rights, human rights, women's human rights rather than the sake of society.

Although the majority of the interviewees admitted the importance of having a ministry responsible for gender-related issues, they mentioned that its name symbolizes the articulation of family into gender politics at the highest state level. As a public officer from the Ministry of the Family acknowledged, the combination of the units of women, family, the elderly and the disabled under the same administrative roof has led to the expression of conflicting principles on gender equality and prevented a coherent agenda on gender equality from being developed. As she expressed it:

> Despite the awareness about women, we have been observing an increasing emphasis on the family in the discourse of the Prime Minister, other Ministers and our Minister [of the Family and Social Policies]. For instance, when one analyses the texts, [one finds that] there is a hidden implication [in the efforts] to solve the problems of the family and to assure a peaceful family. [In this picture], I assume that [the state] is concerned with violence against women, and murders and beatings mainly to protect the family and children [not women as individuals].

An NGO expert addressed the impact of the estrangement between the AKP and the EU on the relations between the national mechanism and women's rights organizations: 'when the AKP first came to power, it avoided pursuing conservative policies on these issues because it aimed at achieving full accession to the EU. So, almost all demands of women's organizations were responded to and quite strong relations were established.' Unlike the 1990s, the government has started to ignore women's rights organizations and cooperation with them has declined significantly, particularly since 2007 (Coşar and Gençoğlu-Onbaşı, 2008, p.326). The government tended to employ conservative consultants for family affairs and to distance itself from feminist circles and non-Islamist feminist civil societal organizations. The Directorate of Religious Affairs is specified as the main ally of the Ministry of the Family and Social Policies. Under the auspices of the Directorate, Family Guidance and Counselling Bureaus (*Aile İrşat ve Rehberlik Bürolari*) have been established to protect and strengthen the family as the most important social institution for protecting individuals and society under the conditions of global change (see Din Hizmetleri Genel Müdürlüğü, 2018). Family Guidance and Counselling Bureaus aim to protect and strengthen the family, and to resolve family problems through Islamic ethics and religious instruction.[4] In this setting, the state's family discourse starts to dominate the institutional structure and policies, and leaves no room for women's rights organizations and groups to voice their demands and influence the policymaking process.

Despite the institutional differences between these cases, both states converge in terms of addressing women's issues with the lens of the family instead of the concerns of gender equality. In both cases, the existing institutions neither promote comprehensive state feminism nor allow any kind of feminism within the state. The administrative governance of gender-related issues is exclusively embedded in family-related institutions that predominantly focus on the social protection of mothers, as the primary caretakers of children, the disabled and the elderly, rather than supporting women's individual rights in accordance with gender equality norms in both cases.

Political Masculinity

The performance of masculinity by political leaders provides a symbolic cover and makes authoritarian discourse and practices acceptable to the masses (Johnson, 2013, p.3). This suggests insights about the linkages between rising authoritarianism and the rise of sexism (neo-traditional/conservative gender climate) in four ways: (1) constructing Putin and Erdoğan as the real and moral representatives of the people, their true values and interests; (2) enabling autocratic leaders to embody society-wide notions of femininity and masculinity; (3) assigning them the right to identify the appropriate notions of femininity and masculinity; and (4) establishing a paternalistic relation with the majority via the prevailing but reconstructed notions of femininity and masculinity – modes of being real/ideal citizens or the reverse (see Muller, 2016).

Based on electoral hegemony and the representative popularity of Putin and Erdoğan, their personalities integrate with the state and nation by consolidating a paternalistic relation between state (male) and nation (female). Masculinity embodied in the personalities of Putin and Erdoğan becomes a powerful vehicle to normatively masculinize the state and to envision it as an ultimate protector and representative of the whole nation. The period of Putin was depicted as a miracle of God by Patriarch Kirill for having enabled the country to exit from the severe crisis of the preceding years with the active participation of the leadership (Bryanski, 2012). Putin personified the consolidation of state power and good management of the state apparatus due to the stability and order established first in Chechnya and then in the whole of Russia (Rogov, 2015, pp.84–5). Erdoğan's success represents that of 'the people' who felt excluded from the Kemalist establishment that was allegedly controlled by secular elites, which terminated with his ascent to national power. He has become the symbol of national pride and strength, due to his ideology of conservative democracy as well as his confident and oppositional stance towards the Western powers including the USA, the EU and Israel.

From the angle that the regimes are merged with the personalities of Putin and Erdoğan, any accusation or critique against Putin and Erdoğan is seen as an assault against the state and nation (see Taş, 2015). Putin's administration tends to defend itself against accusations of corruption and mismanagement by identifying Putin and the ruling elite as moral and national, if not flawless, compared to the opposition parties, which are portrayed as immoral, foreign and fighting only for the sake of power (Gudkov, 2015, p.66). Similarly, Erdoğan portrayed the corruption probe that was conducted against key figures from his administration and family in 2014 as an immoral attack against the whole of the Turkish nation.

A consequent deduction of this reckoning is that the faith of the country is conditional on Putin and Erdoğan holding political office permanently. Putin's political security is presented as synonymous with Russia's security and survival. In 2014, Kremlin Deputy Chief of Staff Vyacheslav Volodin famously declared in the Valdai Discussion Club, 'any attack on Putin is an attack on Russia … There is no Russia today if there is no Putin.' Similarly, as Jenkins (2012) observed, Erdoğan tends to be seen as the embodiment of the national will, with the result that his tastes, prejudices and opinions become those of the nation and therefore whatever he thinks or does, even if not correct, has the support of the Turkish nation. Accordingly, 'if Erdoğan falls, Turkey will fall' (Taş, 2015, p.785).

Putin aligned himself not only with the state but also with society. Putin is considered a democratic ruler by his constituents because he is a popular man, 'a regular Joe', and he thus becomes everyman (Wood, 2016). His tenet that he is the best to rule the country became evident in his speech at a presidential rally in 2012 when he said that 'this was not just about electing the country's president. This was a hugely important test for all of us, for our entire people, a test of our political maturity, independence, and ability to rely on ourselves' (Putin, 2012d). In depicting himself as 'a man of the people' and connecting his life story with the story of the nation (*millet*) (see Hale 2005, p.307), Erdoğan makes it feel as if he knows the people and their values – read as 'common values' – better than anyone else.[5] So, Erdoğan acts as if he knows and is the sole political representative of the moral order of the Turkish nation. This moralizing stance reiterates the legitimacy of the state, personified by Putin and Erdoğan as moral actors who must be responsible for protecting and upholding traditional values and institutions, particularly the family and religion, for the sake of national strength and survival. Accordingly, political masculinity has a function in legitimizing anti-democratic practices or at least making them acceptable for the majority in both Russia and Turkey.

The creation of a masculine and powerful image for Putin and Erdoğan is explicitly gendered and deeply imbued with gender dominance and violence (see Wood, 2016). Political masculinity is determinative in reconstituting hegemonic masculinity and emphasized femininity, in Connell's terms. As Connell (1987) remarks, the victory of hegemonic masculinity requires the creation of a cultural ideal of masculinity, which does not necessarily correspond to the majority of men but to a set of cultural norms and behaviours associated with males (p.185). In addition, both leaders have assumed the right to define proper femininity and masculinity and to justify their definitions on the grounds of national culture and moral values, which are supposed to be shared, accepted and internalized by all in Russian and Turkish society. Putin and Erdoğan install their political masculinity by drawing the picture of a powerful, invincible and macho man, having a fit body and masculine body language, and being dynamic and energetic at all times. Putin's embodiment of the new Russian man relies on society-wide notions of innate biological differences between the sexes, which imagine men as protectors and women as in need of protection, as well as on heteronormativity. Putin has fulfilled the role of a strong man, father, husband and/or grandfather, who does not smoke or drink but who does sport, which is the ideal figure that Russian women in particular want to see (Smolentceva et al., 2017). Similarly, Erdoğan is seen as 'a man of the people', a 'lover of God' and a 'light of hope for the millions', and is presented as genuine and strong enough to truly represent and protect the people (Taş, 2015, p.785). Coupled with being tough, stubborn and bad-tempered, their masculine appearances give the people a feeling of national power and pride, the shelter of a paternalistic relationship, and a sense of connection. The reasons for the strong female support for both leaders should be sought here, despite the reinforcement of a traditional gender order and submissive femininity, which functions at the expense of gender equality (see Tkachenko, 2011). The gendered leadership proves the ground for biological differences between the sexes to produce a legitimate reaction in the media, popular discourse and the culture industry. This has supportive implications for the prevailing tendency to naturalize and legitimize traditional gender roles with reference to biological differences, which marks the prevailing gender regimes in Russia and Turkey.

Part 2

Gender Climate Under Authoritarian Politics in Russia and Turkey

Vulnerability of Russian and Turkish Women in the Labour Market

The promotion of traditional gender roles has been deepening the existing gendered hierarchies related to the composition and patterns of women's employment in both Russia and Turkey. These hierarchies in the labour market have become increasingly enmeshed with the biological differences between the sexes in the sociopolitical climate, in which family values and motherhood are glorified as distinctive national characteristics of Russia and Turkey. Although Russian women have maintained a higher level of attachment to the labour market than Turkish women, as in the Soviet period, the disadvantageous position that both groups of women fall into becomes evident if the gendered structure of employment is taken into account. While the Russian state is concerned to resolve women's double burden with the aim of stimulating fertility rates and strengthening the family, the main problem in Turkey is to accelerate women's entry into the labour force in such a way as to preserve traditional family and gender roles. Whilst recognizing these differences, the Russian and Turkish states reinforce gender-based discrimination in the labour market in reference to conservative and nationalist discourse. The nationalist and conservative discourses promoted by Putin and Erdoğan have the effect of perpetuating traditional roles for women as mothers and wives and undermining women's social status and career prospects. This discourse becomes evident in the enforcement of legislation that contains gender discriminatory regulations and the development of social benefits from a family-oriented perspective. The state's measures concerning women's employment are under the influence of the demographic and moral goals of enhancing fertility and strengthening the family.

The State Approach to Women's Employment in Russia and Turkey

With the ending of the obligation to work following the dissolution of the Soviet Union, women in Russia were rendered free to decide whether to work or stay at home. However, women's participation in the labour force has continued to exhibit a high degree of stability and widespread social acceptance, thanks to the legacy of seven decades of Soviet-ordained gender equality. In contrast to the predictions of the early transition period that women would voluntarily leave the labour force as soon as they were allowed to, women continued to stay in the labour force and were not predominant among the unemployed (Ashwin, 2002). According to World Bank statistics, the average value of female labour force participation was as high as 55.34 per cent between 1990 and 2016 in Russia (the Global Economy, 2018). Various public surveys also confirm the wide public acceptance for women's right to work outside the home and their eagerness to engage in professional activity (RANEPA, 2015, p.54).

Despite this, it is still hard to say that working women in Russia do not encounter any form of discrimination and inequality stemming from gender, marital status or pregnancy. Instead, the composition and patterns of female labour force participation are mainly characterized by women's concentration in gender-appropriate work, gender asymmetry at decision-making levels, job-related barriers and a gender pay gap (Atencio and Posadas, 2015). To deal with the widespread practice of employment discrimination, new legal regulations were enacted in 2013, banning job advertisements that stipulate the desired race, gender, ethnicity, marital status, faith, age or physical appearance (Nechemias, 2014). However, the Russian state resists amending the related articles of the Labour Code that prohibit women's employment in 456 occupations and 38 sectors, and instead continues itself to practise gender-based discrimination in the labour market with the excuse of protecting women's reproductive health (United Nations in the Russian Federation, 2016).

In contrast to the late and early post-Soviet approach, Putin has been seen to acknowledge that 'bringing women back home' is not an attractive and realistic option for Russian women and that the state needs to create the conditions and develop support mechanisms for working women to combine motherhood and the pursuit of professional activity. However, his focus on the status and problems of working women is considerably shaped by the demographic goals of preventing depopulation and increasing fertility, rather than improving gender equality. In his well-known speech in 2006, his primary focus was on the reasons that discourage working women from giving birth to a second child – that is, the loss of economic power and status at home, due to the temporary absence from the labour market (Rotkirch et al., 2007, pp.350–1). Economic incentives for companies to promote part-time employment, flexible working hours and opportunities to work from home, and the development of training opportunities for women returning to work, are mentioned as part of Russia's demographic policy.[1] In the meeting on family, motherhood and childhood policy, Putin (2014b) reasserted the interconnectedness between fertility rates and women's employment: 'we should definitely support those families and those women who want to both raise children and carry on with their careers. A number of factors motivate them: young people do not want to lose their skills, they want to retain their place in the labour market and to progress in their careers.' Russian demographic policy cannot ignore the aspirations of young women beyond motherhood and aims to resolve the tensions stemming from women's double burden, but its measures have not been developed in compatibility with gender equality concerns.

By contrast with Russia, in Turkey female labour force participation has historically been low and the housewifization of women is internalized as the prevailing cultural norm. Although women's employment was legally recognized in the old Civil Code, enacted by the early Republican regime, education was given more attention than employment for the goal of women's equality, and a traditional division of labour was legally and culturally preserved for many decades. This has resulted in a lack of feminization of the labour force with low levels of participation and limited opportunities of employment for women. In 2015, the female labour force participation rate of 32 per cent constituted one of the lowest among Southern European countries, with a concentration of women in the agriculture, service and informal sectors (World Bank, 2018).

The EU accession talks, in conjunction with the determined efforts of the women's rights movement, triggered the achievement of significant legal advances regarding women's employment, with the expectation of an increase in its levels. In the new Civil Code, adopted in 2001, the articles that defined the man as the head of household and obliged women to obtain their husband's permission to work outside the home were abolished (WWHR, 2005, pp.7–9). In a step forward, gender discrimination was recognized as a violation of human rights in the new Labour Law enacted in 2003, which prohibits different treatment on the basis of gender, marital status and pregnancy in setting up contract terms and wages for equal value of job (KSGM, 2008). On the other hand, the state reinforces cultural reservations concerning women's working outside the home, in parallel with its conservative discourse. In the Labour Law, there is still an article that entitles working women to the repayment of premiums and severance payments in cases where they leave their jobs for marriage, which encourages married women to withdraw from the labour force and become housewives (Kılıç, 2008, p.495).

Several legal initiatives were also taken by the AKP government to increase female labour force participation in preparation for EU accession. Under the amendments on the Unemployment Insurance Law No. 4447, the government assigned the Unemployment Insurance Fund to pay the insurance premiums of new employees (young men aged between 18 and 29 and women older than 18) for the first five years of employment (Labour Law, 2008). The government and municipalities provide a significant number of training programmes for women in public training centres, on literacy, embroidery and sewing, care of the elderly, cooking, foreign languages, computer literacy, etc. Nonetheless, these notable improvements have not been coupled with the desired increase in female labour force participation, which was 23.3 per cent in 2005 and 28.8 per cent in 2012 (ASPB, 2012b). According to household labour force survey results, the women's employment rate was still as low as 29.3 per cent and the female labour force participation rate was only 34.3 per cent by 2017 (TÜİK, 2018).

This contradictory picture is mainly related to the absence of a coherent state policy on gender equality. Despite pro-employment initiatives, Erdoğan holds to a more protectionist approach on the basis of women's nature, which constitutes a significant difference from Putin's approach to women's employment as a long-standing tradition and an economic necessity. In his compelling speech at the Women and Justice Summit in 2014, Erdoğan stated that women should not be treated as equal to men in the labour force, as they were in the former communist regimes; on the contrary, they should be favoured with protection for their delicate natures and supported in fulfilling their duties of motherhood, pregnancy and breastfeeding (BBC Türkçe, 2014). However, this kind of explanation serves the purpose of restricting women to the private sphere in Turkey, where women's working outside the home is still an issue of moral concern over the trustworthiness and chastity of women.

Although the Russian and Turkish cases show significant differences concerning the feminization of the labour force, a closer examination of the gendered structure of employment shows that Russian and Turkish working women have similar problems of encountering discriminatory attitudes and inequality stemming from biologically ascribed roles for the sexes in the labour market, particularly under the authoritarian interventions in tandem with a conservative and nationalist discourse. On the one hand, the legal amendments and pro-employment initiatives draw Russia and Turkey closer to internationally accepted standards regarding gender equality in the labour market, but state discourse, the legislation and pro-employment measures contain persistent stereotypes concerning the roles and responsibilities of women and men in family and society. The Russian and Turkish states have made no attempt to prevent women participating in the labour force but the discourse of state-promoted motherhood and its associated incentives no doubt has a considerable impact on women's status and situation in the labour market. When combined with a strong propagation of conservative values and a nationalist narrative, women-friendly incentives cannot serve as the basis for long-term improvement in the status and situation of working women and transformation towards a more egalitarian division of labour. On the contrary, deeply ingrained beliefs about biological differences have been unleashed and have had the effect of restricting women primarily to traditional gender roles. A representative from the Council for the Consolidation of the Women's Movement in Moscow and an academic from the St Petersburg European University observed, respectively:

> Also the ideological situation is very controversial because now we have the very strong influence of the Orthodox Church. It is very very conservative; they do not say [explicitly] that women should stay at home but they support very conservative, gendered images of women, who first of all should be mothers, wives, etc.

> Women have to survive in a market economy with a traditional ideology and [in spite of] the attempts to discriminate by the patriarchal segments of society.

Extended Maternity Leave Schemes in Russia and Turkey

In Russia, the state policies regarding women's employment are mainly motivated by a desire to lower the tension stemming from gender inequality in the labour market, while in Turkey pro-employment initiatives aim to increase the low levels of female labour force participation. However, despite the evident differences in the ideological orientation of state and public acceptance regarding women's employment, combining professional, family and maternal responsibilities is treated as a female issue, impeding gender equality in the labour force, in both countries. The seemingly supportive state measures towards working women for achieving work and family balance are primarily designed to guarantee the desired rates of fertility and labour force participation without challenging gendered hierarchies at home and in the labour force.

During the interviews in both Russia and Turkey, an extended maternity leave scheme was predominantly mentioned as a pro-employment measure that did not transform but reinforced the gendered division of labour. In Russia, state-supported maternity leave was first introduced in 1981 and was extended to three years (half paid, half unpaid) in 2007. This benefit is defined as childrearing leave and issued for both parents in the law but widely known as maternity leave. It amounts to 40 per cent of the salary of mother or father for the first half of the leave and is unpaid for the second half. In Turkey, extending the duration of maternity leave became a matter of discussion under the AKP governments in parallel with their efforts to promote women's employment. Following the end of the sixteen-week birth leave, public employees, regardless of gender, have been entitled to take unpaid maternity leave for up to two years upon request since 2011, while female workers have been entitled to six months of unpaid leave since 2003 (Resmi Gazete, 2016a, b).

Although woman-friendly at first glance, extended maternity leave was criticized during the interviews in Russia and Turkey for relying on the conviction that women are by nature family-oriented and designed to be mothers. It was frequently pointed out that extended maternity leave relies on the idea of a traditional family, depicted as a heterosexual, procreative, married couple, and crystallizes its centrality in social policy by directly addressing women. The regulation of parental leave as optional reinforces traditional roles for women and their vulnerability to gender discrimination in the labour market on account of birth and childcare. There is no paid paternity leave in Russia; male employees are entitled to five days of unpaid leave on request. In Turkey, a ten-day paternity leave was legalized for male public employees only and was conditional on the request of the father, while male workers in the private sector were awarded the entitlement to a five-day leave with pay in 2015.[2] An expert from EGIDA, based in St Petersburg, commented:

If men have to take leave for childcare, the employer will not discriminate between men and women in hiring. This will not make a difference because both will take leave. Nowadays, employers tend to hire more men than women. Men do not need to take this leave. They might not use it. This is the reason for discrimination against women.

An expert from Capital Women's Platform, based in Ankara, established by Islamist feminist women activists, remarked that linking childrearing to motherhood puts women at a disadvantageous position in the labour market:

If you are on unpaid leave for another year, then you will withdraw from work for two years. This means you should probably not find the position you left. This is an important obstacle before woman in terms of her career. In my opinion, it should be distributed between mother and father in a more egalitarian way. It is OK that woman goes breastfeeding for six months, receives her salary or gets on maternity leave for one year but father should care for his child at the end of one year.

In deeply patriarchal cultures such as Russia and Turkey, only the enforcement of parental leave as compulsory will have the effect of transforming cultural barriers that tend to constrain fathers from using optional parental leave, even if they would like to do so. Given the wage disparities between the sexes, the association between men's status in the family and earning, and the widespread understanding of childrearing as a female responsibility, the impact of the legal entitlement of both mothers and fathers to maternity leave on relieving the double burden of Russian women and encouraging the employment of Turkish women outside the home remain limited. Moreover, in Turkey, the fact that maternity leave is unpaid and does not cover male workers in the private sector makes promising outcomes regarding the achievement of gender equality in the labour force unlikely. An academic from St Petersburg European University shared her/his insights as follows:

> [Even] if men want to be involved as fathers on equal terms, society won't allow him to do it if he wants to make a career at the same time, because, for example, if he is a businessman, he cannot share [domestic/care work] [...] A man could want to stay with his children half a day, but flexible working hours would make him a very strange employer or employee. This can put him in an unfair position at his job. This kind of traditionalism is reinforced by the market and by official ideology. Gender equality is a very difficult project for the family.

In the labour market, the generous maternity leave turns into a disincentive for working women to participate in the labour force, and aggravates gender discrimination in hiring, promotion and remuneration in both Russia and Turkey. This measure confirms the confinement of women to care work in connection with biological differences and renders their participation in working life on equal terms practically impossible. Employers often associate the costs of paid leave with female employees and their relations are burdened with the violation of labour legislation. Due to extended maternity leave schemes, private companies prefer not to hire young, married women and/or pregnant women because they are seen as costing more but producing less for the company than their male counterparts (Teplova, 2007). Even in job interviews, Russian women are often asked about marital status and children and an affirmative response has a discouraging impact on the employers' decision to hire (ABA/CEELI, 2006). An expert from EGIDA said:

> In practice, it is nearly impossible for a pregnant woman [to] find a job. If a woman [discloses that she is] pregnant during a job application or interview, or the employer notices this, then she will not be hired. Besides, for women with small children it is difficult to find a job. These women will probably ask for sick leave or leave to care for their children. In other words, they might work less.

A public officer from the Ministry of the Family and Social Policies in Turkey shared her critical but realistic insights about the limitations that long maternity leave creates on hiring women in the public sector:

> She will be away from work for two years. Besides, she will give birth to three children, which makes approximately six years. For example, breastfeeding break

is arranged according to female employees; the exclusion of male employees seems well intentioned. So, these policies might serve to withdraw women from employment. This might not be the real intention. Maybe, the starting point is intended well but I think this is the result. I know so many public officials, who think that they [women] would give birth soon and leave for two to two and a half years but military service is as short as one year and for once, so [they say] I will hire men.

In the labour market, women's position is burdened not only by the predominant gender stereotypes but also by the violations of rights. The ineffective legal enforcement of 'generous' maternity-related rights remains weak to impede gender inequality and discrimination in the labour market. In practice, this has the effect of withdrawing women from the labour force and forcing them to give up their legal rights in order to survive in the private sector or predominate in the public sector despite the low level of earnings. Academics from the Higher School of Economics in Moscow and the Middle East Technical University in Ankara, respectively, stated that:

> Yes, maternity leave [exists] but it doesn't work. If a woman works in a private company, often they use a scheme to make the company [seem like it is] closing down so the employer [doesn't have to pay for benefits] but if she [works for] the state, she [does not have a] high salary.

> Any work place allows women to enjoy this right. In our interviews, we see that the women are forced to make a choice. The employer asks her if she is thinking about using unpaid maternity leave. If she is, then the employer says goodbye. This [using unpaid leave] means she already makes a choice. This is what happens in practice. [...] What workplace would accept this except the public sector? It is only acceptable in the public sector because it is compulsory.

In Russia, the vast majority of the interviewees mentioned numerous illegal violations of social rights in the private sector. According to the Russian Labour Law of 2001, pregnant women can be fired only in the case of the liquidation of the company (ILO, 2001). The loose control and lack of monitoring by the state agencies over the realization of social rights related to maternity creates a window of opportunity that private companies exploit. Following the introduction of paid maternity leave, an increasing number of Russian business owners began to make their companies appear to be going bankrupt, shrinking or closing down in order to avoid the obligation to pay maternity benefit for one and a half years and guarantee the position remaining vacant for the female employee when she returns to work.[3] An academic from St Petersburg European University elucidated how this legal violation takes place:

> For example, a private enterprise employing ten people, with one pregnant woman, could just shut down the enterprise and reopen as a different business, hiring back everyone except the pregnant woman. According to the law that is absolutely legal to do. [This kind of thing is] done because you can't [fire] a pregnant woman

from the workplace, according to the law. But if the enterprise closes, everybody loses his or her job. This is according to the law but there are many many many small tactics of discrimination that are not very visible and that are very difficult to prove in a legal context. [...] So in a sense mostly invisible tactics limit the equal participation of women, but according to law everything is in favour of the women. The practice and the law are quite different.

As an expert from ANNA, a Moscow-based NGO, explained, it is internationally disclosed that the Russian state turns a blind eye to the problems of law enforcement regarding young mothers, as follows:

[Employers] prefer either to fire pregnant women or to make women sign a contract that they will not get pregnant while they work in this position. The state knows this. This was a topic of discussion before CEDAW of the Russian Federation here last year. Basically, governmental agencies said that [...] women have to press charges privately against these companies in a court. According to the legislation, women have to go by themselves to protect their rights themselves.

In the face of increasing numbers of these cases, particularly after the financial crisis of 2008, a civil society movement took place in 2010–11, which organized pickets, rallies, meetings and complaint applications/files to attract public attention to the non-payment of maternity benefits (Chernova, 2012b, p.14). Accordingly, legal amendments were introduced in 2013, replacing the previous payment system, in which the social insurance fund reimbursed the maternity allowances, which were initially paid by employers, through a long and tedious bureaucratic process (Teplova, 2007). In the new payment system, local social insurance fund agencies are rendered responsible for the direct payment of maternity benefits, which, by bypassing employers, simplifies the payment process and guarantees legal protection for equal access to maternity benefits in the case of payment delays, non-payment and/or bankruptcy (Tsentr sotsial'no-trudovykh prav, n.d.-b).

In Turkey, the fact that maternity leave is unpaid and its duration is different for public and private sectors puts female private sector workers in a more vulnerable situation. Given the wide inequalities concerning women's education and training, it would be difficult to say that extended maternity leave equally covers working women even in the private sector. Women with graduate degrees, language skills and technical experience and who occupy top positions can have some bargaining power if another employee could not easily replace them. However, in the informal sector, where women with low levels of education and professional skills are predominantly hired, the turnover rate is quite high and women are seen as unqualified and easily replaceable.[4] An academic from Ankara University depicted the de facto situation in the private sector as follows:

In practice, six-month unpaid leave could not be enjoyed [in the private sector] because the employer threatens to fire [her]. If she provides an expert labour force, which is hard to replace, the employer might permit not for six months but a few months more. Now, there is four-month paid leave; it should be six-month paid leave and six-month unpaid parental leave, which could be used by mother or father. Even this could be an obstacle for women's employment. So, it should be a parental leave.

In Russia, another trick that private companies frequently use in order to avoid the mandatory provision of social benefits is that of 'informal contracts' (Teplova, 2005, p.7). Experts from the Russian women's organizations EGIDA and the Women's Consortium mentioned that they had encountered many cases in which young women were forced to sign informal contracts, declaring that they would not get pregnant for a certain time period after they started work or employers would put a resignation letter into process if they got pregnant (see Smolentceva et al., 2017). A representative from the Council for the Consolidation of the Women's Movement in Moscow observed that:

> If a woman is young and married, she can be told in the first interview 'your skills are good but please write a document showing that you will finish the contract with the company and we will use it when we know you are pregnant'.

Last but not least, the long duration of maternity leave not only makes women less attractive and more expensive workers in the eyes of employers but also lowers their competitiveness, weakens their professional training and qualifications, and restricts opportunities for them to find a new job. The re-training programmes designed to re-adapt working mothers to working life and compensate their loss in competence and skills do not seem to give them a competitive advantage in the labour market (Chernova, 2012b). This reinforces the existing vertical segregation that already prevents both Russian and Turkish women from acquiring senior positions in decision-making and management. Childbirth comes for Russian and Turkish women with a cost of falling behind men in career advancement and occupying secondary positions. Another expert from EGIDA evaluated the negative impact of extended maternity leave on women's career advancement as follows:

> Besides, maternity leave or leave for breast-feeding lasts for one-and-a-half or three years in Russia. So, women are in a disadvantageous position in their career in terms of experience. In this period, women do not get as much work experience as men. When women are on maternity leave, men have many chances to improve [their professional skills]. When they return, women are less qualified and experienced than men [who have not taken any leave]. This affects their job and career. Men can improve their career easily but women make slow progress in their career due to their children.

Gender-Segregated Labour Market in Russia and Turkey

In both Russia and Turkey, state measures targeting working women, based on traditional gender assumptions, do not aim to equalize the rights and opportunities of women in the labour market, and therefore do not bring about a transformative impact on women's employment patterns. Instead, the seemingly 'generous' social benefits, including extended maternity leave, childcare leave and sick leave, reinforce horizontal segregation in the labour market. Despite the high rates of participation, Russian women's employment is mainly characterized by their concentration in gender-appropriate work, which stands at the bottom of the gender status hierarchy with low salaries, low creativity and low prestige (Kozina and Zhidkova, 2006) and a wide gender pay gap (above 30 per cent), one of the highest rates among the high-income countries (Atencio and Posadas, 2015). Similarly, in Turkey, the gender pay gap reaches as high as 42 per cent (AK Parti Kadın Kolları, 2010, p. 5). According to the Social Security Institution, on a daily basis, women earn 4 per cent less than men for work of equal value and this variation rises to 8 per cent in female-dominated sectors such as retail business, education, and health, manufacturing industry, bureau and secretariat management, and counselling management (TEPAV, 2012).

The gender-segregated labour force in Russia and Turkey is structured according to the influence of traditional convictions about motherhood, breadwinners, work-family balance and care work. In both cases, women's choices of work are circumscribed by the need to find a convenient work strategy, which helps women combine work and family responsibilities. Linked to this, a kind of self-limitation becomes evident in the job preferences of women, who mainly prioritize the work and family balance over their self-realization in a suitable profession. Despite lower salaries and status, educated and qualified women frequently choose to work in the public sector as it provides a regular working schedule, which enables them to allocate sufficient time to fulfil care work and domestic duties, and guarantees their access to social rights related to pregnancy and maternity. A researcher from St Petersburg European University shared her/his observations as follows:

> They usually plan according to their care responsibilities. There are different kinds of jobs and [professions]. [The thought process is] 'this job will be convenient for me to have maternity leave [...] If it is a government job, it is [permanent] and I will have benefits but a low salary. The private sector has higher salaries but I will not be paid every social benefit because companies really don't want to pay for everything.' They count everything. And women [turn down] very high-level positions in [...] the private sector and they prefer to go to the governmental sectors because they guarantee all benefits, [even] on maternity leave.

An academic from Ankara University and a representative from Capital Women's Platform in Ankara explained the predominance of Turkish women in the public sector on the basis of similar concerns as Russian women:

> There is the opportunity to enter the professions because having a university degree decreases the pressure on women to concentrate in certain fields, which provides service only women. In other words, she studied for years, got a diploma; so, for sure, she will work. Where? Primarily in the public sector, where the rules are clear. In this regard, the state is a more reliable employer; professional relations are perceived as more institutionalized.

They [the women] tend to work in the sector where they could work easily and peacefully. This is so understandable. For instance, being a teacher is very ideal. There is a three-month vacation. Part-time job. After a while, she can take her child to the school and they can return home together. Because you cannot enjoy your legal rights like breastfeeding break in the private sector as it does in the public sector.

In Turkey, female labour force participation is a multi-dimensional phenomenon that involves both economic and cultural factors. The low level of female participation is related to women's concentration in agriculture as unpaid family workers and to the limited opportunities that are accepted as appropriate for women in the industrial and service sectors. In addition, the reservations that women and their families have about working and interacting with male strangers constitute another obstacle. These sorts of concern, mostly related to protecting the chastity of women, represent a challenge to the aim of increasing and diversifying women's employment in Turkey. An academic from Ankara University, one of the leading experts in Turkish women's employment patterns, offered a crucial insight into the impact of these sorts of obstacle:

Even in industry, the departments that women and men work in are different, even the entry-exit hours differ for men and women. So, a secure area is created in order to minimize the contact and to make the workplace more appropriate for young women [...] In the service sector, home cleaning is based on a woman-to-woman relation, so this is acceptable in conservative patriarchal circles. Except home cleaning, where can women work in the service sector? They can work in service areas, where customers are predominantly men or mixed. Hotel, accommodation facilities, restaurants are not assumed to be appropriate areas for women to work.

Although job opportunities are far more diversified for Russian working women, the association commonly established between being a woman and being a homemaker, at both social and individual levels, pushes them to be more stable and less mobile in the job market, provided that their equal access to social rights and benefits is guaranteed even if at a minimum level. As an academic from the Higher School of Economics in Moscow remarked:

A man can be lazy and he can have a low salary or he can think that this job is not for him and choose [to leave or look for another job]. But women [will take] any kind of job that gives them a salary and at the same time provides them with childcare.

The contradiction is that, while the Russian and Turkish states seem to have the intention of maintaining and encouraging women's attachment to the labour market, they allow the labour market to operate in line with the gender division of labour. In both countries, there is a widespread traditional assumption that men occupy the place of head of household, and should therefore occupy job positions of higher status, prestige and earning than women, while women are expected to run the household on top of working. In this gendered structure of employment, low-paid jobs, which are mostly routine jobs requiring no creativity but attention to detail and standing at the bottom of the gender status hierarchy, are treated as unattractive and even humiliating and not considered favourable or proper for men (Kozina and Zhidkova, 2006, pp.64–6). This paradigm strictly divides the labour force into feminine and masculine spheres and fixes the inferior and subordinate position of women as given in the labour market. Additionally, this sort of traditional assumption leads to an underestimation of female wage work as a secondary, rather than primary, source of income to the household budget and does little to further the social and individual understanding of female wage work as a matter of self-realization in accordance with women's education and life aspirations. An academic from the Higher School of Economics and a feminist activist from Istanbul similarly remarked:

> In public opinion in Russia and in other countries as well, the father or man in the family is the breadwinner. [The man's salary] is taken as the salary of the family; the salary of women is only additional money.
>
> For this reason, as female labour is described within the family, it will always be damaged. It is because she cannot leave domestic responsibilities. Due to these responsibilities, she will be in a weak and disadvantaged position in the labour market. She will continue to be a substitute force. She will have to work in unqualified jobs.

In Turkey, even pro-employment initiatives that include flexible employment, part-time employment and small entrepreneurship by micro-credits rely on traditional roles for men as the primary breadwinners and women as secondary workers. There is no doubt that these measures help women become economically empowered within the family, but they do not ensure a promising change in the status and situation of women in the labour market in Turkey, where most women doing piece work at home tend to identify themselves as housewives and their earnings as contributory to the family budget (Dedeoğlu, 2010). In this setting, these measures have the effect of maintaining housewifization as a way for women and strengthening the gendered structure of the labour force. An academic from Ankara University observed that:

> It is said that [flexible employment] is appropriate for women because there is already a breadwinner [man] at home; if a woman works temporarily, it will be a contribution to the family budget. She could work as a maid in a company for three months and return home. What is meant by flexibility is to employ women in temporary jobs, which do not provide sustainable employment and a chance to have a professional career. However, the main target is to extend this into the whole labour market through women. It seems easier to make it [flexibility] acceptable by women and social reaction [to this] remains limited.

Although men appear to benefit most from the unequal and gendered structure of employment, the reality becomes more complex, if elaborated from an intersectional point of view. It is important to note that the utilization of pro-employment measures is not experienced in the same way by all Russian and Turkish women and very much depends on the social positioning of the agent. In both countries, the working experiences of unskilled, low-qualified and low-educated women are constructed by the intersecting systems of discrimination, derived not only from gender and marital status but also from age, education and class. In a traditionally oriented sociopolitical climate, this has led to questioning the validity of working outside the home on the side of women, who are hired in the service sector and/or in the informal market without access to legal rights and benefits.

The interviewees in Russia interestingly drew attention to the patriarchal revival and, linked to this, a newly emerging phenomenon that women are being indirectly forced to leave the workforce, although women's employment is well settled in the country in economic and cultural terms. As Chandler (2013) and Nechemias (2016) remarked, there is no pressure on women to become full-time homemakers but its increasing recognition and the social benefits available to those women who make this choice create a positive image of the housewife and a source of motivation to stay at home. Thus, most interviewees from both sides saw it as understandable if women prefer to orient themselves towards family and children in a space where they can feel useful, emotionally involved and safe from the double burden of work and family, workplace harassment, sexual harassment and so on. An interviewee from St Petersburg European University stated:

It mostly depends on education, on market capacities, values. But some women without qualifications are forced into these traditional gender roles because they can't find a good and interesting job [that will be] good for self-realization. A job means sufficient money. Why go to work with the thought of alienation? You can work in a job, which you don't like but which brings you money and power, but if it doesn't [bring either of these things], you don't want to do it. With family work, alienation is less often felt because you are involved in it emotionally and it belongs to you.

In Turkey, despite the legal amendments in the Civil Code, the consent of husband or father does still operate as a constraining factor on women's employment. Particularly for lower-class and more traditional families, working outside the home and interacting with strangers can be considered as inappropriate for 'good' women and may not be allowed by the head of the family. In this setting, women tend to do piece work at home, or to work in family workshops and/or workshops in their neighbourhood at low wages and low status without social security coverage (Toksöz, 2012, p.58). The state measures, which are introduced so as to economically empower working women, reinforce the existing cultural challenges against women's working outside the home both for women themselves and for their families. An academic from the Middle East Technical University observed that:

They [women] work in hard conditions, for long hours and without social security coverage. They work for low wages. When the state offers them the same amount of money in return for childcare, they prefer to stay at home. For this reason, women's withdrawal from employment is understandable; this is a rational choice and nobody can judge them for it. It is quite understandable because she works for 11 to 12 hours and earns at most 500 to 600 or 800 liras. If the state pays her, then she works at home in secure and decent conditions because many women report complaints about workplace harassment and so on.

Paradoxically, the positive image of the housewife is an unrealistic prospect for the majority of working women, regardless of age, education and employment status. Despite traditional gender roles being strongly propagated in the media and encouraged discursively and materially by the states, Russian and Turkish families cannot survive without the earnings of women under conditions of declining economic growth and increasing poverty (see Başlevent and Onaran, 2003; Khotkina, 2001). Furthermore, the crisis of the family, inherited from the late-Soviet period, has intensified with alcoholism, male mortality at relatively early ages, divorce or break-up and emergent single motherhood in Russia. As an academic from the Higher School of Economics in Moscow stated, 'Russian women cannot fully rely on their husbands often because he does not earn enough and because she is not sure if he will be here tomorrow as he is'. Overall, this creates a vicious circle, in which women compulsorily show willingness to work on unfavourable terms, which eventually reinforces their secondary status within the labour force in both Russia and Turkey.

Care Work Policies in Russia and Turkey

Despite the efforts to remedy the situation, the severe shortage of public, free and/ or affordable day care centres and pre-school institutions still persists as a major obstacle to the equal participation, competition and progress of women in the labour market. In the Soviet system, the universal provision of monetary support and real services regardless of age, education, position and occupation was a state policy and the care system was institutionalized in the entire country (Chernova, 2012b). As a result of the transition to a market economy in the 1990s, public childcare services were drastically reduced by almost 40 per cent in pre-school institutions in early post-Soviet Russia. While 84 per cent of children over three years old went to pre-schools between 1961 and 1991, 47 per cent of them came to be taken care of at home between 1991 and 2001 (Teplova, 2007, p.293). The number of children on the waiting list for nursery or kindergarten was estimated as approximately one million, with an increase of 600 per cent, by 2006 (Chernova, 2012a, p.87). According to the Federal State Statistics Service, no change was observed in the coverage of children by pre-school education, which was estimated as 67 per cent in 2000, 63 per cent in 2013 (Rosstat, 2015) and 66.3 per cent in 2016 (Rosstat, 2016).

The development of pre-school education, including supporting the establishment of private pre-schools, home-based kindergartens and child day care centres, has become a national priority for the Russian government in recent years (Putin, 2012a). The allocation of a budget equal to 50 billion Russian Rubles (RUB) was announced in 2013 for spending on developing pre-school institutions. The federal government established new rebates to offset day care costs for parents, but the local and regional conditions/specificities continue to constrain access to adequate day care (Chandler, 2013, p.161). As Putin himself affirmed (2014b), by 2014 less than half of all pre-schools in Russia provided care facilities for children under the age of three.

In Turkey, the state has never had a firm commitment to providing public childcare. The general tendency is that women as homemakers and care providers withdraw or step back from the labour force, especially after marriage and childbirth. Despite the recent initiatives to increase women's employment, this perception has not yet changed. Pro-employment initiatives do not go hand in hand with public child and elderly care policies. On the contrary, institutional care is disdained and the familial care of children, the elderly and the disabled is promoted. The statement 'plant a crèche, harvest a nursing home' epitomizes the party's approach to institutional care.

Despite increases in the availability of childcare and pre-school services in Turkey over the last decade, both the supply of services and their utilization remain low. Compared to statistics from 2006, as of 2015 the total number of service providers has increased by 30.5 per cent, and 72.1 per cent of this increase has been through public sector provision. By 2015, a total of 26,972 schools and care centres were in operation in Turkey. Public providers represent 83.8 per cent of all providers of childcare services but most of them do not provide full-time day care and care services for 0-to-5-year-old children. The majority of full-day care services are provided by the private sector. However, they are limited in availability and more expensive than the average household is willing or able to afford. By 2015, 29.5 per cent of children in the 3 to 5 age group in Turkey are estimated to utilize education and care services from early childhood (World Bank, 2015). So, the general tendency is that most women with pre-school-age children do care work at home or count on help from family relatives with little utilization of childcare services in the private sector (Ilkkaracan, 2012).

A vast majority of interviewees in both the public and private sector mentioned that the development of an effective childcare system in quality and quantity proves the most lasting and transformative solution to gender equality in the labour force. Both Russian and Turkish families have unequal access to child day care facilities. In Russia, private day care centres charge fees that are barely affordable for low-income households and single mothers, while public day care facilities generally remain insufficient in numbers to provide full coverage for children, particularly for those under three years old (RANEPA, 2015). Russian interviewees underlined that finding a vacant place in a public childcare facility is such a long and onerous process that women are sometimes drawn to use bribes to register on the waiting lists for pre-schools or day care. A researcher from the St Petersburg European University gave crucial hints about this process:

Women have to use some corruption and go to the director of the kindergarten and ask [them directly], or [subscribe] or put themselves on a waiting list for the kindergarten when they are pregnant. All so that in three years' time, they will have a place for their babies [when their name comes up on the waiting list].

In the absence of opening up sufficient child day care centres and pre-school institutions, as Teplova (2007) depicts, a neo-familial model of care has become a new trend in the post-Soviet era as a result of the complex interaction of deeply embedded traditional values and neo-liberal policies. This model has reinforced the perception of women as the main care providers and has not promoted the redistribution of care work. The grandmothers come to support their single and/or married daughters in unpaid care work in the absence of active support from men in sharing care work and housework and of state support for families with children (Utrata, 2015). An interviewee from the Women's Union, who lived through the Soviet era, shared her personal experience of having assumed the work of caring for her grandchild as her daughter cannot find a suitable day care or pre-school. However, the lack of opportunity to rely on support from family members or older relatives created a serious problem for young parents.

While neo-familialism is a post-Soviet phenomenon in Russia, housewifization and familialism as the model for care work are the prevailing cultural norms in Turkey. The unequal division of domestic chores and care work reduces the attractiveness of working life for married women. According to the Population Household Survey, single and younger women participate more in the labour force than married women (TÜİK, 2011, p.131). Even for women with higher education, being a housewife can be preferred over work and they may withdraw from the labour force for childrearing.[5] For most women, particularly for those with low levels of education, the difference between earnings and the cost of care is too low to motivate women to stay in the labour force or pay for childcare and kindergarten services. If not quitting the job at least for a temporary period, working mothers have to rely on family support from their mothers or mothers-in-law. A representative from Capital Women's Platform in Ankara commented as follows:

> Generally, they [working mothers] get support from their mothers [for childcare]. Their mothers take care of their children. Otherwise, she has to pay a third of her salary for nursery or crèche. Actually, affording the expense of crèche and nursery is not enough because child's entry-exit hours might not match with the mother's working hours.

Although 61.2 per cent of women outside the labour force still declared homemaking as the reason for their non-participation (ASPB, 2012b), the Turkish state does not seem determined concerning the development and implementation of public care policies as a way of resolving the main factors that impede a considerable increase in female employment. An academic from the Middle East Technical University stated that:

> You can call them passive policies because they do not say that women should stay at home but they say that women should care for the disabled people, the children. The crèches of SHÇEK [Institution of Social Services and Child Protection] were closed. There is no institutionalization in care work. The existing institutions are being destroyed. Senior centres were closed down. New ones are not opened up. When all these are coupled, there is no room left for women to go outside the house.

According to the Labour Code, employers who hire between 100 and 150 female workers are obliged to establish a nursing room for infants to be cared for and breastfed. If the number is more than 150, then employers have to find both a nursing room and a childcare centre for children aged between 0 and 6. Male workers can utilize these services provided that they are divorced or widowed. The criteria of number and eligibility reflect the traditional conviction that care work is a female duty and obligation. As long as this requirement is not regardless of gender and number, its implementation turns into a disadvantage for women in the labour force. Female workers become a costly and unattractive labour force that employers prefer not to hire or employers appeal to small tactics such as keeping the number slightly under the legal limit, in order to escape this obligation.

Pro-employment initiatives have been supported with the reformulation of the family as the main unit of care, through pro-family discourse and the introduction of new material benefits for in-home care by women. The state has chosen to compensate for the shortage of public care by introducing a new social policy called cash transfer. This benefit is paid directly to housewives in return for their caring for children, the elderly and the disabled at home (Buğra 2012, p.27). This means that, under the guise of supporting mothers, the state thereby incorporates social policy into the wide network of family ties, hinders the institutionalization of care services and institutionalizes familialism as the main unit of care. This attitude to the family was not invented by the AKP but it has institutionalized family relations to lift social burdens from the state. An academic from Hacettepe University evaluated the role of the family as follows:

> Family is functionalized in a more effective way than former governments and state policies. For instance, there was no payment for care services before. It has become a natural part of social policy. We objected many times to the transformation of KSGM into the Ministry of the Family. This was not simply symbolic. The establishment of the Ministry of the Family and Social Policies signified the unity between social policy and the family on the institutional level. This is not in accordance with conservative and traditional understanding, either. Cash benefit for care services is an example. The family is a union of love. All of us are a part of a family. On the one hand, there is an ideological discourse saying that mothers take care of their children, the elderly, etc. On the other hand, they [the government] are aware that this does not work that way in practice. That is why they support family care instead of public care and allocate a budget.

Promoting familialism ideologically and materially as a model of care work indicates that the Turkish state acknowledges the impossibility of running a household on a single wage and intends to relieve the economic problems of low-income families where women are mostly out of the formal labour force. This sort of protectionist policy targeting women from lower-class families enabled the government to keep its ties strong with its conservative constituency and meet their welfare needs. However, this protectionist orientation does not target the empowerment of women outside the family. A feminist activist from Ankara mentioned that 'they [the state] have been redefining the family. They have been redefining women within the family. They have been stimulating a form of empowerment but this is not the kind of empowerment that we seek. So, the issue of family is related to the current approach on woman.'

6

Pro-Natalism and the Rediscovery of Motherhood

In Russia and Turkey, a neo-traditional and neo-conservative gender climate is clearly embodied in the design of pro-natal policies. Many interviewees from both sides brought up the combination of nationalism, patriotism, morality and accusations of criminality in the formulation of pro-natal policies. Despite significant differences regarding demographic problems and the situation of the family, both the Russian and Turkish states gender the demographic and moral situation by linking national survival to asymmetrical gender roles ascribed to biologically determined differences. Moreover, a pro-natal discourse and policies surrounding reproductive behaviour, abortion, birth control and maternity have gained momentum, accompanied with a discourse of strengthening the family in both cases.

The demographic decline in Russia that dates back to the late-Soviet period has worsened with low birth rates and abnormal death rates from the mid-1990s to the mid-2000s. The population of Russia decreased from 148.7 million in 1992 to 143.2 million in 2005.[1] The death rate was 50 per cent higher in 1997 than in 1987 (2.3 million as opposed to 1.5 million), while the birth rate dropped to 1 million (Eberstadt, 2004, pp.9–10). By 2005, the negative difference between the number of deaths and births was estimated at 11.2 million (Putin cited in Cook, 2011, p.1). The demographic decline has been an issue of national priority for Putin from the very beginning. In January 2000, Putin stated that the social crisis characterized by demographic problems and moral degradation posed a serious threat to Russia's national security and sovereignty (MFA, 2000). In the Concept of Demographic Development for the Russian Federation through 2015, issued in 2001, the preconditions for achieving a higher birth rate are outlined as supporting family values and increasing family welfare, including housing conditions, material prosperity, conditions for raising several children and so on (Demoscope, 2001). In the president's address to the Federal Assembly in 2006, Putin (2006a) indicated support for working women, who have to combine work and family obligations, to encourage childbirth with the introduction of material measures including maternity capital and new child benefits. Supporting large families with at least three minors was inscribed into the pro-natal policy with the introduction of regional maternity capital funded by regional authorities, allocation of land and additional tax incentives to parents (Medvedev, 2010). 'Strengthening the family' is addressed in the Concept of Family Policy to 2025 with suggestions to reduce the number of divorces with higher divorce taxation, to reduce extra-marital birth rates and abortion, and to increase birth rates in wedlock with support for larger families.

In Turkey, in contrast to Russia, the fertility rate is not low. Although demographic projections point to a decreasing population growth rate, the fertility rate per woman was estimated as 2.10 by 2016, which is still higher than the average rate in Europe (TÜİK, 2017). Despite these figures, Erdoğan has recently initiated a pro-natal policy with the double aims of preventing the aging of the population and bringing up a pious generation. At the Women's Day Celebration in 2008, Erdoğan made an unexpected declaration and suggested women should have at least three children. He explained this declaration and further ones concerning abortion, family planning and C-section deliveries as indicating a desire to safeguard the strength and survival of the Turkish nation and avoid the problem of an aging population that is currently confronting Western countries (Taylor, 2014). At the International Family and Social Policies Summit, Erdoğan said that 'at least three children are necessary in each family, because our population risks aging. We are still on the good side, as we still own a young and dynamic population. But we are slowly aging. Currently, the whole Western world is trying to cope with this problem' (*Hürriyet Daily News*, 2013).

Additionally, the traditional family marked by conservative lifestyle preferences is promoted as the spiritual foundation of society, which will prevent moral degradation at both the individual and the social level and act as a shelter against social risks. A strengthening of the family discourse and policy has been put into practice with a new population policy that targets higher birth rates with a set of incentives, including maternity leave, child and family benefits, the option to take early retirement, reductions in income tax for workers, marriage credits, more flexible working conditions in the public sector, and the development of a family- and child-friendly social and cultural environment (Yılmaz, 2015, p.381). The Ministry of the Family and Social Policies organizes seminars on premarital education and family education in various provinces and in public institutions. The Ministry also conducts pilot projects to provide counselling for married couples before and during the divorce process. Lastly, in January 2015, a new programme called the 'Programme for the Protection of the Family and Dynamic Population Structure' (*Aile ve Dinamik Nüfusun Korunması Programı*) was introduced for protecting the family and the dynamic structure of the population by providing family education and consultancy services, extending maternity-related rights, disseminating pre-school services, and introducing new material incentives for family welfare and childcare (Onuncu Kalkınma Planı, 2015). The fact that this programme offers new incentives primarily for working women, including extending maternity leave for foster mothers, part-time work options and a lump-sum payment for giving birth, reveals the linkages between sustaining the dynamic structure of the population and the reproductive behaviour of working women.

Although both the Russian and Turkish states advocate a discourse of strengthening the family to resolve demographic problems, the phenomenon of the family shows differences in Russia and Turkey. In Russia, the fragility of family relations, stemming from the over-burdened lives of working women and the estrangement of men from family life, has been inherited from the late-Soviet days. The demographic crisis, combined with a sharp increase in divorce rates, juvenile delinquency and alcoholism, is attributed to the weakening influence of the family as a source of socialization and moral control, leading to a reassessment of gender roles. In the early 1990s, the public debate was devoted to the issue of re-establishing 'correct' gender identities, behaviours and division of labour under the guidance of biological traits (Kay, 2002, p.58). Under the rule of Putin, state support for working mothers, which had been a characteristic of the Soviet regime, returned to the national agenda primarily because of their reproductive capacities rather than because of their contribution to the economy (Chandler, 2013, p.120). An academic from the Russian Academy of Sciences in Moscow and a gender expert from the UNDP in Moscow remarked, respectively:

> Our state, our ideologists decided to support the traditional values. They decided to support not women, as it was in the Soviet period, but the family, the absolutely traditional family, not couples that are perhaps educating children and raising children but just registered family relations.

> The family issue is discussed when demography and health issues are discussed because of the deterioration of public health and alcoholism, there is a threat to birth rates and general mortality. The government looks to the family as in need of support. When family issues are adequately addressed, some other issues will fall into place. Meaning there would be generally more attention to family health, women's health, to the impact on birth rate and child health in the end. It triggers the whole stuff, the other positive developments if one is getting it right. If you see comments on the family in this context, by now there is a lot of awareness of this link. The politicians generally started in child health and give attention to it. I think this is the point that we enter in our discussion on women.

In contrast to Russia, in Turkey the emphasis on strengthening the family does not point to the erosion of the traditional family but corresponds to a paradigm shift in delineating the 'ideal Turkish family'. The transformation of Turkish society in the direction of secular and Western-oriented modernization did not lead to a weakening in the special role and function of the family. Family life, including gender roles, sexuality and reproduction, was re-regulated with the legal reforms that established equality between the sexes before the law, while considerably preserving traditional norms regarding morality, modesty and chastity of women. So, there has been a continuity concerning the privileged role that the family occupies in the reorganization of society, along either secular or conservative lines (Yılmaz, 2015). Under Erdoğan's rule, the conservative family discourse is shaped by the religious dogma that men and women, by nature, are complementary to each other, which makes seeking out equality between the sexes as of no significance. Two academics from Hacettepe University and Istanbul University observed, respectively:

> Instead of modernist and developmentalist discourse, now there is more traditionalist and conservative language.

The family has been prioritized since the Republican period. It is not specific to the AKP period. However, there are very serious differences [between these periods]. I think that the current period is a turning point in the gender regime. There are different forms in defining woman on the basis of the family. In other words, the [AKP] government and the new discourse do not even recognize equality before the law. The distinguishing feature of the Kemalist period was its intense efforts to westernize women. However, social dynamics are extremely important. The nature of the family and the way in which gender relations are established in the family are decisive.

Despite the similarities regarding the nationalist and conservative content of their pro-natal policies, Putin and Erdoğan's discourses are differently motivated. For Erdoğan, a pro-natal policy reflects his ambitions to avoid an aging population – identified as an advantage against the West – and to raise a pious generation to have the whip hand over those segments aspiring to secular values and ethnic concerns. Referring to *fitrat*, Erdoğan has characterized women who do not comply with motherhood as 'half persons' who abstain from maternity and deny their femininity (Bruton, 2016). His pro-natal discourse carries an apparently humiliating and blaming subtext for women who do not follow pro-natal policies, on the basis of their not acting in conformity with religious dictates. By contrast, Putin aims to reverse the negative demographic trend with a public discourse that encourages women to give birth to more children, and appreciates them for doing so, on the basis of patriotism, national survival and long-standing Russian traditions of love for children, loyalty, compassion and selfless support. The key nodes of Putin's approach to the demographic crisis can be identified as national security, family policy and moral degradation. The rationale behind his approach and policies is that, in order for Russian sovereignty to be restored, not only does the state apparatus need to be strengthened and economic stability achieved but the growth of procreation, moral restoration and the welfare of the family also need to be assured.

Both Putin and Erdoğan's ways of resolving demographic problems have a gender-neutral language, ignoring the realities of gendered inequalities in family, the labour market and society. A concern with gender inequality and discrimination that mainly stems from traditional gender roles is not observed in either Putin or Erdoğan's speeches and policies. Pro-natal policies designed to increase fertility rates do not challenge but deepen gendered hierarchies in the economy, politics and at home. The Russian state's approach to gender equality with a view to the social protection of motherhood and reproductive rights has impeded initiatives for the advancement of women and the provision of equal opportunities.

The Conceptualization of Motherhood by the Russian and Turkish States

The assumption that biologically determined differences between men and women have greater implications for the distribution of roles influences the ways of resolving demographic problems in both Russia and Turkey. As long as the demographic crisis is gendered, biological differences will be used to delineate the acceptable images of femininity and masculinity. Motherhood is treated as the primary social role and function of being 'a proper woman', and this treatment is justified through female biological traits. Being portrayed as naturally emotional, gentle and soft versus rational, selfish and wild, women are presumed to be more properly suited to the role of taking care of their family. Then, establishing strong family ties and a warm home environment is seen as women's primary duty; home–family is claimed as women's natural and non-negotiable life space and motherhood as women's natural destiny (Kay, 2000, pp.29–30). A feminist activist from Moscow pointed out that:

> There is an underlying assumption that the genders are different [and that this] is a natural way of life that does not quite mean that they are not equal but [rather that] they are different, and with these differences [certain inequalities, discrepancies or certain elements of different stages of life] may come. As I said, there is an assumption that women are more responsible for children and care of the children, which is again taken for [granted] as natural. For a woman, having, raising and starting a family is naturally interesting, important and valuable.

In this framing, motherhood is to a large extent connected with essentialist ideas about predestination and the ability of a woman to be a mother and such ideas are offered as explanations of their greater involvement in running the household and in childcare, while fatherhood is defined in terms of earning the family's livelihood. An academic from St Petersburg European University stated:

> The portrayal of women [in the post-Soviet time] is primarily as mothers, [which the government has promoted] in the past [few] years. [...] Women are mostly connected [to the home] in Russia. When women's images are primarily related to family obligations and as mothers, [the obligation to work] is secondary compared to the family.

In both Russia and Turkey, traditional and conservative gender discourse and policies link population decline, family decline and the decline of the moral order. This linking relies on the conviction that women have a finer sense of morality and justice because of female biological traits. Women are assumed to be morally superior to men, due to 'the maternal role and its subsequent nurturing and caring characteristics, which were ascribed to all women regardless of their actual maternal status', and therefore more responsible for safeguarding the future of the national and moral order (Kay, 2000, pp.29–30). An academic from the Russian Academy of Sciences in Moscow evaluated the focus on demography in Russia as follows:

> Now, if we're considering Russia, the state has some gender [policies] but they are very controversial. Now the focus of these policies is mainly demographic. There is a lot of moral panic about the demographic situation and the low birth rate. So, the focus of politics is demography.

Both Russian and Turkish states assume the responsibility for protecting women but this protective role is linked to the aim of guaranteeing the security of the family and society rather than recognizing women as individuals. The status, rights and interests of women are restricted to the area of the family and the role of motherhood. The linking has the effect of ignoring women's self-realization as individuals and their emancipation from the family. Women's self-realization is primarily portrayed as motherhood. An academic from St Petersburg European University and a public officer from the Ministry of the Family and Social Policies in Ankara observed, respectively, that:

> National politics always has a gender dimension. The demographic problem is a particular one: women are assessed as reproductive resources. The church is happy about it; it's very strict about who are bad women and who are good women. Demography and reproduction are state issues because that is how the state sees the demographic problem. If the state sees the demographic problem as a migration issue, this is another story. Part of the demographic problem is reproduction and women. They used to be productive and reproductive. But now they almost forget about their productive roles. Reproduction is not a private but a political issue.

> Despite the awareness about women, we have been observing an increasing emphasis on the family in the discourse of the Prime Minister, other Ministers and our Minister [of the Family and Social Policies]. For instance, when one analyses the texts, it is found out that there is a hidden implication [in the efforts] to solve the problems of the family and to assure a peaceful family.

In both Russia and Turkey, challenging Western culture is extremely important in the construction of traditional and conservative discourse, which emphasizes the traditional family and motherhood as distinguishing indicators of the Russian and Turkish cultures. For instance, the image of women who chase after professional aspirations and consequently avoid or delay childbirth is presented as a destructive influence of Western culture. Western ideas are considered to bring egotism for women and to be destructive of the Russian nation and culture. An academic from the Russian Academy of Sciences in Moscow commented that:

> Our government, all these ideologists, they all are speaking about a demographic crisis and they see a connection between Western feminism and this demographic crisis. They say that Western feminism is the [reason] for the decreasing number of children because every woman would like to realize herself. She is thinking about her self-realization. When she is 20, 30, 35 years old and even when she is 40, she is not ready to have children and [now] very few women are ready to have more than two children.

In Turkey, the neo-conservative critique of Republican modernization creates the fiction that the natural harmony between the sexes was destroyed and the family weakened because of the Western-oriented Republican reforms, despite the family having been a permanent feature of the Republican regime. Social and moral troubles are related to the loss of power and importance of the family, due to Western aspirations. So, the emphasis on the traditional family structure is renewed, as if it had been lost or broken in Turkish society, to deal with social troubles and, more importantly, to preserve Turkish national authenticity. An academic from the Middle East Technical University shared her/his insights about the incorporation of the family in social policies:

> In Turkey, the family has always been a cherished institution but in the last decade, gradually a discourse on how the family institution has been underrated or ignored was incorporated in the state policies. And a glorification of the family institution, which I sometimes call 'family fetishism', has started. Now, I see it on the TV spots of the Ministry of the Family and Social Policies.

In both cases, the growing power of the Orthodox Church and the Directorate of Religious Affairs reinforces the national and moral dimension of the pro-natal debate. In Russia, the Orthodox Church draws attention to moral decline on the basis of the erosion of traditional family values and identifies feminism that equates with liberal values, reading gender equality as a threat to the national security of Russia. The accusation of the Orthodox Church that single women are egotistical reinforces the nationalist understanding of the demographic crisis. In Turkey, similarly, to oppose the portrayal of women within the family as having a duty to reproduce has been considered an attack on the unity of the nation and 'moral' values. In 2008, the Directorate of Religious Affairs denounced 'feminism as an immoral' position (Altunok, 2016, p.142). Backed up with religious beliefs, pro-natal discourse and policies privilege motherhood as a marker of difference that targets those who are allegedly anti-national, immoral and not part of 'the people'. Maternity is identified as a sacred duty that needs to be undertaken for the sake of the Russian and Turkish nations rather than an individual matter. In other words, religious values and norms strengthen the hands of the Russian and Turkish states to avoid any challenge to traditional and conservative discourse and policies that are hardly designed in conformity with gender equality concerns, and enable them to justify their authoritarian interventions into reproductive behaviours. As academics from St Petersburg European University and Hacettepe University, respectively, remarked:

> On the one hand, [we have] the patriarchal type of neo-traditionalism, which is easily identified with the politics of the Russian Orthodox Church and Russian nationalism. They come together and nationalism is always quite traditional. The church ideology [is such that] they emphasize gender boundaries, they essentialize gender, and they try to moralize gender roles and sexuality and women's reproductive capacities. Family becomes very feminine and their femininity is also very traditional because when you speak about family, they have a very archaic understanding of what family is. When we speak about sexual life, they have very moral lines [which are] very different from real practices in understanding what should be 'proper' sexual life, [the division of men's and women's roles], and what

[makes a] 'good' man or woman. That is neo-traditionalism. It is very vocal in the Russian church. The church is getting more power ideologically and politically because politicians want to build up the national idea and also to have ideological legitimacy.

Here, we are talking about a sort of conservatism, which is embedded in masculinity. In the 2000s, masculinity has continued. However, it is different from the one we had in the early Republican period, which maintained equality on the basis of citizenship along with the criteria of chastity, motherhood and honour. Rather, we have been witnessing a form of conservatism, which defines women on the basis of religio-morality. I need to emphasize its religious basis in order to reveal the differentiation between the moral rules and the ethics. In doing so, it gives reference to and prioritizes the religion-based moral principles.

In this setting, the family is sanctified and idealized as if it were a sphere independent of any power struggle and violence. This impossible ideal is imposed over women as a sacred role and obligation. In this ideal picture, the rights and interests of 'woman' as an individual are sacrificed for an ultimate goal. Embracing traditional values is proposed as a solution to all socio-economic and cultural problems that both countries have to deal with. Various different forms of family life associated with class affiliation and economic and social status have appeared. Academics from the Middle East Technical University in Ankara and the Russian Academy of Sciences in Moscow made similar remarks on the imagined role of the family, respectively:

In Turkey, the family is always presented as a happy and peaceful place and traditionally great emphasis has been placed on this institution. Also, we see that lately the extended family model is often emphasized. For instance, not only mothers, fathers and dependent children but grandmothers, grandfathers, uncles, and aunts are included in the TV spots put out by the Ministry of the Family and Social Policies; there are many people inside that intertwined ribbon depicting the family in these TV spots. There is a glorification of the family institution and a perception of women as simply extensions of this institution. Women are given the responsibility to take care of and ensure that this glorious institution continues in a healthy way. The family is not only a very important institution but also its continuation until eternity depends on 'our women acting with the right values'. This approach constantly refers to women as 'our women' (as I deliberately emphasized) and the word 'our' implies ownership. The responsibility for the continuation of the family institution and that of being the key agent to provide happiness to all members of the family, including the elderly, the children and the disabled, are laid on women in this parlance.

Demographics are presented by the leaders of the country, by Putin and Medvedev or whoever is around now, as a solution or as a potential solution to all the problems [the country is facing]. The scheme is very simple if not to say simplistic. There are fewer and fewer people and your demography is falling. If they can stabilize [the population], things will be better. If women suddenly begin to have more children, everything will be resolved: economic and social issues will become better as long as women keep having more and more children, [because] we have more people. This is the main premise.

Abortion Policy in Russia and Turkey

Regarding reproductive rights, the regulation of access to abortion emerged as the most salient issue in Russia and Turkey. In both countries, restricting abortion is proposed as a resolution to provide the conditions for women to opt to give birth and thus prevent a demographic crisis. Russia has one of the highest rates of abortion in the world, despite the considerable decrease achieved from more than 2 million in 2001 to 929,963 in 2014. The high rate is related to the perception of abortion as a contraceptive method, due to the limited access to modern contraceptive devices since Soviet days. A law banning abortion has not yet been issued, but the Russian state has followed the path of tightening the abortion regime since 2003 to deal with the high rate of abortion (Johnston, 2018). The conditions for terminating pregnancies in the second trimester were restricted in 2004. On 3 December 2007 the State Duma introduced a decree entitled 'On approving the list of medical conditions for artificial pregnancy termination' and prohibited access to abortion on the formerly acceptable social grounds of poverty and unemployment. Another measure introduced in 2008 makes counselling about the risks of having an abortion compulsory, along with signed consent by women who choose to terminate their pregnancy (Cook, 2011, pp.7–8). In 2011, the State Duma introduced new restrictions on abortion that limits the timeframe for abortions to up to 12 weeks of pregnancy, or up to 22 weeks in the case of pregnancy resulting from rape, and at any point in the event of medical complications. The law also requires a waiting period of 2–7 days before abortions can be performed and obliges pregnant women to see the foetus on ultrasound and have counselling before terminating the pregnancy (Rossiiskaia Gazeta, 2011).

The interviewees pointed to the increasing visibility of the Orthodox in anti-abortion campaigns that urge the government to ban abortion nationwide (RT, 2017). In the 2011 amendments, the proposals, backed by the Orthodox Church, to disqualify abortion as a medical service in the national health plan and to require the consent of the husband for married women and that of parents for teenage girls before abortion were not included in the law (RBTH, 2014). However, in 2015, new legislation to restrict access to abortion was proposed by the Duma's Committee on Issues of Women, the Family and Children, in cooperation with the Orthodox Church (National Right to Life News, 2015). Most of the interviewees stated that the state has intentionally involved the Orthodox Church to revive family values and glorify motherhood and added a moral and religious dimension to the nationalist debate about reproductive rights. As they argued, this has had the impact of justifying the criminalization and stigmatization of abortion via moral and national references in public opinion. In doing so, they said, the state distracts public opinion from social ills such as unemployment, poverty, the deterioration of education and healthcare services, the short supply of day care centres and urban housing, the lack of sex education, and the prevalence of alcoholism and domestic violence, which they cited as the main reasons for the low fertility rates.

> Women don't want to give birth to many children because they are not sure about their future. If they are living in poverty, they don't want to create more poor people. They [may also] want to give [their children] a good education and they can't rely on men. The big problem is that the Orthodox Church is unfortunately getting more and more influence in my country. The Church [supports] the prohibition of abortion.

In contrast to Russia, Turkey has maintained a liberal regime regarding access to abortion and use of contraceptive devices. In 1983, abortion was legalized until the end of the tenth week of pregnancy for non-medical reasons, was legally permissible through 20 weeks in the case of sexual assault, and without limits if the health or life of the woman or the foetus was in danger. Married women and minors are obliged to obtain consent for the abortion from the spouse or parent, respectively. According to World Health Organization statistics, the number of abortions at all ages remained less than 100,000 annually between 2002 and 2013 (WHO, 2018). However, it was, unexpectedly, brought up by Erdoğan in 2012 after thirty-five civilians, who were initially suspected of being Kurdish militants, were killed in an air attack along the south-eastern border. He linked this incident with abortion and called it 'murder' (Radikal, 2012). In pro-state circles, his aim was treated as being to change the public agenda and deflect the reactions against the attack rather than to limit the reproductive rights of women. However, as many of the interviewees noted, this explanation revealed the significance of women's bodily autonomy and reproductive rights for political concerns. Upon his speech, a draft law on abortion was proposed by the AKP. If passed into law, it would give medical staff the option to refuse to perform abortions on the grounds of personal belief or conscience. Although, in Turkish culture, abortion is not condemned as a sin, it is seen as a moral transgression.[2] Indeed, some interviewees from the Islamist women's movement admitted that many women from conservative circles have at least one abortion over the course of their lives. The previous legislation concerning abortion remained intact in the face of an immediate public outcry. However, since then, de facto limitations have been imposed on access to abortion derived from the attitude of medical staff and arbitrary violations of the law at the majority of state hospitals.[3]

Erdoğan's personal prejudice against C-sections establishes another form of state intervention in women's reproductive rights. According to him, C-sections are a threat to the survival of the Turkish nation because women, fearing that repeat Caesarean deliveries might cause health damage, tend to restrict the number of deliveries to two (CNNTÜRK, 2013).[4] He has also characterized birth control as treason and accused those who advocate birth control of seeking the Turkish nation's extinction (Taylor, 2014). Lastly, he has renewed his opposition to birth control on the basis of religious dictates (Diken, 2016). In parallel to his explanations, the General Directorate of

Family Planning, which provided information to women about birth control and distributed contraceptive devices, has been closed down. An academic depicted this shift as a passive pro-natal policy that does not explicitly denounce birth control but causes women to lose easy and free access to contraceptive devices:

> Regarding health services, the General Directorate of Family Planning was closed. This means that there is no longer a population policy; we do not teach birth control. Such a decision was made and this is an important decision. It is a very institutional decision. This is a passive pro-natal policy because it does not clearly declare that I will not provide you with a family planning service. However, with the closure of the General Directorate, women who would like to have birth control are discouraged, on the one hand. On the other hand, with the statement of three children, reproduction is encouraged.

These legal regulations and the leaders' speeches regarding the reproductive rights of women reflect traditional and conservative gender discourses in tandem with the authoritarian interventions of both states. In this framing, women demanding abortion are condemned as sinful, murderous and unpatriotic and blamed for defying religious and moral values at a societal level, even if the procedure continues to be legal. As most interviewees from Russia and Turkey pointed out, the de facto restrictions, such as emotional manipulation, humiliation, poor service conditions and lack of anaesthesia at public hospitals, are designed to deter women from seeking abortion and at the same time illustrate the power of state discourse to manage the social perceptions of women who do not comply with the notion of 'good' femininity and the state's disciplinary power over reproductive decisions to achieve a higher rate of fertility and to protect religious values.

Furthermore, not all Russian and Turkish women are exposed to these restrictions in the same way. If elaborated from an intersectional point of view, their experiences are very much shaped by class differences and regional disparities. The mandatory waiting period and the exclusion of anaesthesia from insurance coverage in Russia, the limitations on C-sections in Turkey, the poor and unhygienic conditions and violation of legal rights regarding abortion at state hospitals in both countries largely affect poor and rural women and women in vulnerable situations, while middle- and upper-class and urban women can avoid these restrictions and receive high-quality service without insult, humiliation or pain in private clinics. Moreover, in Turkey, state hospitals practise a punitive measure – that is, the disclosure of abortion care to women's husbands and parents without their consent, which constitutes a violation of women's rights and autonomy concerning sexuality and reproductive rights. This punitive measure puts young and single women, who can barely afford the costs of obtaining abortion in private clinics, in a very difficult situation. An expert from a crisis centre based in St Petersburg observed that:

> It includes a week of silence to think about the abortion [and decide whether or not to do it]. It will absolutely work against women's health because for women who are from poor families, who have no money or who live in rural areas, it

is impossible to visit the gynaecologist again after a week. During the week [of silence], a state-supported crisis centre calls women to manipulate them into not having the abortion. [These crisis centres] have [a lot of] resources. They do consultations on not having abortions, rejecting abortion, and blaming women for abortion. They say abortion is killing [...] If you want to have an abortion without any problem, you should go to a private clinic and pay around 175 dollars. This way, you don't have to wait one more week. You pay for everything and everything is good with anaesthesia. [With this sort of restriction] people think that women could have more children but for women from the middle class it isn't difficult to go have an abortion in a private clinic.

Traditional and conservative gender discourse connects the reproductive behaviour of women to the question of the maintenance of the Russian and Turkish nation and state. The above-mentioned restrictions mean laying a bio-political claim on women's bodies, which is formulated in reference to national, religious and moral ambitions. Drawing on the empirical findings, it is possible to argue that the Russian and Turkish states have intentionally revised legal amendments, policies and practices in reference to a moral and national narrative, which may ultimately deter women from seeking abortion care and discourage physicians from providing a service to them because they are fearful of the penalty. However, reducing abortion rates by tightening pregnancy termination terms does not necessarily lead to a direct increase in fertility rates.

Maternity Capital in Russia

In Russia, another state benefit that all interviewees mentioned is maternity capital. Maternity capital was introduced in 2007 and later renamed family capital.[5] It is a certificate and entitlement for mothers who give birth to a second or third child. Since 2015, maternity (family) capital amounts to RUB 453,026, index-linked to inflation, and is paid to mothers when the child reaches the age of three. The money will not be paid in cash but in a voucher and is restricted to three possible uses: the purchase or improvement of an apartment, the mother's pension savings or the child's education costs. Single-parent households with one child, which are quite common, are not eligible for the maternity capital benefit. Its purpose was explained as intended to resolve the dilemma of unpaid care work for women who either choose to quit work and stay at home with children or forego having children to advance their careers (Rotkirch et al., 2007, p.353).

However, almost all interviewees were highly critical of the maternity capital benefit for being gender-framed. In his annual speech in May 2006, when maternity capital was first mentioned, Putin (2006a) referred to young families as synonymous with mothers and did not say a word about the role of men as husbands and fathers in childbirth, childrearing and family life. Mothers and families are defined as the target group of the incentives and support programmes for encouraging the birth rate, particularly for the second and third child. In this framing, women are still designated as those who undertake the bulk of childcare and are recognized as struggling with the conflicting claims of work and family. The benefit does not encourage a more equitable gendered division of labour at home, but rather aims to help women who have to leave the job market to care for children or avoid giving birth to a second child.

> Maternal capital is gendered. It is maternal. It should be parental and include men, too. This compensates women's leave from work and professionalizes the housewife. For this purpose, if the state is traditional, it is too [little] for mothers. Women have to work sooner or later to earn money for their family.

Maternity capital reflects the Russian state's interest in setting the norms regarding family structure and reproductive behaviours. With this benefit, the state showed its commitment to mainly support a certain type of family, consisting of two parents with two or more children, and seems to negatively perceive or ignore single-child families. Another academic from St Petersburg European University remarked:

> I think there is a kind of picture of a very specific kind of family with very specific needs and very specific resources. They had a very particular type of family in mind when they implemented this policy. Of course, [this type] is a heterosexual family with a man as the breadwinner and a woman, well-educated but mostly a housewife, who is ready to leave her job and stay at home with their children.

Maternity capital might affect reproductive decision-making only slightly, if at all, because it assumes a certain type of family that has access to socio-economic resources. Many interviewees pointed out that class differences and regional disparities are not necessarily considered in estimating its amount. Maternity capital, they argued, would help middle- and upper-class families who already have an apartment to upgrade with the benefit, although it is hardly enough to buy an apartment in Moscow or St Petersburg, compared to rural areas, with this amount of money. On the other hand, for low-income families, who do not have any assets or income to convert capital into more housing space, financing the current needs of the new-born is a more urgent issue than investing for the future education of children. An expert from the Consortium of Women's Non-Governmental Associations in Moscow evaluated maternity capital as follows:

> And [the young families] couldn't use this money for their own reasons like buying clothes for children or for food for the family. They have to use it for three reasons and this money is not [sufficient]. In Russia, RUB 300,000 is not enough for [buying] a house. Maybe it is [a sufficient amount of] money for education but every family needs to eat and [every child needs clothes] now, not three years later. That's why maternity capital isn't a way to solve this demographic problem.

A small group of academics from the European University at St Petersburg, who were involved in research to measure the impact of maternity capital on reproductive decision-making, noted that working women needed institutional support, including public childcare, health care and education, more than they needed a lump-sum payment, although maternity capital would be better than nothing for them.

> It is like having a meal: you have the normal meal, the meat and everything, and after that [you have] this small piece of chocolate. This maternal leave is like a piece of chocolate. It is good and [it is available] but that is not enough. You still need the normal meal; you need the whole system to work properly so you can trust this institution.

Combatting Domestic Violence in Russia and Turkey

Domestic violence appears as the most visible indicator of rising gender inequality in both Russian and Turkish societies. Although the Russian and Turkish cases show differences in terms of the legal regulation of domestic violence, they converge on understanding it from a family-oriented perspective. The lack of an understanding of domestic violence as a violation of women's rights constitutes one of the strongest traits of the neo-traditional/conservative gender climates in both cases. In the 1990s, the Russian government legally regulated the privatization of domestic violence. Proscribing state intervention regarding the violation of women's rights in the private sphere was justified under the guise of privacy, which was considerably violated during the Soviet era (Johnson, 2009, p.30). With the campaigns initiated especially by women's organizations over the decade, domestic violence was named for the first time and identified as a specific violation of human rights (Johnson, 2007, p.381). Thanks to these efforts, the issue of domestic violence was placed on the agenda three times. In 1993, the Women of Russia Party proposed a draft law but it did not succeed. In 1997, the bill was again on the agenda of the Duma but again was not issued. A package of bills addressing domestic violence was introduced once more in 1999 but child abuse was at the forefront of the package. The most productive proposal was in the 2001 five-year plan introduced by the Ministry of Labour and Social Development addressing various aspects of violence in the family, including the founding of government crisis centres and shelters (p.384). As a legal expert from the Consortium of Women's Non-Governmental Associations in Moscow put it:

> There was a draft law. Not one, we had about forty draft laws. Not one was adopted because our parliament says that we have legislation; we have a criminal court and you can use this legislation in domestic violence. But the police who sit every day who look at these problems every day say that our legislation isn't good. We have to get special legislation for domestic violence.

Despite these efforts, domestic violence is not legally recognized as a violation of women's human rights in conformity with gender equality norms, despite the long-standing demands of the feminist movement and women's NGOs (Johnson, 2009).

During the 2011–13 interviews, almost all interviewees touched upon the lack of adequate legislation and the reluctance of the Russian parliament to issue a specific law punishing domestic violence. An expert from Crisis Centre, based in St Petersburg, remarked that:

> Now, we are trying to [propose] a new law on violence against women. Unfortunately, the project [draft] of the new law is very old, old-fashioned, not progressive, and absolutely [contrary to] new trends and international conventions. The Istanbul Convention is progressive and strong concerning violence against women but the law prepared by the Russian government goes against this trend. It was written by the Duma deputies. We tried to send our [comments] on this new law. They were all rejected. We prepared lots of suggestions last year, from many many organizations in Russia, but they were rejected. We don't like the law on domestic violence. It didn't contain more than model suggestions. It is just [so that people can] say "yes Russia has a law on domestic violence", but it isn't comprehensive or modern. [In the draft law] you see mostly prevention, but there is no [...] system of effective promotion, punishment of perpetrators, or safety.

The absence of a specific law removes the accountability of the perpetrators, enables them to repeat violence against family members and leaves victims without any protection. As a result, the legal process does not work efficiently or fast enough to punish perpetrators immediately and protect victims of domestic violence. Even if the victim appeals to the court, 'in view of the gaps in legislation, it is extremely difficult to prove crimes of domestic violence (even physical violence, which has ensuing visible evidence)' (ANNA, 2010, pp.10–11). An expert from UNDP in Moscow described the impact of the lack of a specific law as follows:

> The courts are late on the stage. The evidence isn't collected. The issue is that many court cases come to court so late. When they come to the court, the evidence is insufficient and cannot be subsumed OK under the law.

Many interviewees from Russia complained that the government declares that the existing laws, especially the Penal Code, are sufficient to criminalize and punish domestic violence. However, there are no provisions that explicitly define and punish all forms of domestic violence in the Penal Code. Moreover, after the amendments to the Penal Code in 2003, most cases of domestic violence are defined as private prosecutions, in which the victims are deprived of state protection and must act in a prosecutorial capacity themselves (ANNA, 2010). This legal amendment makes the existing situation more complicated by the fact that domestic violence is widely perceived by law-enforcement officers and people themselves as a private conflict between spouses but not as a violation of human rights (UNDP, 2010, p.54).

> Not one [law on domestic violence] was adopted because our parliament says that we have legislation; we have a criminal court and you can use this legislation in domestic violence. We have to get special legislation for domestic violence.

Coupled with a lack of expertise and technical capacity, the lack of legal regulation allows law-enforcement bodies to act with reluctance and procrastination in treating domestic violence as a crime, collecting the necessary evidence, and proving it in court. The interviewed experts from the Women's Consortium, who were involved in training the law-enforcement bodies on handling domestic violence, cited these bodies' own complaints that the existing laws make the investigation process rather complicated. It becomes extremely difficult to prove crimes of domestic violence and the relationship between perpetrator and victim in court. Senior experts from ANNA mentioned that the lack of legal regulation removes the accountability of the perpetrators, enables them to repeat their violence and leaves the victims without protection.

Another deficiency of the legal situation in Russia is the lack of knowledge about domestic violence cases that should be categorized by marital status, education, occupation, domicile, etc., which is essential for creating efficient policies to prevent and combat domestic violence. There are no nationwide, reliable statistics on the incidence of domestic violence reports, investigations, prosecutions and convictions. According to the report prepared by the Consortium of Women's NGOs, the statistics presented by the government cover only those cases which occur within wedlock, although the number of couples living in unregistered unions amounted to 24 per cent of the total number of families by 2012. According to the figures by 2013, only 17 per cent of crimes took place against women within wedlock while 64 per cent were outside wedlock. These statistics only estimate criminal cases where a conviction was reached rather than the number of calls made to law-enforcement bodies. Considering that almost 60 to 70 per cent of women do not report the abuse they face, the credibility of these figures is weak (STOPWAV, 2014). The fact that statistical data covers only women in registered marriages provides an overview of the scale of the problem in Russia but at the same time indicates that the state treats violence that women suffer from a family-oriented perspective.

An expert from UNDP in Moscow underlined the importance of ensuring efficient follow-up and monitoring mechanisms to track domestic violence cases nationwide:

> One probably has to say that many of the achievements have also not been followed up, not even in terms of reliable figures. You need statistics to be kept up and you need reporting from the republics to the centre in order to keep a body of statistical knowledge on these issues like access to jobs, I mean, what you have on the situation of gender issue. Even the incidence of domestic violence for quite a while and even now has not been really statistically followed up. At least not consistently for all the republics and so on and so on the statistical material you have and you can ... is not really comprehensive at all. It is never really reliable statistics because there might be one or two republics that have never reported ... We can't be sure of the overall figure. That is one issue.

Although part of the problem may be attributed to the deficiencies of state mechanisms, including the absence of a specific gender violence law, the lack of sufficient crisis centres, unreliable data, a traditional and conservative gender discourse, promoted by the Russian state, have reinforced the persisting stereotypes and beliefs about innate gender differences, which see men as dominant and women as subordinate and needing protection. This has had the effect of normalizing gender violence in public, in the media and at state level in reference to traditional family values, which mainly connote to those proclaimed by the Orthodox Church. An expert from Crisis Centre based in St Petersburg commented that:

> The [available] information about violence in the family is fake. It isn't true. There is manipulation and disinformation about domestic violence. The government said very openly that they would not run a comprehensive project [draft law] against domestic violence. They rejected the issue [completely]. We have [a traditional family model]: high status of males, and fathers or husbands who control children and women and who have the power. The government invites conservative men from religious circles to give speeches and wishes to prevent the influence of outside agencies, such as pedagogical influences, on the family.

In tandem with the nationalist narrative under Putin, which stands Russia against Western countries on the basis of the advocacy of traditional family values, Russia has increasingly moved further away from combatting domestic violence. According to this narrative, the traditional family, which is built upon hierarchical relations between husband, wife and children, is an indicator of Russian national authenticity and sovereignty. Against this backdrop, the pressure from any international organizations, including UN agencies, to recognize domestic violence is regarded as an international imposition. These sorts of 'imported' steps from the West are believed to destroy the traditional family structure as the foundation of the Russian nation and state. Many interviewees reported that, because of these concerns, the Russian state shows weak liability and commitment to international obligations under CEDAW and is very reluctant to take the preventative measures suggested by the UN authorities. For instance, the Duma did not ratify the Convention on Preventing and Combatting Violence against Women and Domestic Violence of the Council of Europe, known as the Istanbul Convention (STOPWAV, 2014). As experts from ANNA stated, the shadow reports to be submitted to the UN bodies have never been prepared on time:

> Russia also signed CEDAW, [so if we follow the convention], this means that the Russian government took on the obligation to fulfil and implement all the provisions stipulated in the convention. There is the very important [obligation] that the government creates a national mechanism for gender equality. Unfortunately, the government did not adopt it. During the Putin era, many kinds of backlash happened. Among this backlash is the annihilation of the commission which existed within the frame of the presidential administration. It was not a very powerful administration but it existed. It was something like a forum. It was the year [2006] that the president spoke about women's situation and conditions in our country, and the commission was under the president. It was annihilated when Putin was the president, along with the one under the Prime Minister. It was much [worse] in the Ministry of Social Development and Health. It was reorganized and was a big department in the frame of a previous Ministry. Now only one person

is more or less [working on] women's issues (Academic from Russian Academy of Sciences in Moscow).

The Russian state keeps its distance from women's NGOs that are connected with the global feminist movement and insist on catching up with the international standards stipulated by CEDAW and the Istanbul Convention. The crisis centres, most of which used to be autonomous, with little or no funding from government and connected to the global women's movement, have become dominated by the government agencies and then come to adopt a gender-neutral approach to domestic violence, which sees domestic violence as deriving from family conflicts rather than gender-based inequality (Johnson and Saarinen, 2013). Many representatives from women's rights organizations stated that their involvement in legal consultancy, activity planning and law-making regarding preventing domestic violence remains quite limited. As an expert from a crisis centre based in St Petersburg remarked:

> Now, we are trying to [propose] a new law on violence against women. Unfortunately, the project [draft] of the new law is very old, old-fashioned, not progressive, and absolutely [contrary to] new trends and international conventions. The Istanbul Convention is progressive and strong concerning violence against women but the law prepared by the Russian government goes against this trend. It was written by the Duma deputies. We tried to send our [comments] on this new law. They were all rejected. We prepared lots of suggestions last year, from many many organizations in Russia, but they were rejected. We don't like the law on domestic violence. It didn't contain more than model suggestions. It is just [so that people can] say 'yes, Russia has a law on domestic violence', but it isn't comprehensive or modern. [In the draft law] you see mostly prevention, but there is no [...] system of effective promotion, punishment of perpetrators, or safety.

Another crucial actor of public debate on domestic violence is the Orthodox Church. The representatives of the Church argued that using the concept of domestic violence in the legal framework conflicts with the state's pro-family discourse and should be discredited because of its connections with the ideas of radical feminism.[1] The recent attempts to criminalize domestic violence were pushed back under the influence of Putin's personal beliefs and of the opposition of pro-family groups defending Orthodox values (Johnson, 2016). In 2016, battery committed by family members was criminalized for a short period through amendments to the Criminal Code. These amendments effectively criminalized domestic violence but were annulled because of pro-family concerns (about interference in family matters, protecting the status of the husband and so on) in January 2017 (Johnson, 2016). In 2017, domestic violence was decriminalized by the Duma on the basis of advocacy for the traditional Russian family, which is presented as based on hierarchical relations between the sexes (Walker, 2017). The amendment treats 'moderate' violence within families as an administrative rather than a criminal offence, punishable by a fine rather than a jail sentence. With this amendment, any violence that does not cause serious medical harm (defined as requiring hospital treatment), such as bruises, scratches or slaps, is no longer criminal.

The case can be made a criminal one if the beating is repeated within a year (Walker, 2017). In passing this amendment, the Russian government used the concept of the traditional family as a legitimate ground for decriminalizing domestic violence.

In Turkey, unlike Russia, domestic violence against women as a form of violation of individual rights and of discrimination against women is recognized at the state level. A comprehensive law, programmes and action plans to combat domestic violence have been prepared, thanks to the legal harmonization process with the EU and the efforts of women's rights movements. Turkey was the first country to ratify the Istanbul Convention with no reservations in 2011 (Acar and Altunok, 2013, p.18). In 2012, a new law called the Law on the Protection of the Family and Prevention of Violence against Women was enacted. Despite significant legal improvements and campaigns for the prevention of violence against women, however, the steady increase of femicide has not been stopped.[2] As a Turkish feminist activist remarked on this contradictory picture:

> On the one hand, the law on violence was enacted; the women's organizations have become more active and made violence against women visible. On the other hand, violence against women and murders have been increasing. All this cannot be explained with the increase in the [public] visibility of women. It can be associated with the gender policy of the state. They [the state] have been redefining the family. They have been redefining women within the family. They have been stimulating a form of empowerment but this is not the kind of empowerment that we seek. So, the issue of family is related to the current approach on women.

Most interviewees explained this contradictory situation through the state's protectionist approach to combat domestic violence. The Turkish state mainly aims to eliminate the adverse effects of domestic violence on the family union. The protectionist approach is linked to woman's roles within the family that require the state to protect women as the nation's sacred mothers and devoted wives, not as individuals deserving of equal human rights. A senior expert who has been actively working in UN bodies on violence against women commented:

> Actually, there is a serious struggle to combat violence against women. The government's violence against women policies mainly aim to protect women. [...] Theirs is a protectionist approach, which is linked to women's roles within the family (sacred mother, devoted sister image), and with the approach 'do not touch our mothers and sisters'. This is not a gender equality-based approach.

Domestic violence has been addressed at the state level but the state contains domestic violence within family policy. This illustrates that domestic violence is not regarded as violation of women's individual rights. An expert from the Foundation of Women's Solidarity, one of the leading institutions in this field, remarked that the protectionist approach becomes evident in the title of the last law issued for preventing domestic violence in 2012. In the first draft prepared by the women's rights organizations, the term family was not included in the title. Family was added by the Prime Ministry, despite the strong objection of the feminist groups.

> The Turkish government's approach to violence against women is definitely not based on a discourse originating from the individual's rights. Yet, the world has already passed this point. All contemporary international standards with respect to violence against women accept this phenomenon's relationship with inequality between women and men. Now, this is admitted by international conventions. Turkey […] ratified the legally binding Istanbul Convention on this issue. So, what does this mean? Unless you combat every dimension of inequality, inequality in politics, inequality in employment etc., and unless you maintain the equality of women and men in every field, it is hard to expect a serious improvement in the prevalence of violence against women; the protectionist approach, by itself, is just not enough.

Two National Action Plans were specifically prepared on combatting domestic violence. The first plan was prepared within the framework of the 'Combatting Domestic Violence Project', which was conducted by KSGM, funded by the EU and supported by the UNFPA. It covered the period 2007–10. Enacting necessary legal amendments, strengthening institutional mechanisms, organizing and implementing attainable protective services for victims and providing rehabilitation services for victims and perpetrators are defined as the objectives of the plan to combat domestic violence against women (KSGM, 2007). The second plan is put into action to ensure the continuation of legal and practical advances achieved in combatting domestic violence for the period of 2012–15. It has been updated in accordance with the Istanbul Convention. Its targets are defined as furthering legal regulations, eliminating deficiencies in implementation, raising awareness in society, increasing intra-institutional cooperation, improving protective and empowering measures for the victims, and providing more efficient health services for the victims (ASPB, 2012a).

Despite these advances, most interviewees stated that, at the state level, domestic violence is not seen as resulting from hierarchical relations between the sexes. Rather, as observed in the approach of the Ministry of the Family and Social Policies, it is considered a criminal issue resulting from psychological problems, poor communication among family members, alcoholism and so on. A researcher from the Middle East Technical University observed that:

> The problem is that the issue of violence against women is currently considered as a criminal issue. This is an issue of security and should be solved in this way. The police go to the [crime scene] and intervene in it. The police say do not beat your wife, in the simplest term, of course, if he can. The issue is structural though. In the current treatment, this issue is not perceived in structural terms but in cultural or individual terms. In this understanding, men beating their wives are assumed to be marginal subjects. It is believed that they beat their wives because of being alcoholics and/or mentally ill. So, they are suggested to get therapy.

It is not inaccurate to say that the so-called preventative measures against domestic violence constitute a dimension of pro-family discourse, projects and incentives, which are motivated with the aim of strengthening the family through improving family welfare, education and intra-family communication. An academic from Ankara University stated that:

> A very complex policy to prevent domestic violence has developed with pluses and minuses. There have been women's shelters, ŞÖNİMs [Violence Prevention and Monitoring Centres] and regulations. The Directorate of Religious Affairs and the General Staff have been involved in the process. They have all started programmes about the prevention of domestic violence against women. At the state level, the issue of women's rights has turned into an issue of the modernization and reformation of the family, the issue of the prevention of domestic violence and the maintenance of family peace. So, women's rights [...] have become a part of a family policy rather than a specific women's rights issue because there is actually nothing done regarding the violence against women except the family.

This protectionist approach is fortified by bringing religious instructions to the fore in the regulation of family affairs. To this end, Family Guidance and Counselling Bureaus (*Aile İrşat ve Rehberlik Bürolari*) were established under the Directorate of Religious Affairs in 2003 and have worked in close cooperation with the Ministry of the Family and Social Policies. However, some interviewees criticized this increasing involvement because the Directorate adopts a patriarchal interpretation of religion and approaches domestic violence from a protectionist and family-oriented viewpoint. Serious improvement in the prevalence of violence against women is unlikely when the problem is combatted using only a religiously supported protectionist approach that does not overlap with a gender equality-based approach. A feminist activist and lawyer, who voluntarily takes the cases of women who are exposed to domestic violence, observed that:

> The source of violence against women is the inequality between women and men and this is an issue of power, which is established on the basis of the body of woman. Unless you attempt to remove this power and you admit that women and men are really equal, you do not have a political will to end male violence against women. This government never had such a political will and still has not [...] the cases have been increasing because an interpretation which is based on male superiority has been brought up. This interpretation is claimed to be religious although it is based on the male interpretation of Islam. Besides, this interpretation has been presented as if it is the sole interpretation of Islam, and the children have been indoctrinated with this [male] interpretation.

In Turkey's strongly traditional society, it is unlikely that the actions of most police, prosecutors and judges are not based on commonly held beliefs about women's subordinate position in the family. The legal advances might help the social absorption of values regarding gender equality, only if supported by political discourse and structural reforms in conformity with gender equality concerns. So, the advocacy of a conservative discourse, based on protecting the family union and natural harmony between the sexes in reference to religion, directly and indirectly prevents the efficient enforcement of domestic violence legislation. A lawyer dealing with cases of domestic violence reported that the judges of family courts are usually required to be married with children, which is believed to provide a representative model to the spouses in conflict. Perhaps not unrelatedly, it is not uncommon for them to try to convince spouses in domestic violence cases to continue with their marriage. Another interviewee from academe observed that this sort of practical criteria creates an impact of cultural and emotional manipulation on the lawsuit process:

> There are family courts where being a judge requires being at a specific age, having a family, having a child. The judges are expected to convince the spouses to continue the marriage, if possible. Therefore, the law does not question the family as it is. In other words, even if a woman is beaten, she is not to take any course which would endanger the children and the family, and which would break the family union.

Some structural reforms make the violation of internationally recognized legislation that Turkey is to abide by possible. As the interviewees from Purple Roof, the most nationally well-known private women's shelter in İstanbul, and the Foundation for Women's Solidarity stated, public employees assume the role of mediator and stand between victim and perpetrator in the shelters run by the state. This arrangement is in direct conflict with the Istanbul Convention that Turkey is a part of and it does eliminate perpetrator accountability. An academic who has been closely monitoring the activities of public shelters remarked:

> The number of female employees in the Directorate of Religious Affairs has enormously increased because female employees have been hired in Family Guidance and Counselling Offices. They have been providing consultancy and support services to women. There is more than one in every city. There is an idea to unite and incorporate these offices with the ŞÖNİMs. This would be appropriate because the ŞÖNİMs are not so different from the Family Guidance and Counselling Offices. They have been doing a terrible job by providing services to women and men in the same place. To the end of combatting violence, the victim and the perpetrator are given services in the same place! Why do they do this? In fact, the aim is to reconsolidate the family. That is why feminists are on tenterhooks.

Besides, the legal process does not function efficiently and fast enough to immediately punish the perpetrators and provide the victims of domestic violence with timely protection. The number of shelters is as low as 120, which only meets 63 per cent of the need, and they are not easily accessible. There is a lack of well-trained law-enforcement officers to ensure the success of protective measures. In most cases, the officers may not cooperate to provide victims with legal and psychological consultation (see Institute of Population Studies, 2014). This has a discouraging effect for women who are exposed to violence to ask for help. A feminist activist who works as a volunteer at Purple Roof, closely interacted with these women and shared her/his insights as follows:

> In the middle of this tough process, women could give up and say that I give up and go back home or they go to a shelter but after seeing the conditions of and the treatment in the shelter, they would prefer to go back to their homes. For instance, the ŞÖNİMs are mostly out of town. The shelter is not the only need in combatting violence. The women who appealed to the Purple Roof mostly do not want [to go to] the shelter. However, the social solidarity centres provide these women with limited support; they do not deal with them and direct them to the shelter. So, this does not offer a solution. As I said, the shelters and the social solidarity centres are out of town. The rules are left on paper. It seems that women are not encouraged to come and appeal. The woman can be running away from home; she can have no money and can come from far away with poor transportation. All this affects the women's daily life. Unfortunately, there are no facilitative efforts to handle these [troubles].

Unlike Russia's legal framework that decriminalizes domestic violence, Turkey has achieved significant legal advances on domestic violence. However, the state discourse emphasizing biological differences and family union trivializes the legal framework and decreases its deterrent effect. When it comes to the obedience of women in the family union, a similar dynamic that normalizes it, respectively, on the basis of the traditional family structure and religious dictates becomes evident in both Russia and Turkey.

Concluding Remarks

The hypotheses that were laid out at the beginning posited that the state has an interest of legitimacy in gender, which can be extended to family, demography, morality and national unity. The analysis of the Russian and Turkish cases show that gender constitutes an important dimension of political struggle for hegemony. The socio-economic and political gain that a state stands to derive from reinforcing specific gendered categories plays a key role in determining the state's tendency to pursue progressive, conservative, pro-natal or anti-natal policies regarding gender. The concepts of gender order and gender climate allowed me to elaborate on the orientation of political discourse on gender, which relies on the tripodal relationship between state, gender and legitimacy. In both Russia and Turkey, the wider political context, which is depicted with either modernizing efforts or rising authoritarian tendencies, has an influence over the creation of the prevailing gender climate, in which the underlying gender order is revisited to configure the appropriate rhetoric and attitudes about gender.

Gender Climate in the Soviet and early Republican Periods

A political agenda for women's rights and status dated back to the early westernizing efforts that had been pursued in the pre-revolutionary periods in Tsarist Russia and the Ottoman Empire. The importance of women's education was acknowledged for social progress and prosperity. Women's role as mothers of future generations gained significance as part and parcel of westernizing reforms. However, the early progressive reforms moved back and forth. They encountered strong resistance from the conservative sides and remained limited in their reach to the peasantry in both Tsarist Russia and the Ottoman Empire. The radical rupture that was characterized by the endowment of equal rights for men and women happened with the establishment of the Soviet and early Republican regimes. The Soviet and early Republican regimes were modernization projects albeit in different routes – respectively, communist and capitalist. Women's equality occupied the centre of both modernization projects. The prevailing gender climates that emerged during the Soviet and early Republican periods were organized around the state-led ideology of women's equality, which are referred to in academic literature as early instances of state feminism. This ideology paved the way for introducing legal and social reforms that assured women's equality before the law, public visibility, access to education and employment outside the home. The difference, though, was that women's emancipation was assumed to occur through education in the Turkish case while it was through work in the Soviet case.

The Soviet and Republican cases illustrate that gender identities and relations became a sphere of political struggle over modernizing the respective countries. The Soviet and early Republican gender climates represented the motivation of modernist efforts to break the old social relations and to establish a new social system. In the immediate post-revolutionary period, the Communist Party attempted to destroy the pre-revolutionary culture in order to consolidate their hegemonic rule. The disruption would symbolize the triumph of the new regime because the reproduction of future communist generations – ideal comrades who might not resist the new Soviet order – was in the hands of women (Ashwin, 2000, pp.1–3). Similarly, the Republican revolution confronted the Ottoman past that was characterized by the dominance of religion in state affairs and public life. To ensure a break with the past, the revolution aimed at social transformation, in which women were given a special place. Women's liberation would signify the achievements of the secular and national pillars of the new regime. In both cases, the role of cultural reproduction was emphasized for women, who had to raise children loyal to the communist and secular-national premises of the Soviet and Republican regimes.

However, the radical break that was set forth by the Soviet and the early Republican gender climates is best described as 'continuity in rupture' and/or 'oscillation between modernity and tradition'. The traditional gender categories continued to play a determining role despite the radical attempts to break with pre-revolutionary culture. The underlying pre-revolutionary gender order was reconstituted in accordance with the communist and secular/national interests and concerns of the newly established states. Although the Soviet and the early Republican reforms introduced radical shifts to the prevailing gender climate, the patriarchal gender order was largely preserved. Soviet and Turkish women were liberated to a large extent thanks to the attainment of formal equality before the law but traditional norms and patterns were considerably preserved in the organization of the public sphere, education system, labour force participation, family relations and political participation.

The instance of rupture in continuity that characterized the interaction between gender order and gender climate also stemmed from the focus of Soviet and Republican leaders on capitalism and religion as the main sources of women's inequality and oppression. Neither of them could seize the patriarchal gender order as the main source of women's subordination to male authority. The Soviet and Republican revolutionaries assumed women would be liberated through the breaking of the socio-economic order organized around capitalism and religion, respectively, and the establishment of a new legal framework and set of institutional structures. They were unable to notice that pre-revolutionary society had been full of traditional gendered patterns stemming not only from capitalism and religion but also from the domination of masculinity. On the contrary, despite all radical efforts, the underlying norms and patterns regulating gender categories were inherited to a great extent from the pre-revolutionary past in both regimes.

In the light of these presumptions, I shall argue that such arguments as instrumentalization of women and/or using women as window-dressing regarding the gender regime established by the Soviet and Republican revolutions might seem as reductionist as the emancipatory argument, which contends the full liberation of women thanks to the Soviet and Republican egalitarian rhetoric and policies. These arguments do not allow us to examine the interplay between state and gender in a particular context. It was not women but gender and gender relations which were utilized by the newly established states to consolidate a new social, economic and political order. So, the legal amendments and other measures taken to ensure women's rights could not be regarded as a simple derivative of state policies. They pertained to the constitution of a hegemonic gender climate, and the establishment of new notions of femininity and masculinity at the intersection of the underlying gender order and the new socio-economic and political conditions.

Neo-Traditional/Conservative Gender Climate in Russia and Turkey

As Kay suggests, if the gender order is patriarchal, then the gender climate could ensure an evolutionary change towards a more egalitarian discourse or unleash the traditional norms and patterns. The Russian and Turkish cases oscillate between these two instances. The motivation of catching up with Western levels regarding women's rights led to the pursuit of an egalitarian discourse and policies during the Soviet and early Republican times. However, the recent situation illustrates that the experience of state feminism and the long history of women's rights have not transformed into a shift on the state level towards considering women as individuals or establishing a more egalitarian gender climate. Although the function that gender categories fulfilled remains the same with the Soviet and Republican regimes, the state-led ideology of women's equality has been gradually abandoned at state level throughout the recent decade. Instead, the gender climates in Russia and Turkey have been organized on the grounds of neo-traditional and neo-conservative premises that propose a masculinist reinterpretation of gender order around nationalist and conservative political discourses.

The neo-traditional/conservative orientation of the current gender climates is mostly related to the interests and concerns of the state under the rules of Putin and Erdoğan. The need to reinforce ties with the majority coalition and sustain their support has become a concern for Putin and Erdoğan as their regimes have tended to drift towards authoritarianism. Under the conditions of the deteriorating relations with the West and the emergence of internal opposition, they have increasingly built their claim of legitimacy on the representation of the 'real' Russian and Turkish people. Against this backdrop, traditional gender norms and values have regained importance to signify national authenticity against Western culture and to identify the symbolic borders of the Russian and Turkish nations. The underlying gender order, which is believed to contain the core values and relationships vital for national unity, power and survival, is revisited to reconfigure the real and true beliefs of the Russian and Turkish people. With the aid of traditional gender norms, both the Russian and Turkish states imagine an abstract homogenous unity and render these norms commonly accepted within this unity, despite the wide ethnic, religious and social diversities across these countries. The masculinist reinterpretation of traditional gender norms that strictly order society on the basis of certain norms, roles and identities for all also help these authoritarian regimes repress diversity, pluralism and gender equality, and thus avoid any demand for regime transformation.

Rising authoritarianism in Russia and Turkey has intensified the efficacy and forcefulness of a gender climate that calls for the regulation of women's sexualities, reproductive rights and their position in the familial realm and labour market in reference to national authenticity, religious values and moral concerns. In both countries, women are treated as a specific political group for the purpose of guaranteeing the survival of the Russian and Turkish nations, preserving Russian and Turkish cultural values, and transmitting them to future generations. The notion of 'good' femininity has been revived on the grounds of motherhood, and motherhood is portrayed as the biologically prescribed (and thus indisputable) civic and natural duty of women. The articulation of the 'good' woman reflects the aim of re-establishing proper gender relations in reference to Russian and Turkish traditional values and customs. The heterosexual family with children is assumed to be the natural and proper form, with the result that alternative familial forms, such as cohabitation, same-sex relations and so on, are marginalized. In this framing, the vision of the traditional family is imposed on the people, as though it were embraced by all segments of Russian and Turkish societies, and as though it conformed perfectly to their social realities. Highlighting the biological differences with reference to the masculinist reinterpretation of religion and traditional values helps political authorities normalize and justify any form of gender-related discrimination, and limit the expression of gender variations.

Bringing gender into the operation of authoritarianism via the concept of gender climate helps us grasp the damaging reflections over gender equality created by the encounter between the legitimacy concerns of rising authoritarianism and the underlying gender order. Almost all incentives touching upon women's interests and situation in the family, the labour market and society are reformulated around a family-oriented approach in such a way as to reinforce biological differences and use them to naturalize discriminatory attitudes and practices against women. Pro-natal policies are primarily designed as a response to the Russian and Turkish states' decision to try to reverse the demographic indicators and to prevent the so-called moral decline against the devastating impact of cultural globalization. Pro-employment initiatives of the Turkish state and the efforts that aim to relieve the double burden of Russian women reinforce gendered hierarchies in the labour market and prove to regulate women's employment outside the home in accordance with family roles and responsibilities. Social policies are primarily directed towards women as a special group in need of state protection and have supported them primarily as mothers through special protections and benefits in both cases. Domestic violence is not treated as a violation of women's individual rights but as a phenomenon that should be tolerated as part of the traditional family structure in Russia or to be resolved from the angle of protecting the family union in Turkey.

Another profound impact of authoritarian politics on gender climate is traced in the extension of state power into intimate spheres and individual choices – about marriage, divorce, sexual relations and orientation, abortion and reproduction – for the sake of national survival. In both of the countries studied here, the political authorities tend to force women and men to fulfil the state's ambitions through the provision of incentives or disincentives, including surveillance power, persuasive tactics, material benefits and, if necessary, discipline, as seen in the regulation of abortion policy and the promotion of motherhood. Relying on deeply rooted patriarchy and paternalism, both leaders maintain that the state is responsible for protecting and upholding traditional values and institutions (such as the family) for the survival of the nation and the preservation of moral authenticity. The interventions of the state, therefore, tend to meet with warm approval among the majority of Russian and Turkish citizens. As Sperling (2015) indicates, this sort of strategy helps state policies achieve a cultural resonance that strengthens the ties between state and citizenry, thereby strengthening the states' legitimacy as good and moral actors. Moreover, the leaders have designated their regimes as ones that would/could defend and protect the 'commonly held' traditional values that characterize the real Russian and Turkish people against the deleterious influence of Western norms and values.

In neo-traditional/conservative gender climates, a family-oriented approach is favoured against gender equality and the discursive utilization of women's bodies and sexualities has appeared as a significant tool to consolidate the representative claims of both regimes. The legitimacy and visibility gained by biological differences between the sexes are the distinguishing features of neo-traditional/conservative gender climates. However, there are certain differences derived from differing political dynamics and cultural diversities. Putin assumes to unite all people around a civic national identity, while a religiously imbued Turkish national identity has become hegemonic under the rule of Erdoğan. Nationalism coincides with tradition and religious values in both cases but the emphasis on religion as the primary reference point of national identity allows increasing control and restrictions on women via body politics in Turkey. From a comparative perspective, it is possible to say that the gender climate in Turkey does encourage community pressure and moral control over women's sexuality (including sexual intercourse out of wedlock, cohabitation, single motherhood and divorce) and bodily autonomy through imposing certain dress codes and codes of behaviour (including laughing or kissing in public spaces, the visibility of pregnant women, smoking). In contrast, as Nechemias (2016) remarked, the degree of religiosity shows little relationship to gender attitudes in Russia; women's sexuality is much more liberated and moral toleration of premarital sex, cohabitation and a revealing dress code is higher in Russia. However, the Orthodox Church contributes to a gender climate in which alternative forms of femininity are less heard and gender equality loses its importance. Both cases show that the use of traditional and religious references in tandem with authoritarian practices brings about not only the extension of state authority into intimacy through the provision of incentives or disincentives but also unleashes the traditional forces to control women's sexuality and bodily autonomy.

Last but not least, the orientation of gender climate also depends on the absence or presence of patriarchal features, feminist movements and cultural forces opposing sexism and misogyny in the social context. In Russia and Turkey, where feminism never became mainstream and has never been thoroughly understood by the masses, the opportunities to counteract state-sponsored discriminatory policies against women by relying on the promises of gender equality remain to a large extent unappealing. Moreover, the masculinist discourse of Putin and Erdoğan stigmatizes feminist ideas that oppose the imposition of appropriate notions of femininity and masculinity and marginalizes them as foreign, immoral and unpatriotic.

Appendix A

Interview List in Moscow and St Petersburg

Centre for Supporting Women's Initiatives, Moscow
Consortium of Women's Non-Governmental Associations, Moscow
Council for the Consolidation of the Women's Movement, Moscow
European University at St Petersburg
Higher School of Economics National Research University, Moscow
Moscow Centre for Gender Studies, Moscow
National Centre for the Prevention of Violence (ANNA), Moscow
Russian Academy of Sciences, Moscow
St Petersburg Public Organization Juridical Aid for Socially Unprotected People (EGIDA), St Petersburg
Union of Russian Women, Moscow
UN Refugee Agency, Moscow
UN Women Regional Office for Eastern Europe and Central Asia, Moscow
Women's Crisis Centre, St Petersburg

Appendix B

Interview List in Ankara and İstanbul

Ankara University, Ankara
Capital Women's Platform, Ankara
Women's Solidarity Foundation, Ankara
General Directorate of Women's Status, Ankara
Hacettepe University, Ankara
Istanbul University, Istanbul
Middle East Technical University, Ankara
Turkish Women's Union, Ankara
The Association for the Support and Training of Women Candidates, Ankara
United Nations Population Fund, Ankara
Yıldız Technical University, Istanbul

Appendix C

Interview Questionnaire

1. How do you identify the main characteristics of gender politics in Turkey/Russia?
2. What are the main differences between the pre-1980 period and the post-1980 period regarding the Turkish/Russian state's approach to the gender question?
3. What are the main discourses about gender in Turkey/Russia?
4. What are the main priorities of the Turkish/Russian state regarding women?
5. How do you identify the main characteristics of masculinity and femininity?
6. How do you evaluate the approach of the Turkish/Russian state to the family and motherhood?
7. What is the situation of women in the labour force in Turkey/Russia?
8. What is the situation of women in politics in Turkey/Russia?
9. What do you think about the women's movement in Turkey/Russia?
10. How do you evaluate the legal amendments or decrees issued in recent years?

Notes

Introduction

1 For the history of the women's movement in Turkey, see Engel (2004); Kadıoğlu (1994); Pushkareva (1997); Zihnioğlu (2003).

Chapter 3

1 Vladimir Surkov's book, which was entitled *Putin: His Ideology*, was published in 2006.
2 It is important to understand the particularities of conservatism in Turkish political history. In the context of modernization, conservatism emerged as critical of Western-style modernization and secularism. It relies on the ideas of Ottoman-Turkish nationalism and religion as a value system, and adopts capitalism as an economic model. The defenders of this sort of conservatism consider Islam as a moral system and do not aim to establish an Islamic state. See Atacan (2005, p.195).
3 In 1998, Leyla Şahin, a female university student, brought a case against Turkey because of the headscarf ban at the ECHR. In 2004, the court decided that the ban was not a violation of human rights and could be justified on the basis of the protection of the secular regime where the majority of the population is Muslim (Hürriyet, 2005a).

Chapter 4

1 In the old Penal Code, adultery was identified as a criminal act, with different treatments and penalties for men and women, at the expense of the latter. The Constitutional Court effectively decriminalized it for both men and women, in 1996 and 1998 respectively. In accordance with the harmonization of the legal framework with the EU *acquis*, adultery is not included in the new Penal Code that was enacted in 2004.
2 For the party's understanding of family as an institution of social security, see the 2002 Election Manifesto, the 2003 AKP Government Programme, the 2012 party programme and the 2012 64th Government Programme.
3 In 2018, the Ministry of the Family and Social Policies was administratively restructured as the Ministry of the Family, Labour and Social Services. For the vision of the ministry, visit https://ailetoplum.aile.gov.tr/kurum-hvakkinda.
4 For an example of the activities conducted by Family Guidance and Counselling Bureaus, see İstanbul Müftülüğü (2008).
5 As someone born into a lower-class family, with a poor educational background and then having been imprisoned for his political principles, Erdoğan is viewed by many as

a symbol of victory against the allegedly secular elites, particularly the higher echelons of the bureaucracy, the army and, to some extent, the Western-oriented industrial bourgeoisie.

Chapter 5

1   The demographic policy came into force in 2007 as Presidential Decree No.1351 of 9 October 2007 'On approval of the Concept of Demographic Policy of the Russian Federation for the period up to 2025.'

2   A draft law proposing unpaid and non-transferable parental leave for both spouses was prepared in 2005, but this proposal was dropped from the government's agenda due to the opposition of the leading employers' association (TİSK) (Dedeoğlu, 2012, p.284).

3   Centre for Social and Labour Rights, a Moscow-based NGO, provides legal counselling and support for working women who do not receive payment of benefits related to maternity and childcare due to the liquidation of the company, the disappearance of the employers and/or the abundance of the firm. See Tsentr sotsial'no-trudovykh prav (n.d.-a).

4   In Turkey, women's employment in the informal sector increased by 64.9 per cent between 2000 and 2006, while it was around 15 per cent between 1989 and 2000 (Dedeoğlu, 2010). By 2001, the rate of women involved in the informal sector was as high as 58 per cent and women predominated over men in the informal sector on the basis of sector, status at work and wage (Ka-Der, 2012).

5   The labour force participation of women with higher education declined from 79.7 per cent in 1989 to 69.8 per cent by 2006 (Ecevit, 2008, p.130). There is an increase of 17.8 per cent in the non-participation of women in higher education between 2011 and 2012 (TEPAV, 2012).

Chapter 6

1   According to the World Health Organization, the population of Russia was 143,202 in 2005 and 143,221 in 2006 (WHO, 2007, p.82; 2008, p.100).

2   The Hanafi school of Islam, prevalent in Turkey, allows abortion until the end of four months (120 days) if the life or health of the woman or foetus is threatened.

3   A women's rights organization called Morçatı conducted research on access to abortion at state hospitals. Although it is still legal to terminate an unwanted pregnancy until the end of the tenth week, among thirty-seven state hospitals in Istanbul that the staff contacted, only three of them agreed to provide a non-emergency termination; seventeen said that they could provide the service only if there was a medical emergency; the remaining twelve refused to carry out termination for whatever reason (Morçatı, 2015).

4   Upon these statements, the Public Health Law (*Umumi Hıfzısıhha Kanunu*) restricted Caesarean sections to strict medical reasons and outlawed Caesarean sections on demand. For the Public Health Law, see http://www.resmigazete.gov.tr/eskiler/2012/07/20120712-12.htm (accessed 6 March 2016).

5   For the Maternity Capital Law, see http://www.pfrf.ru/en/matcap/(accessed 30 November 2018).

Chapter 7

1   For detailed explanations of the Russian Orthodox Church's position on domestic violence, see Shadrina (2015).
2   Female victims of murder increased from 66 to 953 (an increase of 1,400 per cent) between 2002 and 2009. In 2014 alone, there was a 31 per cent increase in violence against women compared to the previous year.

Bibliography

ABA/CEELI (2006). *CEDAW Assessment Tool Report for the Russian Federation.* Washington, DC: American Bar Association and Central European and Eurasian Law.

Abadan-Unat, Nermin (1981). 'Social Change and Turkish Women'. In Nermin Abadan-Unat (ed.). *Women In Turkish Society.* Leiden: E.J. Brill, pp. 5–36.

Abadan-Unat, Nermin (1991). 'Educational Reforms: The Impact of Legal reforms on Turkish Women'. In N.R. Keddie and B. Baron (eds). *Women in Middle Eastern History: Shifting Boundaries in Sex and Gender.* London: Yale University Press, pp. 177–94.

Acar, Feride (1991). 'Women in the Ideology of Islamic Revivalism in Turkey: Three Islamic Women's Journals'. In R. Tapper (ed.). *Islam in Modern Turkey: Religion, Politics and Literature in a Secular State.* London: I.B. Tauris, pp. 280–303.

Acar, Feride (1995). 'Women and Islam in Turkey'. In Şirin Tekeli (ed.). *Women in Modern Turkish Society.* NJ: Zed Books, pp. 46–65.

Acar, Feride (2000). 'Turkey'. In M. McPhedran, S. Bazilli, M. Ericson, A. Byrnes (eds). *The First CEDAW IMPACT STUDY Final Report.* York: Center for Feminist Studies, York University and the International Women's Rights Project.

Acar, Feride, and Altunok, Gülbanu (2012). 'Understanding Gender Equality Demands in Turkey: Foundations and Boundaries of Women's Movements'. In Saniye Dedeoğlu and E. Adem Yavuz (eds). *Gender and Society in Turkey: The Impact of Neoliberal Policies, Political Islam and EU Accession.* London: I.B. Tauris, pp. 31–45.

Acar, Feride, and Altunok, Gülbanu (2013). 'The "politics of intimate" at the intersection of neo-liberalism and neo-conservatism in Turkey'. *Women's Studies International Forum,* 41, 14–23.

Acuner, Selma (1999). *Türkiye'de Kadın-Erkek Eşitliği ve Resmi Kurumsallaşma Süreci.* Ankara: Ankara Üniversitesi Sosyal Bilimler Enstitüsü Yayınlanmamış Doktora Tezi.

Acuner, Selma (2002). '90'lı Yıllar ve Resmi Düzeyde Kurumsallaşmanın Doğuş Aşamaları'. In Aksu Bora and Asena Günal (eds). *90'larda Türkiye'de Feminizm.* İstanbul: İletişim, pp. 125–58.

Akdoğan, Yalçın (2004). *AK Parti ve Muhafazakar Demokrasi.* İstanbul: Alfa Yayınları.

Akdoğan, Yalçın (2006). 'The Meaning of Conservative Democratic Identity'. In M. Hakan Yavuz (ed.). *The Emergence of A New Turkey, The Emergence of A New Turkey. Islam, Democracy and the AK Parti.* Salt Lake City: University of Utah Press, pp.49–65.

AKP (2002). *Kalkınma ve Demokratikleşme Programı.* [Online]. Available at: https://acikerisim.tbmm.gov.tr/xmlui/bitstream/handle/11543/926/200205071. pdf?sequence=1&isAllowed=y [Accessed 21 September 2018].

AK Parti Kadın Kolları (2010). *Kadın-Erkek Eşitliği Çalıştay Raporu.* [Online]. Available at: https://www.academia.edu/36017218/Kad%C4%B1n_-Erkek_E%C5%9Fitli%C4%9 Fi %C3%87al%C4%B1%C5%9Ftay_Raporu [Accessed 21 September 2018].

Aksoy, Hürcan Aslı (2015). 'Invigorating Democracy in Turkey: The Agency of Organized Islamist Women'. *Politics & Gender,* 11, 146–70.

Aktürk, Şener (2017). 'Turkey's Role in the Arab Spring and the Syrian Conflict'. *Turkish Policy Quarterly,* Winter, 15 (4), 87–95.

Aldıkaçtı Marshall, Gül (2013). *Shaping Gender Policy in Turkey. Grassroots Women Activists, the European Union and the Turkish State.* Albany: SUNY Press.

Al Jazeera Turk (2014). *Erdoğan AB önce aynaya baksın,* 17 December 2014. [Online]. Available at: http://www.aljazeera.com.tr/haber/erdogan-ab-once-aynaya-baksin [Accessed 21 March 2016].

Allison, Roy (2009). 'The Russian Case for Military Intervention in Georgia: International Law, Norms and Political Calculation'. *European Security,* 18 (2), 173–200.

Al Monitor (2013). *Erdogan Blames International Conspiracy for Protests,* 14 June 2013. [Online]. Available at: http://www.al-monitor.com/pulse/originals/2013/06/erdogan-gezi-conspiracy-taksim-governance-authoritarian-akp.html#ixzz538F1sK9h [Accessed 21 October 2016].

Alpan, Başak (2016). 'From AKP's "Conservative Democracy" to "Advanced Democracy": Shifts and Challenges in the Debate on "Europe"'. *South European Society and Politics,* 21 (1), 15–28.

Altunisik, Meliha B., and Martin, Lenore G. (2011). 'Making Sense of Turkish Foreign Policy in the Middle East under AKP'. *Turkish Studies,* 12 (4), 569–87.

Altunok, Gülbanu (2016). 'Neo-conservatism, Sovereign Power and Bio-power: Female Subjectivity in Contemporary Turkey'. *Research and Policy on Turkey,* 1 (2), 132–46.

Anderson, John (2007). 'Putin and the Russian Orthodox Church: Asymmetric Symphonia?'. *Journal of International Affairs,* 61 (1), 185–95.

ANNA (2010). *Violence against Women in the Russian Federation. Alternative Report to the United Nations Committee on the Elimination of Discrimination Against Women 46th Session. Examination of the 6th and 7th reports submitted by the Russian Federation.* [Online]. Available at: http://www2.ohchr.org/english/bodies/cedaw/docs/ngos/ANNANCPV_RussianFederation46.pdf [Accessed 26 April 2011].

Anthias, Floya, and Yuval-Davis, Nira (1989). 'Introduction'. In Nira Yuval-Davis and Floya Anthias (eds). *Woman-Nation-State.* New York: Palgrave Macmillan, pp. 1–15.

Arat, Yeşim (1993). 'Women's Studies in Turkey: From Kemalism to Feminism'. *New Perspectives on Turkey,* 9, 119–35.

Arat, Yeşim (1994). 'Toward a Democratic Society: The Women's Movement in Turkey in the 1980s'. *Women's Studies International Forum,* 17 (2–3), 241–48.

Arat, Yeşim (1998). 'Feminists, Islamists, and Political Change in Turkey'. *Political Psychology,* 19 (1), 117–31.

Arat, Zehra (1994a). 'Kemalism and Turkish Women'. *Women & Politics,* 14 (4), 57–80.

Arat, Zehra (1994b). 'Turkish Women and the Republican Reconstruction of Tradition'. In Fatma Muge Gocek and Shiva Balaghi (eds). *Reconstructing Gender in the Middle East. Tradition, Identity and Power.* New York: Colombia University Press, pp. 57–81.

Ashwin, Sarah (2000). 'Introduction: Gender, state and society in Soviet and post-Soviet Russia'. In Sarah Ashwin (ed.). *Gender, State and Society in Soviet and Post-Soviet Russia.* London: Routledge, pp. 1–29.

Ashwin, Sarah (2002). 'The Influence of the Soviet Gender Order on Employment Behaviour in Contemporary Russia'. *Sociological Research,* 41 (1), 21–37.

ASPB (2012a). *Kadına Yönelik Şiddetle Mücadele Ulusal Eylem Planı 2012–2015.* Ankara: T.C. Aile ve Sosyal Politikalar Bakanlığı Kadının Statüsü Genel Müdürlüğü. [Online]. Available at: http://www.kadininstatusu.gov.tr/upload/kadininstatusu.gov.tr/mce/2012/kadina_yonelik_sid_2012_2015.pdf [Accessed 31 August 2013].

ASPB (2012b). *Türkiye'de Kadının Durumu*. Ankara: T.C. Aile ve Sosyal Politikalar Bakanlığı Kadının Statüsü Genel Müdürlüğü. [Online]. Available at: http://www. kadininstatusu.gov.tr/upload/kadininstatusu.gov.tr/mce/2012/trde_kadinin_ durumu_2012_ekim.pdf?p=1 [Accessed 31 August 2013].

Atacan, Fulya (2005). 'Explaining Religious Politics at the Crossroad: AKP-SP'. *Turkish Studies*, 6 (2), 187–99.

Atencio, Andrea, and Posadas, Josefina (2015). *Gender Gap in Pay in the Russian Federation Twenty Years Later, Still a Concern*. The World Bank Poverty Global Practice Group Policy Research Working Paper 7407. [Online]. Available at: http://documents. worldbank.org/curated/en/838301468185384790/pdf/WPS7407.pdf [Accessed 12 December 2018].

Atkinson, Dorothy (1978). 'Society and the Sexes in the Russian Past'. In Dorothy Atkinson, Alexander Dallin, and Gail Warshofsky Lapidus (eds). *Women in Russia*. Sussex: Harvester Press, pp. 3–38.

Attwood, Lynne (1996). 'Young People, Sex and Sexual Identity'. In Hilary Pilkington (ed.). *Gender, Generation and Identity in Contemporary Russia*. London: Routledge, pp. 95–120.

Attwood, Lynne (1999). *Creating the New Soviet Woman. Women's Magazines as Engineers of Female Identity, 1922-53*. London: Mac Millan Press.

Averre, Derek (2007). 'Sovereign Democracy and Russia's Relations with the European Union'. *Demokratizatsiya*, 15 (2), 173–90.

Aydın-Düzgit, Senem (2016). 'De-Europeanisation through Discourse: A Critical Discourse Analysis of AKP's Election Speeches'. *South European Society and Politics*, 21 (1), 45–58.

Aydın-Düzgit, Senem, and Kaliber, Alper (2016). 'Encounters with Europe in an era of Domestic and International Turmoil: Is Turkey a de-Europeanising Candidate Country'. *South European Society and Politics*, 21 (1), 1–14.

Başkan, Birol (2017). 'Islamism and Turkey's Foreign Policy during the Arab Spring'. *Turkish Studies*, 19 (2). doi: 10.1080/14683849.2017.1405346.

Başlevent, Cem, and Onaran, Özlem (2003). 'Are Married Women in Turkey More Likely to become Added or Discouraged Workers?'. *Labour*, 27 (3), 439–58.

Baydar, Gülsüm (2002). 'Tenuous Boundaries: Women, Domesticity and Nationhood in 1930s Turkey'. *Journal of Architecture*, 7 (3), 229–44.

Baykan, Ayşegül, and Ötüş-Baskett, Belma (1999). *Nezihe Muhittin ve Türk Kadını. 1931: Türk feminizminin düşünsel kökenleri ve feminist tarih yazıcılığından bir örnek*. İstanbul: İletişim.

BBC Türkçe (2014). Erdoğan: Kadın-erkek eşitliği fıtrata ters, 24 November 2014. [Online] Available at: http://www.bbc.com/turkce/haberler/2014/11/141124_ kadininfitrati_erdogan [Accessed 2 September 2017].

BBC Türkçe (2015). *Erdoğan: Milli irade istikrarı seçti*, 2 November 2015. [Online]. Available at: http://www.bbc.com/turkce/haberler/2015/11/151102_erdogan_secim_ yorum [Accessed 21 June 2016].

Bebel, August (2005). *Women and Socialism*. [Online]. Available at: https://www.marxists. org/archive/bebel/1879/woman-socialism/ch07.htm [Accessed 10 October 2018].

Berman, Harold J. (1946). 'Soviet Family Law in the Light of Russian History and Marxist Theory'. *Yale Law Journal*, 56 (1), 26–57.

Bianet (2018). 'Çiçek'ten flört ve feminizm tanımları', 29 November 2018. [Online]. Available at: http://www.bianet.org/bianet/bianet/14696-cicek-feminizm-sapiklik-flort-fahiseliktir [Accessed 12 December 2018].

Bilinov, Maksim (2014). 'New Family Code to Protect Family, Religious Values – Key Lawmaker'. *RT*, 4 March 2014. [Online]. Available at: https://www.rt.com/politics/russia-family-code-traditions-764/[Accessed 25 July 2016].

Birdal, Mehmet Sinan (2013) 'Queering Conservative Democracy'. *Turkish Policy Quarterly*, 11 (4), 119–29.

Birgün (2015). *Erdoğan: Milli irade istikrarı seçti*, 1 November 2015. [Online]. Available https://www.birgun.net/haber-detay/erdogan-milli-iradenin-tavrina-saygi-duymamiz-gerekecek-93971.html [Accessed].

Bitten, Natasha, and Kerimzade, Tatiana (2013). 'The Duma and Russian Orthodox Church vs Feminism', Open Democracy, 14 October 2013. [Online]. Available at: https://www.opendemocracy.net/5050/natasha-bitten-tatiana-kerim-zade/duma-and-russian-orthodox-church-vs-feminism [Accessed 21 September 2017].

Bogner, Alexander, and Menz, Wolfgang (2009). 'The Theory-Generating Expert Interview: Epistemological Interest, Forms of Knowledge, Interaction'. In Alexander Bogner, Beate Littig, and Wolfgang Menz (eds). *Interviewing Experts*, Basingstoke: Palgrave MacMillan, pp. 43–80.

Borenstein, Eliot (2006). 'Selling Russia. Prostitution, Masculinity, and Metaphors of Nationalism after Perestroika'. In Helena Goscilo and Andrea Lanoux (eds). *Gender and National Identity in Twentieth Century Russian Culture*. DeKalb: Northern Illinois University Press, pp. 174–95.

Bozkır, Gürcan (2000). 'Türk Kadınlar Birliği'. *Toplumsal Tarih Dergisi*, 75 (13), 21–6.

Bridger, Sue (1992). 'Young Women and Perestroika'. In Linda Edmondson (ed.). *Women and Society in Russia and the Soviet Union*. Cambridge: Cambridge University Press, pp. 178–201.

Bridger, Sue, Kay, Rebecca, and Pinnick, Kathryn (1996). *No More Heroines? Russia, Women and the Market*. London: Routledge.

Bruton, F. Brinley (2016). 'Turkey's President Erdoğan Calls Women Who Work "Half Persons"'. *NBC News*, 8 June 2016. [Online]. Available at: http://www.nbcnews.com/news/world/turkey-s-president-erdogan-calls-women-who-work-half-persons-n586421 [Accessed 11 August 2016].

Bryanski, Gleb (2012). 'Russian patriarch calls Putin era "miracle of God"'. *Reuters*, 8 February 2012. [Online]. Available at: https://uk.reuters.com/article/uk-russia-putin-religion/russian-patriarch-calls-putin-era-miracle-of-god-idUKTRE81722Y20120208 [Accessed 12 December 2018].

Buci-Glucksmann, Christine (1984). 'Hegemony and Consent: A Political Strategy'. In A. Showstack Sassoon (ed.). *Approaches to Gramsci*. London: Writers and Readers, pp. 116–26.

Buckley, Mary (1989). *Women and Ideology in the Soviet Union*. Ann Arbour: University of Michigan Press.

Buckley, Mary (1992). 'Political Reform'. In Mary Buckley (ed.). *Perestroika and Soviet Women*. Cambridge: Cambridge University Press, pp. 54–71.

Buckley, Mary (1993). *Redefining Russian Society and Polity*. San Francisco & Oxford: Westview Press.

Buckley, Mary (1997). 'Adaptation of the Soviet Women's Committee: deputies' voices from "Women of Russia"'. In Mary Buckley (ed.). *Post-Soviet Women: from the Baltic to Central Asia*. Cambridge: Cambridge University Press, pp. 157–85.

Buğra, Ayşe (2012). 'The Changing Welfare Regime of Turkey: Neoliberalism, Cultural Conservatism and Social Solidarity Redefined'. In *Gender and Society in Turkey: The Impact of Neoliberal Policies, Political Islam and EU Accession*. London: I.B. Tauris, pp. 15–30.

Bykova, Marina (2004). 'Nation and Nationalism. Russia in Search of its National Identity'. In Gerrit Steunebrink and Evert van der Zweerde (eds). *Civil Society, Religion, and the Nation. Modernization in Intercultural Context: Russia, Japan, Turkey*. Amsterdam and New York: Rodopi, pp. 29–50.

Çavdar, Gamze (2010). 'Islamist Moderation and the Resilience of Gender: Turkey's Persistent Paradox'. *Totalitarian Movements and Political Religions*, 11 (3–4), 341–57.

Cameron, David R., and Orenstein, Mitchell A. (2012). 'Post-Soviet Authoritarianism: The Influence of Russia in Its Near Abroad'. *Post-Soviet Affairs*, 28 (1), 37–41.

Chaisty, Paul and Whitefield, Stephen (2013). 'Forward to Democracy or Back to Authoritarianism? The Attitudinal Bases of Mass Support for the Russian Election Protests of 2011–2012'. *Post-Soviet Affairs*, 29 (5), 387–403.

Chandler, Andrea (2013). *Democracy, Gender and Social Policy in Russia: A Wayward Society*. New York: Palgrave Macmillan.

Chernova, Zhanna (2012a). 'New Pronatalism?: Family Policy in Post-Soviet Russia'. *REGION: Regional Studies of Russia, Eastern Europe, and Central Asia*, 1 (1), 75–92.

Chernova, Zhanna (2012b). 'Parenthood in Russia: From the State Duty to Personal Responsibility and Mutual Cooperation'. *Anthropology of East Europe Review*, 30 (2), 1–19.

Cizre, Ümit (2004). 'Problems of Democratic Governance of Civil-Military Relations in Turkey and the European Union Enlargement Zone'. *European Journal of Political Research*, 43 (1) January, 107–25.

Cizre, Umit (2014). 'Understanding Erdoğan's Toxic Recrimination in Turkey'. Open Democracy, 13 February 2014. [Online]. Available at: https://www.opendemocracy.net/umit-cizre/understanding-erdoğan's-toxic-recrimination-in-turkey [Accessed 18 December 2018].

Clark, William A. (2013). 'The 2012 Presidential Election in Russia: Putin Returns'. *Electoral Studies*, 32, 374–77.

CNNTürk (2011). *Başbakan: 'O kadın, kız mıdır kadın mıdır?*, 4 June 2011. [Online]. Available at: https://www.cnnturk.com/2011/yazarlar/06/04/basbakan.o.kadin.kiz.midir.kadin.midir/618955.0/index.html [Accessed 6 April 2017].

CNNTÜRK (2013). *Erdoğan'dan kürtaj ve sezaryen yorumu*. 19 June 2013. [Online]. Available at: http://www.cnnturk.com/2013/guncel/06/19/erdogandan.kurtaj.ve.sezaryen.yorumu/712176.0/index.html [Accessed 2 August 2016].

Colton, Timothy J., and Hale, Henry E. (2014). 'Putin's Uneasy Return and Hybrid Regime Stability'. *Problems of Post-Communism*, 61 (2), 3–22.

Connell, R. W. (1987). *Gender and Power*. Stanford, CA: Stanford University Press.

Connell, R. W. (1990). 'The State, Gender, and Sexual Politics: Theory and Appraisal'. *Theory and Society*, 19 (5), 507–44.

Constitutional Court of Turkey n.d., [Online]. Available at: http://www.constitutionalcourt.gov.tr/inlinepages/publications/pdf/introductoryBooklet.pdf [Accessed 12 October 2018]

Cook, Linda (2011). 'The Political Economy of Russia's Demographic Crisis: States, Markets, Mothers and Migrants'. In Neil Robinson (ed.). *The Political Economy of Russia*. MD: Lowman and Littlefield Publishers, pp. 97–120.

Cornell, Svante E. (2014). 'Erdoğan's Looming Downfall Turkey at the Crossroads'. *Middle East Quarterly*, Spring 21 (2). [Online]. Available at: http://www.mcforum.org/3767/erdogandownfall?keepThis=true&TB_iframe=true&height=450&width=600&caption=Middle+East+Forum+%3A%3A+Writings#_ftnref5 [Accessed 18 December 2018].

Coşar, Simten, and Özman, Aylin (2004). 'Centre-right Politics in Turkey after the November 2002 General Election: Neo-liberalism with a Muslim Face'. *Contemporary Politics*, 10 (1), 57–74.

Coşar, Simten (2007). 'Women in Turkish Political Thought: Between Tradition and Modernity'. *Feminist Review*, 86, 113–31.

Coşar, Simten (2012). 'The AKP's Hold on Power: Neoliberalism Meets the Turkish-Islamic Synthesis'. In Simten Coşar and Gamze Yücesan-Özdemir (eds). *Silent Violence. Neo-liberalism, Islamist Politics and the AKP Years in Turkey*. Ottawa: Red Quill Books, pp. 67–92.

Coşar, Simten, and Gençoğlu-Onbaşı, Funda (2008). 'Women's Movement in Turkey at a Crossroads: From Women's Rights Advocacy to Feminism'. *South European Society and Politics*, 13 (3), 325–44.

Coşar, Simten, and Yeğenoğlu, Metin (2011). 'New Grounds for Patriarchy in Turkey? Gender Policy in the Age of AKP'. *South European Society and Politics*, 16 (4), 555–73.

Çakır, Serpil (1994). *Osmanlı Kadın Hareketi*. İstanbul: Metis Yayıncılık.

Çınar, Menderes (2006). 'Turkey's Transformation under the AKP Rule'. *The Muslim World*, 96 July, 469–86.

Çitçi, Oya (2011). '1979'dan 2010'a Neoliberal Dönemde Kadın Memurlar'. In *Birkaç Arpa Boyu. 21. Yüzyıla Girerken Türkiye'de Feminist Çalışmalar*. Koç University Press, pp. 415–60.

Dağı, İhsan D. (1996). 'Democratic Transition in Turkey, 1980-83: The Impact of European Diplomacy'. *Middle Eastern Studies*, 32 (2) (April), 124–44.

Dağı, İhsan (2005). 'Transformation of Islamic Political Identity in Turkey: Rethinking the West and Westernization'. *Turkish Studies*, 6 (1), 21–37.

Dağı, İhsan (2008). 'Turkey's AKP in Power'. *Journal of Democracy*, 19 (3), 25–30.

Dedeoğlu, Saniye (2010). 'Visible Hands–Invisible Women: Garment Industry Production in Turkey'. *Feminist Economics*, 16 (4), 1–32.

Dedeoğlu, Saniye (2012). 'Equality, Protection or Discrimination: Gender Equality Policies in Turkey'. *Social Politics*, 19 (2), 269–90.

Demoscope (2001). 'Kontseptsiya demograficheskogo razvitiya Rossiiskoi Federatsii na period do 2015 goda', 24 September 2001. [Online]. Available at: http://www.demoscope.ru/weekly/knigi/koncepciya/koncepciya.html [Accessed 29 January 2018].

Diken (2016). *Erdoğan tazeledi: hiçbir Müslüman aile doğum kontrol anlayışının içinde olamaz*, 30 May 2016. [Online]. Available at: http://www.diken.com.tr/erdogan-tazeledi-hicbir-musluman-aile-dogum-kontrolu-anlayisinin-icinde-olamaz/[Accessed 21 April 2017].

Din Hizmetleri Genel Müdürlüğü (2018). *Aile ve Dini Rehberlik Daire Başkanlığı*. [Online]. Available at: http://www2.diyanet.gov.tr/DinHizmetleriGenelMudurlugu/Sayfalar/Gorevler.aspx) [Accessed 30 November 2018].

Diner, Çağla, and Toktaş, Şule (2010). 'Waves of Feminism in Turkey: Kemalist, Islamist and Kurdish Women's Movements in an Era of Globalization'. *Journal of Balkan and Near Eastern Studies*, 12 (1), 41–57.

Dodge, Norton T. (1966). *Women in the Soviet Economy. Their Role in Economic, Scientific, and Technical Development*. Baltimore: Johns Hopkins University.

Durakbaşa, Ayşe (1997). 'Kemalism as Identity Politics in Turkey'. In Zehra F. Arat (ed.). *Deconstructing Images of 'The Turkish Woman'*. New York: St. Martin's Press, pp. 139–55.

Durakbaşa, Ayşe (1998). 'Cumhuriyet Modern Kadın ve Erkek Kimliklerinin Oluşumu: Kemalist Kadın Kimliği ve 'Münevver Erkekler'. In *75 Yılda Kadınlar ve Erkekler*. Koç University Press, pp. 29–50.

Eberstadt, Nicholas (2004). 'Russia's Demographic Straightjacket. *SAIS Review*, 2, 9–25.

Ecevit, Yıldız. (2008). İşgücüne Katılım ve İstihdam'. In TÜSİAD KAGİDER, *Türkiye'de Toplumsal Cinsiyet Eşitsizliği. Sorunlar, Öncelikler ve Çözüm Önerileri*. İstanbul: Graphis, pp.113–214.

Ecevit, Yıldız (2012). 'Feminist Sosyal Politika Bağlamında, Türkiye'de Çocuk Bakımı ve Eğitimine İki Paradigmadan Dogru Bakmak'. In Ahmet Makal and Gülay Toksöz (eds). *Geçmişten Günümüze Türkiye'de Kadın Emeği*. Ankara: Ankara Üniversitesi Yayınevi, pp. 201–19.

Edmondson, Linda (1996). 'Equality and Difference in Women's History: Where Does Russia Fit In?'. In Rosalind Marsh (ed.). *Women in Russia and Ukraine*. Cambridge: Cambridge University Press, pp. 94–110.

Ellis, Robert (2015). 'It Isn't Their Differences that Have Put Russia and Turkey at Loggerheads – It's the Similarities between Putin and Erdogan'. *Independent*, 2 December 2015. [Online]. Available at: www.independent.co.uk/voices/it-s-not-their-differences-that-have-put-russia-and-turkey-at-loggerheads-it-s-the-similarities-a6757456.html [Accessed 25 July 2016].

Engel, Barbara Alpern (2004). *Women in Russia 1700–2000*. Cambridge: Cambridge University Press.

Engels, Friedrich (2010). *The Origin of the Family, Private Property and the State*. [Online] Available at: https://www.marxists.org/archive/marx/works/download/pdf/origin_family.pdf [Accessed 10 October 2018].

Erdoğan, Recep Tayyip (2005a). *Speech at the 'Alliance of Civilisations: Turkey's Role' Meeting*. [Online]. Available at: http://www.akparti.org.tr/site/haberler/basbakan-erdogan-turkiyenin-ab-uyeliginin-gerceklestigigun-medeniyetler-ca/5686#1 [Accessed 21 October 2017].

Erdoğan, Recep Tayyip (2005b). *Speech at the Opening of the High Level Group Meeting of the Alliance of Civilisations Initiative*, 27 November 2005. [Online]. Available at: http://unaoc.org/repository/First%20HLG%20Meeting%20Opening%20Statement%20-%20Prime%20Minister%20Recep%20Tayyip%20Erdogan.doc.pdf [Accessed 21 October 2017].

Erdoğan, Recep Tayyip (2006). 'Conservative Democracy and the Globalisation of Freedom'. In M. Hakan Yavuz (ed.). *The Emergence of a New Turkey. Islam, Democracy and the AK Parti*. Salt Lake City: University of Utah Press, pp. 333–40.

Esen, Berk, and Gumuscu, Sebnem (2016). 'Rising Competitive Authoritarianism in Turkey'. *Third World Quarterly*, 37 (9), 1581–606.

Esen, Berk, and Gumuscu, Sebnem (2017a). 'A Small Yes for Presidentialism: The Turkish Constitutional Referendum of April 2017'. *South European Society and Politics*, 22 (3), 303–26.

Esen, Berk, and Gumuscu, Sebnem (2017b). 'Turkey: How the Coup Failed?'. *Journal of Democracy*, 28 (1), January, 59–73.

Evans, Alfred B. (2008). 'President Putin's Legacy and Russia's Identity'. *Europe-Asia Studies*, 60 (6), 899–912.

Farnsworth, Beatrice Brodsky (1978). 'Bolshevik Alternatives and the Soviet Family: The 1926 Marriage Law Debate'. In Dorothy Atkinson, Alexander Dallin, and Gail Warshofsky Lapidus (eds). *Women in Russia*. Sussex: Harvester Press, pp.139–65.

Ferree, Myra Marx, Risman, Barbara, Sperling, Valerie, Gurikova, Tatiana, and Hyde, Katherine (1999). 'The Russian Women's Movement: Activists' Strategies and Identities'. *Women & Politics*, 20 (3), 83–109.

Flenley, Paul (2008). 'Russia and the EU: The Clash of New Neighbourhoods'. *Journal of Contemporary European Studies*, 16 (2), 189–202.

Freedom House Survey (1998). [Online]. Available at: https://freedomhouse.org/report/
freedom-world/freedom-world-1998 [Accessed 21 October 2017].

Freedom House Survey (2018). [Online]. Available at: https://freedomhouse.org/sites/default/
files/FH_FITW_Report_2018_Final_SinglePage.pdf [Accessed 21 October 2017].

Gal, Susan, and Kligman, Gail (2000). *The Politics of Gender after Socialism. A
Comparative-Historical Essay*. Princeton, NJ: Princeton University Press.

Gelman, Vladimir (2014). 'The Rise and Decline of Electoral Authoritarianism'.
Demokratizatsiya, 22 (4), Fall, 503–22.

The Global Economy (2018). *Russia: Female Labor Force Participation*. [Online]. Available
at: http://www.theglobaleconomy.com/Russia/Female_labor_force_participation/
[Accessed 12 December 2018].

The Global Gender Gap Report (2007). Geneva: World Economic Forum.

The Global Gender Gap Report (2012). Geneva: World Economic Forum.

The Global Gender Gap Report (2017). Geneva: World Economic Forum.

Goldman, Marshall I. (2004). 'Putin and the Oligarchs'. *Foreign Affairs*, 83 (6), 33–44.

Goldman, Wendy (1993). *Women, the State and Revolution. Soviet Family Policy and Social
Life, 1917–1936*. New York: Cambridge University Press.

Goldman, Wendy (1996). 'Industrial Politics, Peasant Rebellion and the Death of the
Proletarian Women's Movement in the USSR'. *Slavic Review*, 55 (1), 46–77.

Gorbachev, Mikhail S. (1987). *Perestroika. New Thinking for Our Country and the World*.
New York: Harper & Row.

Göçer-Akder, Derya, and Özdemir, Zelal (2015). 'Comparing International Dimensions
of Revolutionary Situations: The Cases of Egypt 2011 and Turkey 2013'. *Journal of
Contemporary Central and Eastern Europe*, 23 (2–3), 181–94.

Göle, Nilüfer (1997). 'Secularism and Islamism in Turkey: The Making of Elites and
Counter-Elites'. *Middle East Journal*, 51 (1), 46–58.

Gretskiy, Igor, Treshchenkova, Evgeny, and Golubev, Konstantin (2014). 'Russia's
Perceptions and Misperceptions of the EU Eastern Partnership'. *Communist and Post-
Communist Studies*, 47 (3–4), 375–83.

The Guardian (2013). 'Feminism Could Destroy Russia, Russian Orthodox Patriarch
Claims'. 9 April 2013. [Online]. Available at: https://www.theguardian.com/world/2013/
apr/09/feminism-destroy-russia-patriarch-kirill [Accessed 21 January 2017].

The Guardian (2014). Recep Tayyip Erdoğan: '"Women Not Equal to Men"'. 24 November
2014. [Online]. Available at: https://www.theguardian.com/world/2014/nov/24/turkeys-
president-recep-tayyip-erdogan-women-not-equal-men [Accessed 21 January 2017].

The Guardian (2018). Turkey's Erdogan says Country Should Make Adultery Illegal and
Listening to EU on Matter Was a "Mistake"'. 27 February 2018. [Online]. Available at:
http://www.independent.co.uk/news/world/middle-east/turkey-adultery-cheating-crime-
president-recep-erdogan-eu-infidelity-law-a8230281.html [Accessed 21 March 2018].

Gudkov, Lev (2015). 'Resource of Putin's Conservatism'. In Leon Aron (ed.). *Putin's Russia.
How It Rose, How It Is Maintained, and How It Might End*. Washington, DC: American
Enterprise Institute, pp. 52–72.

Gultekin-Punsmann, Burcu (2010). 'Linking Turkey's EU Accession Process and the ENP
Regional Initiative: Necessary Cross-Border Cooperation with South Caucasus'. In
Bezen Balamir-Coşkun and Birgül Demirtaş-Coşkun (eds). *Neighbourhood Challenge:
European Union and Its Neighbours*. Boca Raton: Universal Publishers, pp. 379–96.

Hale, Henry (2010). 'Eurasian Polities as Hybrid Regimes: The Case of Putin's Russia'.
Journal of Eurasian Studies, 1 (1), January, 33–41.

Hale, William (1993). *Turkish Politics and the Military.* London: Routledge.

Hale, William (2005). 'Christian Democrats and the AKP: Parallels and Contrasts'. *Turkish Studies*, 9 (2), 293–310.

Hale, William (2006). 'Christian Democracy and the JDP. Parallels and Contrasts'. In M. Hakan Yavuz (ed.). *The Emergence of a New Turkey. Islam, Democracy and the AK Parti.* Salt Lake City: University of Utah Press, pp. 66–87.

Hale, William, and Özbudun, Ergun (2010). *Islamism, Democracy and Liberalism in Turkey. The Case of the AKP.* London and New York: Routledge.

Haukkala, Hiski (2008). 'The Russian Challenge to EU Normative Power: The Case of European Neighbourhoood Policy'. *The International Spectator*, 43 (2), 35–47.

Henderson, Sarah L. (2003). *Building Democracy in Contemporary Russia: Western Support for Grassroots Organizations.* Ithaca, NY: Cornell University Press.

Huntington, Samuel P. (1993). 'The Clash of Civilizations?'. *Foreign Affairs*, 72 (3) (Summer), 22–49.

Hutcheson, Derek S. and Petersson, Bo (2016). 'Shortcut to Legitimacy: Popularity in Putin's Russia'. *Europe-Asia Studies*, 68 (7), 1107–26.

Hürriyet (2005). *Erdoğan: Müslüman değil, muhafazakar demokratız*, 26 April 2005. [Online]. Available at: http://www.hurriyet.com.tr/erdogan-musluman-degil-muhafazakar-demokratiz-314711 [Accessed 11 November 2017].

Hürriyet (2005). *AIHM, Leyla Şahin'in türbanla ilgili itirazını reddetti*, 10 November 2005. [Online]. Available at: http://www.hurriyet.com.tr/gundem/aihm-leyla-sahinin-turbanla-ilgili-itirazini-reddetti-3504033 [Accessed 11 November 2017].

Hürriyet (2008). *Batının ahlaksızlığını aldık*, 24 January 2008. [Online]. Available at: http://www.hurriyet.com.tr/gundem/batinin-ahlaksizligini-aldik-8092765 [Accessed 12 December 2018].

Hürriyet Daily News (2013). *Turkish PM Erdoğan Reiterates His Call for Three Children.* 3 January 2013. [Online]. Available at http://www.hurriyetdailynews.com/turkish-pm-erdogan-reiterates-his-call-for-three-children-38235 [Accessed 7 August 2019].

Hürriyet Daily News (2014). *Turkish President Erdoğan says gender equality is against nature*, 24 November 2014. [Online]. Available at http://www.hurriyetdailynews.com/turkish-president-erdogan-says-gender-equality-against-nature-74726 [Accessed 12 December 2018].

Ilkkaracan, Pınar (2007). *Reforming the Penal Code in Turkey: The Campaign for the Reform of the Turkish Penal Code from a Gender Perspective.* [Online]. Available at http://www.ids.ac.uk/ids/Part/proj/pnp.html [Accessed 10 October 2018].

İlkkaracan, İpek (2012). 'Why So Few Women in the Labour Market in Turkey?'. *Feminist Economics*, 18 (1), 1–37.

İlkkaracan Ajas, İpek (2012). 'Feminist Politik İktisat ve Kurumsal İktisat Çercevesinde Türkiye'de Kadın İstihdamı Sorununa Farklı Bir Yaklaşım'. In *Geçmişten Günümüze Türkiye'de Kadın Emeği içinde.* Imge Bookstore, pp. 201–19.

ILO (2001). 'Labour Code of the Russian Federation of 31 December 2001'. [Online]. Available at: http://www.ilo.org/dyn/natlex/docs/WEBTEXT/60535/65252/E01RUS01.htm [Accessed 17 December 2018].

Inglehart, Ronald, and Norris, Pippa (2009). 'The True Clash of Civilisations'. *Foreign Policy*, 4 November 2009. [Online]. Available at: https://foreignpolicy.com/2009/11/04/the-true-clash-of-civilizations/ [Accessed 6 November 2018].

İnsel, Ahmet (2003). 'The AKP and Normalizing Democracy in Turkey'. *South Atlantic Quarterly*, 102 (2/3), Spring/Summer, 293–308.

Institute of Population Studies (2014). *Domestic Violence Against Women in Turkey Summary Report*. [Online]. Available at: http://www.hips.hacettepe.edu.tr/ING_SUMMARY_REPORT_VAW_2014.pdf [Accessed 21 December 2018].

Issoupova, Olga (2000). 'From Duty to Pleasure? Motherhood in Soviet and post-Soviet Russia'. In Sarah Ashwin (ed.). *Gender, State and Society in Soviet and Post-Soviet Russia*. London: Routledge, pp. 30–54.

İstanbul Müftülüğü (2008). *İstanbul Müftülüğü Aile İrşat ve Rehberlik Bürosu* [Online]. Available at: http://www.istanbulmuftulugu.gov.tr/aile-irsat-ve-rehberlik-burosu/faaliyetler/506-istanbul-muftulugu-aile-irsat-ve-rehberlik-burosu.html [Accessed 12 October 2016].

Jenkins, Gareth (2012). 'Erdogan's Volatile Authoritarianism: Tactical Ploy or Strategic Vision?'. *Turkey Analyst*, 5 December 2012. [Online]. Available at: https://turkeyanalyst.org/publications/turkey-analyst-articles/item/329-erdogans-volatile-authoritarianism-tactical-ploy-or-strategic-vision [Accessed 21 March 2018].

Johnson, Janet Elise (2007). 'Domestic Violence Politics in Post-Soviet States'. *Social Politics: International Studies in Gender, State & Society*, 14 (3), 380–405.

Johnson, Janet Elise (2009). *Gender Violence in Russia. The Politics of Feminist Intervention*. Bloomington: Indiana University Press.

Johnson, Janet Elise, and Saarinen, Aino (2013). 'Twenty-First-Century Feminisms under Repression: Gender Regime Change and the Women's Crisis Centre Movement in Russia'. *Signs*, 38 (3), Spring, 543–67.

Johnson, Janet Elise (2013). 'The Gender of Institutionalized Corruption in Russia'. *Prepared for delivery at the 2013 Annual Meeting of the American Political Science Association*, Chicago, 29 August – 1 September.

Johnson, Janet Elise (2014) 'Pussy Riot as a Feminist Project: Russia's Gendered Informal Politics'. *Nationalities Papers*, 42 (4), 583–90.

Johnson, Janet Elise (2016). 'Gender Equality Policy: Criminalizing and Decriminalizing Domestic Violence'. *Russian Analytical Digest*, 200. [Online]. Available at: www.css.ethz.ch/en/publications/rad.html [Accessed 11 August 2017].

Johnson, Janet Elise, and Novitskaya, Alexandra (2016). 'Gender and Politics'. In Stephen K. Wegren (ed.). *Putin's Russia: Past Imperfect, Future Uncertain*. Lanham, MD: Rowman & Littlefield, pp. 215–32.

Johnston, Robert (2018). *Historical Abortion Statistics, Russia*. [Online]. Available at: http://www.johnstonsarchive.net/policy/abortion/ab-russia.html [Accessed 30 November 2018].

Ka-Der (2012). *Kadın İstatistikleri 2011–2012*. [Online]. Available at: http://cms2.ka-der.org.tr/images/file/635106274401809552.pdf [Accessed 29 November 2013].

Kabasakal-Arat, Zehra (2003). 'Where to look for the truth: Memory and Interpretation in Assessing the Impact of Turkish Women's Education'. *Women's Studies International Forum*, 26 (1), 57–68.

Kadıoğlu, Ayşe (2005). 'Civil Society, Islam and Democracy in Turkey: A Study of Three Islamic Non-Governmental Organizations'. *The Muslim World*, 95, January, pp. 23–41.

Kadıoğlu, Ayşe (1998). 'Cinselliğin İnkarı: Büyük Toplumsal Projelerin Nesnesi Olarak Türk Kadınları'. In Ayşe Berktay Hacımirzaoğlu (ed.). Istanbul: Tarih Vakfı Yayınları, pp. 29–50.

Kadıoğlu, Ayşe (1994). 'Women's Subordination in Turkey: Is Islam Really the Villain?'. *Middle East Journal*, 48 (4), 645–60.

Kadir Has Üniversitesi (2016). *Türk Dış Politikası Kamuoyu Algıları Araştırması*. [Online]. Available at: http://www.khas.edu.tr/news/1367 [Accessed 21 November 2018].

Kadir Has Üniversitesi (2017). *Türk Dış Politikası Kamuoyu Algıları Araştırması*. [Online]. Available at: http://www.khas.edu.tr/news/1588 [Accessed 21 November 2018].

Kandiyoti, Deniz (1987). 'Emancipated but Unliberated? Reflections on the Turkish Case'. *Feminist Studies*, 13 (2) Summer, 317–38.

Kandiyoti, Deniz (1989). 'Women and the Turkish State: Political Actors or Symbolic Pawns?'. In Floya Anthias and Nira Yuval-Davis (eds). *Woman-Nation-State*. London: Palgrave Macmillan, pp. 126–49.

Kandiyoti, Deniz (1991a). End of Empire: Islam, Nationalism and Women in Turkey. In Deniz Kandiyoti, (ed.). *Women, Islam and the State*. Philadelphia: Temple University Press, pp. 22–47.

Kandiyoti, Deniz (1991b). 'Introduction'. In Deniz Kandiyoti (ed.). *Women, Islam and the State*. London: MacMillan, pp. 1–21.

Kandiyoti, Deniz (1997). 'Gendering the Modern. On Missing Dimensions on the Study of Turkish Modernity'. In Sibel Bozdoğan and Reşat Kasaba (eds). *Rethinking Modernity and National Identity in Turkey*. Seattle and London: University of Washington Press, pp. 113–32.

Kandiyoti, Deniz (2016). 'Locating the Politics of Gender: Patriarchy, Neoliberal Governance and Violence in Turkey'. *Research and Policy on Turkey*, 1 (2), 103–18.

Karakaya, Naim, and Özhabeş, Hande (2013). *Judicial Reform Packages: Evaluating Their Effect on Rights and Freedoms*. TESEV Democratisation Program Policy Report Series. İstanbul: TESEV Yayınları. [Online]. Available at: http://tesev.org.tr/wp-content/uploads/2015/11/Judicial_Reform_Packages_Evaluating_Their_Effect_On_Rights_And_Freedoms.pdf [Accessed 20 December 2018].

Kay, Rebecca (2000). *Russian Women and Their Organizations. Gender, Discrimination and Grassroots Women's Organizations, 1991–96*. London: MacMillan Press.

Kay, Rebecca (2002). 'A Liberation from Emancipation? Changing Discourses on Women's Employment in Soviet and Post-Soviet Russia'. *Journal of Communist Studies and Transition Politics*, 18 (1), 51–72.

Kazantsev, Andrey (2007). 'Sovereign Democracy: The Structure and Socio-Political Functions of the Concept'. *Forum of the Newest Eastern European History and Culture - Russian Edition* No. 1.

Keyman, E. Fuat and Icduygu, Ahmet (2003). 'Globalization, Civil Society and Citizenship in Turkey: Actors, Boundaries and Discourses'. *Citizenship Studies*, 7 (2), 219–34.

Keyman, E. Fuat, and Gumuscu, Sebnem (2014). *Democracy, Identity and Foreign Policy in Turkey. Hegemony through Transformation*. London: Palgrave Macmillan.

Kiblitskaya, Marina (2000). 'Russia's Female Breadwinners: The Changing Subjective Experience'. In Sarah Ashwin (ed.). *Gender, State and Society in Soviet and Post-Soviet Russia*. London: Routledge, pp. 55–70.

Kılıç, Azer (2008). 'The Gender Dimension of Social Policy Reform in Turkey: Towards Equal Citizenship?'. *Social Policy and Administration*, 42 (5), 487–503.

Kırkıpınar, Leyla (1998). 'Türkiye'de Toplumsal Değişme Sürecinde Kadın'. In *75 Yılda Kadınlar ve Erkekler*. Koç University Press, pp. 13–27.

Khotkina, Zoya (1994). 'Women in the Labour Market: Yesterday, Today and Tomorrow'. In Anastasia Posadskaya (ed.). *Women in Russia. A New Era in Russian Feminism*. London and New York: Verso, pp. 85–108.

Khotkina, Zoya (2001). 'Female Unemployment and Informal Employment in Russia'. *Problems of Economic Transition*, 43 (9), 20–33.

Klinova, B. (1995). 'Women and Legal Rights in Russia'. In Vitalina Koval (ed.). *Women in Contemporary Russia*. Oxford: Berghahn Books, pp. 47–60.

KONDA (2016). *KONDA Barometresi Temalar, 15 Temmuz Darbe Grişimi.* [Online].
Available at: http://konda.com.tr/wp-content/uploads/2017/07/KONDA1608_15_
TEMMUZ_DARBE_GIRISIMI.pdf [Accessed 11 November 2018].

Konstantinova, Valentina (1994). 'No Longer Totalitarianism, But Not Yet Democracy:
the Emergence of an Independent Women's Movement in Russia'. In Anastasia
Posadskaya (ed.). *Women in Russia. A New Era in Russian Feminism.* London: Verso,
pp. 57–73.

Kozina, Irina, and Zhidkova, Elena (2006). 'Sex Segregation and Discrimination in the
New Russian Labour Market'. In Sarah Ashwin (ed.). *Adapting to Russia's New Labour
Market: Gender and Employment Behaviour.* London: Routledge, pp. 52–79.

Köksal, Duygu (1998). 'Yeni Adam ve Yeni Kadın: 1930'lar ve 40'larda Kadın, Cinsiyet ve
Ulus'. *Toplumsal Tarih,* 51, March, 31–35.

Kramer, Mark (2014). 'Why Russia Intervenes'. *Perspectives on Peace and Security,* August.
[Online]. Available at: https://perspectives.carnegie.org/us-russia/wp-content/
uploads/2014/09/Why-Russia-Intervenes-n.pdf [Accessed 21 April 2014].

Kremlin.ru (2014). *Vladimir Putin Presented the Order of Parental Glory,* 2 June 2014.
[Online]. Available at http://en.kremlin.ru/events/president/news/45820 [Accessed
2 September 2017].

Kremlin.ru (2016). *Order of Parental Glory Awarded at the Kremlin,* 1 June 2016. [Online].
Available at: http://en.kremlin.ru/events/president/news/52064 [Accessed 2 September
2017].

KSSGM (2004). *Response to the Republic of Turkey to the Implementation of the Beijing
Platform for Action.* Ankara: Republic of Turkey General Directorate on the Status and
Problems of Women. [Online]. Available at: http://www.un.org/womenwatch/daw/
Review/responses/TURKEY-English.pdf [Accessed 26 December 2013].

KSGM (2007). *Combating Domestic Violence against Women National Action Plan 2007–
2010.* 2007. Ankara: The Republic of Turkey Prime Ministry General Directorate on
the Status of Women. [Online]. Available at: http://www.kadininstatusu.gov.tr/upload/
kadininstatusu.gov.tr/mce/eski_site/Pdf/kyais-uep-eng.pdf [Accessed 15 December 2013].

KSGM (2008). *National Action Plan Gender Equality 2008–2013.* Ankara: The Republic
of Turkey Prime Ministry General Directorate on the Status of Women. [Online].
Available at: http://www.huksam.hacettepe.edu.tr/English/Files/NAP_GE.pdf
[Accessed 1 December 2013].

Kumari, Jayawardena (2016). *Feminism and Nationalism in the Third World.* London and
New York: Verso.

Kuzio, Taras (2015). 'Nationalism and Authoritarianism in Russia: Introduction to the
Special Issue'. *Communist and Post-Communist Studies,* 49 (1), 1–11.

Labour Law. (2008). [Online]. Available at: http://www.tbmm.gov.tr/kanunlar/k5763.html
[Accessed 30 November 2018].

Lapidus, Gail W. (1975). 'Political Mobilization, Participation, and Leadership: Women in
Soviet Studies'. *Comparative Politics,* 8 (1), 90–118.

Lapidus, Gail W. (1977). 'Sexual Equality in Soviet Policy. A Developmental Perspective'.
In *Women in Russia,* pp. 116–30.

Lapidus, Gail Warshofsky (1978a). 'Sexual Equality in Soviet Policy: A Developmental
Perspective'. In Dorothy Atkinson, Alexander Dallin, and Gail Warshofsky Lapidus
(eds). *Women in Russia.* Sussex: Harvester Press, pp.115–38.

Lapidus, Gail Warshofsky (1978b). *Women in Soviet Society, Equality, Development and
Social Change.* Berkeley, Los Angeles and London: University of California Press.

Lapidus, Gail W. (1982). 'Introduction. Women, Work, and Family: New Soviet Perspectives'. In Gail W. Lapidus (ed.). *Women, Work, and Family in the Soviet Union*. New York: M. E. Sharpe, pp. ix–xlvi.

Lapidus, Gail W. (1993). 'Gender and Restructuring: the Impact of Perestroika and its Aftermath on Soviet Women'. In Valerie M. Moghadam (ed.). *Democratic Reform and the Position of Women in Transitional Economies*. Oxford: Claredon Press, pp.137–61.

Laruelle, Marlene (2015). 'Russia as a "Divided Nation," from Compatriots to Crimea: A Contribution to the Discussion on Nationalism and Foreign Policy'. *Problems of Post-Communism*, 62 (2), 88–97.

Laurelle, Marlene (2017). 'The Kremlin's Ideological Ecosystems: Equilibrium and Competition'. *PONARS Policy Memo 483*, November. [Online]. Available at: http://www.ponarseurasia.org/memo/kremlins-ideological-ecosystems-equilibrium-and-competition [Accessed 26 November 2017].

Lenin, Vladimir I. (1933). *The Emancipation of Women: From the Writings of V.I. Lenin*. [Online]. Available at: https://www.marxists.org/archive/lenin/works/subject/women/abstract/99_dcr7.htm [Accessed 10 October 2018].

Lenin, Vladimir I. (2004). *On the Emancipation of Women*. Hawaii: University Press of the Pacific.

Levada Centre (2012). 'Stabilisation vs. Democracy'. 5 April 2012. [Online]. Available at: https://www.levada.ru/en/2016/04/05/stabilization-vs-democracy/ [Accessed 30 October 2018].

Levada Centre (2016). 'Church'. 5 April 2016. [Online]. Available at: https://www.levada.ru/en/2016/04/05/church/ [Accessed 30 October 2018].

Levitsky, Steven, and Way, Lucan (2002). 'The Rise of Competitive Authoritarianism'. *Journal of Democracy*, 13 (2), 51–65.

Lipovskaya, Olga (1997). 'Women's groups in Russia'. In Mary Buckley (ed.). *Post-Soviet Women: From the Baltic to Central Asia*. Cambridge: Cambridge University Press, pp. 186–200.

Lissyutkina, L. (1993). 'Soviet Women at the Crossroads of Perestroika'. In Nanette Funk and Magda Mueller (eds). *Gender Politics and Post-Communism: Reflections from Eastern Europe and the Former Soviet Union*. London and New York: Routledge, pp. 274–86.

Luhn, Alec (2014). 'Russian Opposition Leader Jailed in Bolotnaya Square Protest Case'. *the Guardian*, 24 July 2014. [Online]. Available at: http://www.theguardian.com/world/2014/jul/24/russian-opposition-leader-jailed-bolotnaya-square-sergei-udaltsov-putin [Accessed 2 September 2017].

Marsh, Rosalind (1995). 'Anastasia Posadskaia, the Dubna Forum, the Independent Women's Movement'. In Rosalind Marsh (ed.). *Women in Russia and Ukraine*. Cambridge: Cambridge University Press, pp. 286–97.

Marsh, Rosalind (1998). 'Women in Contemporary Russia and the Former Soviet Union'. In Rick Wilford and Robert L. Miller (eds). *Women, Ethnicity and Nationalism. The Politics of Transition*. London and New York: Routledge, pp. 87–119.

Massell, Gregory J. (2015). *The Surrogate Proletariat. Moslem Women and Revolutionary Strategies in Soviet Central Asia, 1919-1929*. Princeton, NJ: Princeton University Press.

McAllister, Ian, and White, Stephen (2008). 'It's the Economy, Comrade!' Parties and Voters in the 2007 Russian Duma Election'. *Europe-Asia Studies*, 60 (6), August, 931–57.

McDermid, Jane and Hillyar, Anna (1999). *Midwives of the Revolution. Female Bolsheviks and Women Workers in 1917.* London: UCL Press.

McFaul, Michael (2007). *Rebuilding the Iron Curtain Testimony before the House Committee on Foreign Relations.* Carnegie Endowment for International Peace, 17 May 2007. [Online]. Available at: http://carnegieendowment.org/2007/05/17/russia-rebuilding-iron-curtain-pub-19202 [Accessed 21 February 2018].

Medvedev, Dimitri (2010). 'Presidential Address to the Federal Assembly', 30 November 2010. [Online]. Available at: http://en.kremlin.ru/events/president/transcripts/messages/9637 [Accessed 1 February 2018].

Mengi, Ruhat (2005). '"Kadın çalışmasın" la başlıyor her şey!'. [Online]. *Gazete Vatan,* 1 March 2005. Available at: http://haber.gazetevatan.com/0/48156/4/yazarlar [Accessed 30 November 2018].

Meuser, Michael, and Nagel, Ulrike (2009). 'The Expert Interview and Changes in Knowledge Production'. In *Interviewing Experts.* London: Palgrave Macmillan, pp. 17–42.

MFA (2000). 'National Security Concept of the Russian Federation', 10 January 2000. [Online]. Available at: http://www.mid.ru/en/foreign_policy/official_documents/-/asset_publisher/CptICkB6BZ29/content/id/589768 [Accessed 29 January 2018].

Ministry of Culture and Tourism (n.d.). [Online]. Available at: http://www.kultur.gov.tr/EN,104191/turkish-women.html. [Accessed 12 December 2018].

Morçatı (2015). *Ücretsiz, Güvenli, Erişilebilir Kürtaj Hakkının Takipçisiyiz.* 3 February 2015. [Online]. Available at: https://www.morcati.org.tr/tr/ana-sayfa/301-ucretsiz-guvenli-erisilebilir-kurtaj-hakkinin-takipcisiyiz [Accessed 24 April 2017].

Müftüler-Baç, Meltem (2011). 'Turkish Foreign Policy Change, Its Domestic Determinants and the Role of the European Union'. *South East European Politics and Society,* 16 (2) June, 279–91.

Muller, Jan Werner (2016). *What is Populism?* Philadelphia: University of Pennsylvania Press.

Murvayeva, Marianna (2014). 'Traditional Values and Modern Families: Legal Understanding of Tradition and Modernity in Contemporary Russia'. *Journal of Social Policy Studies,* 12 (4), 625–38.

Najmabadi, Afsaneh (2006). 'Gender and Secularism of Modernity: How Can a Muslim Woman Be French?'. *Feminist Studies* 32 (2), 239–55.

National Right to Life News (2015). *Russia: Church and State Sign Agreement to Prevent Abortion.* 1 July 2015. [Online]. Available at: http://www.nationalrighttolifenews.org/news/2015/07/russia-church-and-state-sign-agreement-to-prevent-abortion/#.VoChzoS4k_U [Accessed 2 September 2017].

Nechemias, Carol (2009). 'Russia's Drift towards Authoritarianism: The Impact on Women's Reproductive Rights'. *Paper presented at the ECPG Conference in Belfast, Northern Ireland,* 21 January 2009.

Nechemias, Carol (2014). 'Women in the Russian Labour Force: A Retreat from Equality?'. *Prepared for presentation at the workshop, "Global Women's Work in Transition," The Liechtenstein Institute on Self-Determination,* 25–26 September 2014, Princeton University.

Nechemias Carol (2016). 'The Putin Era and Gender Equality: A Patriarchal Renaissance?'. *Paper prepared for presentation at 16th Annual International Aleksanteri Conference, Life and Death in Russia,* 26–28 October 2016, the University of Helsinki and the Finnish Centre of Excellence in Russian Studies.

Oğuzlu, Tarık (2008). 'Middle Easternization of Turkey's Foreign Policy: Does Turkey Dissociate from the West?'. *Turkish Studies,* 9 (1), 3–20.

Okara, Andrey (2007). 'Sovereign Democracy: A New Russian Idea or a PR Project?'. 8 August 2007. [Online]. Available at: http://eng.globalaffairs.ru/number/n_9123 [Accessed 21 November 2017].

Onuncu Kalkınma Planı (2015). *Ailenin ve Dinamik Nüfus Yapısının Korunması Programı Eylem Planı*. [Online]. Available at: http://www.dap.gov.tr/IMG_CATALOG/dosya/ailenin-ve-dinamik-nufus-yapisinin-korunmasi-programi-eylem-planipdf.pdf [Accessed 17 December 2018].

Öncü, Ayşe (1981). 'Turkish Women in Professions: Why so Many?'. In Nermin Abadan-Unat (ed.). *Women in Turkish Society*. Leiden: E.J. Brill, pp. 181–93.

Onis, Ziya (1997). 'The Political Economy of Islamic Resurgence in Turkey: The Rise of the Welfare Party in Perspective'. *Third World Quarterly*, 18 (4), 743–66.

Öniş, Ziya (2003). 'Domestic Politics, International Norms and Challenges to the State: Turkey-EU Relations in the post-Helsinki Era'. *Turkish Studies*, 4 (1), 9–34.

Öniş, Ziya (2009). 'Conservative Globalism at the Crossroads: The Justice and Development Party and the Thorny Path to Democratic Consolidation in Turkey'. *Mediterranean Politics*, 14 (1), 21–40.

Öniş, Ziya (2011). 'Multiple Faces of the "New" Turkish Foreign Policy: Underlying Dynamics and a Critique'. *Insight Turkey*, 13 (1), 47–65.

Öniş, Ziya (2012). 'Turkish and the Arab Spring: Between Ethics and Self-Interest'. *Insight Turkey*, 14 (3), 45–63.

Öniş, Ziya (2013). 'Sharing Power: Turkey's Democratization Challenge in the Age of the AKP Hegemony'. *Insight Turkey*, 15 (2), 85–102.

Öniş, Ziya (2015). 'Monopolising the Centre: The AKP and the Uncertain Path of Turkish Democracy'. *The International Spectator*, 50 (2), 22–41.

Öniş, Ziya, and Keyman, Fuat (2003). 'Turkey at the Polls: New Path Emerges'. *Journal of Democracy*, 14 (2), 95–107.

Öniş, Ziya, and Yılmaz, Şuhnaz (2009). 'Between Europeanization and Euro-Asianism: Foreign Policy Activism in Turkey during the AKP Era'. *Turkish Studies*, 10 (1), 7–24.

Özbay, Ferhunde (1990). 'The Development of Studies on Women in Turkey'. In Ferhunde Özbay (ed.). *Women, Family and Social Change in Turkey*. Bangkok: UNESCO, pp. 1–12.

Özbudun, Ergun (2006). 'From Political Islam to Conservative Democracy: The Case of the Justice and Development Party in Turkey'. *South European Society and Politics*, 11 (3–4), 543–57.

Özbudun, Ergun (2014). 'AKP at the Crossroads: Erdoğan's Majoritarian Drift'. *South European Society and Politics*, 19 (2), 155–67.

Özbudun, Ergun (2015). 'Turkey's Judiciary and the Drift Toward Competitive Authoritarianism'. *International Spectator*, 50 (2), 42–55.

Özturk, Ahmet Erdi, and Gözaydın, İştar (2017). 'Turkey's Constitutional Amendments: A Critical Perspective'. *Research and Policy on Turkey*, 2 (2), 210–24.

Papkova, Irina (2011). *The Orthodox Church and Russian Politics*. Washington, DC: Woodrow Wilson Centre Press; Oxford: Oxford University.

Pateman, Carole (1988). *The Sexual Contract*. Cambridge: Polity.

Person, Robert (2015). 'Potholes, Pensions, and Public Opinion: The Politics of Blame in Putin's Power Vertical'. *Post-Soviet Affairs*, 31 (5), 420–47.

Person, Robert (2017). 'Balance of Threat: The Domestic Insecurity of Vladimir Putin'. *Journal of Eurasian Studies*, 8 (1) January, 44–59.

Posadskaya, Anastasia (1994). 'A Feminist Critique of Policy, Legislation and Social Consciousness in Post-Socialist Russia'. In *Women in Russia. A New Era in Russian Feminism*. London: Verso, pp.164–82.

Pravitelstvo Rossiiskoy Federatsiyi (2017). *Natsionalnaya Strategiya deyctviy v interesah zhenshin na 2017–2022 godyı*. [Online]. Available at: http://static.government.ru/media/files/njlkIvH7WCvOIYRmcucV4jdNihEmTOUe.pdf [Accessed 30 November 2018].

Pushkareva, Natalia (1997). *Women in Russian History. From the Tenth to the Twentieth Century*. New York: M.E. Sharpe.

Putin, Vladimir V. (1999). *Russia at the Turn of the Millennium*, 30 December 1999. [Online]. Available at: http://pages.uoregon.edu/kimball/Putin.htm [Accessed 8 October 2017].

Putin, Vladimir V. (2003). *Poslanie Federal'nomu Sobraniyu Rossiiskoi Federatsii*, 16 May 2003. [Online]. Available at: http://kremlin.ru/events/president/transcripts/21998 [Accessed 28 October 2017].

Putin, Vladimir V. (2005a). *Interv'yu amerikanskomu telenanalu "Foks N'yus"*, 17 September 2005. [Online]. Available at: http://kremlin.ru/events/president/transcripts/23178 [Accessed 27 October 2017].

Putin, Vladimir V. (2005b). *Interv'yu "Radio Slovenksogo" i Slovatskoi telekompanii STV*, 22 February 2005. [Online]. Available at: http://kremlin.ru/events/president/transcripts/22837 [Accessed 27 October 2017].

Putin, Vladimir V. (2005c). *Zayavlenie dlya pressy i otvety na voprosy na sovmestnoi s Prezidentom SShA Dzordzhem Bushem press-konferentsii*, 24 February 2005, Bratislava. [Online]. Available at: http://kremlin.ru/events/president/transcripts/22840 [Accessed 27 October 2017].

Putin, Vladimir V. (2006a). *Annual Address to Assembly*, 10 May 2006. [Online]. Available at: http://en.kremlin.ru/events/president/transcripts/23577 [Accessed 27 January 2018].

Putin, Vladimir V. (2006b). *Interview with NBC Television Channel (USA)*, 12 July 2006. [Online]. Available at: http://en.kremlin.ru/events/president/transcripts/23699 [Accessed 21 November 2017].

Putin, Vladimir V. (2006c). *Interview with TF1 Television Channel (France)*, 12 July 2006. [Online]. Available at: http://en.kremlin.ru/events/president/transcripts/23700 [Accessed 21 November 2017].

Putin, Vladimir V. (2008) *Putin's Prepared Remarks at 43rd Munich Conference on Security Policy. Text of Putin's speech at NATO Summit*, Bucharest, 2 April 2008. [Online]. Available at: https://www.unian.info/world/111033-text-of-putins-speech-at-nato-summit-bucharest-april-2-2008.html [Accessed 21 October 2017].

Putin, Vladimir V. (2012a). *Address to the Federal Assembly*, 12 December 2012. [Online]. Available at: http://en.kremlin.ru/events/president/transcripts/17118 [Accessed 10 January 2018].

Putin, Vladimir V. (2012b). *Rossiya i menyayushchiisya mir*. Moskovskie Novosti, 27 February 2012. [Online]. Available at: http://www.mn.ru/politics/20120227/312306749.html [Accessed 11 October 2017].

Putin, Vladimir V. (2012c). *Russia: The Ethnicity Issue Prime Minister Vladimir Putin's Article for Nezavisimaya gazeta*. 23 January 2012. [Online]. Available at: http://archive.premier.gov.ru/eng/events/news/17831/, [Accessed 23 November 2017].

Putin, Vladimir V. (2012d). *Speech at a rally in support of presidential candidate Vladimir Putin*, Moscow, 4 March 2012. [Online]. Available at: http://en.kremlin.ru/events/president/news/14684 [Accessed 12 October 2017].

Putin, Vladimir V. (2013a). *Poslanie Prezidenta Federal'nomu Sobraniyu*, 12 December 2013. [Online]. Available at: http://kremlin.ru/events/president/news/19825 [Accessed 23 November 2017].

Putin, Vladimir V. (2013b). *Zasedanie mezhdunarodnogo diskussionnogo kluba "Valdai"*, 19 September 2013. [Online]. Available at:, http://kremlin.ru/transcripts/19243 [Accessed 23 November 2017].

Putin, Vladimir V. (2014a). *Obrashchenie Prezidenta Rossiiskoi Federatsii. 18 marta 2014 goda.* [Online]. Available at: http://kremlin.ru/news/20603 [Accessed 22 October 2017].

Putin, Vladimir V. (2014b). *Speech at State Council Presidium meeting on family, motherhood and childhood policy*, 17 February 2014. [Online]. Available at: http://en.kremlin.ru/events/president/transcripts/20265 [Accessed 10 January 2018].

Racioppi, Linda, and O'Sullivan-See, Katherine (1995). 'Organizing Women before and after the Fall: Women's Politics in the Soviet Union and Post-Soviet Russia'. *Signs: Journal of Women in Culture and Society*, 20 (4), 818–50.

Racioppi, Linda and O'Sullivan See, Katherine (1997), *Women's Activism in Contemporary Russia.* Philadelphia: Temple University Press.

Radikal (2012). *Her kürtaj bir Uludere'dir*, 27 May 2012. [Online]. Available at: http://www.radikal.com.tr/turkiye/basbakan_her_kurtaj_bir_uluderedir-1089235 [Accessed 6 April 2016].

Radio Free Europe/Radio Liberty (2017). *Putin Signs Controversial Law Tightening Internet Restrictions*, 30 July 2017. [Online]. Available at: https://www.rferl.org/a/russia-putin-signs-vpn-law-internet/28648976.html [Accessed 21 October 2018].

RANEPA (2015). *Critical 10 Years. Demographic Policies of the Russian Federation: Successes and Challenges.* Moscow: "Delo" Publishing House.

RBTH (2014). *Russia Seeks to Further Decrease Abortion Rates*, 28 January 2014. [Online]. Available at: https://www.rbth.com/society/2014/01/28/russia_seeks_to_further_decrease_abortion_rates_33543.html [Accessed 17 December 2018].

Resmi Gazete (2016a). 'Analık İzni veya Ücretsiz İzin Sonrası Yapılacak Kısmi Süreli Çalışmalar Hakkında Yönetmelik'. 13 April 2016. [Online]. Available at: http://www.resmigazete.gov.tr/eskiler/2016/11/20161108-11.htm [Accessed 17 December 2018].

Resmi Gazete (2016b). 'Kamu Personeli Genel Tebliği'. 8 November 2016. [Online]. Available at: http://www.resmigazete.gov.tr/eskiler/2016/04/20160413-10.htm [Accessed 17 December 2018]

Reuters (2013). *Turkey's Erdogan says "dark alliances" Behind Graft Inquiry*, 21 December 2013. [Online]. Available at: https://www.reuters.com/article/turkey-corruption/update-3-turkeys-erdogan-says-dark-alliances-behind-graft-inquiry-idUSL6N0K002S20131221 [Accessed 21 October 2016].

Riabova, Tatyana, and Riabov, Oleg (2002). 'U NAS SEKSA NET: Gender, Identity and Anti-Communist Discourse in Russia'. In Alexander A. Markarov (ed.). *State Politics and Society: Issues and Problems with Post-Soviet Development.* Iowa City: Centre for Russian, East European and Eurasian Studies in the University of Iowa, pp. 29–38.

Riabova, Tatiana, and Riabov, Oleg (2014). 'The Remasculinization of Russia? Gender, Nationalism and the Legitimation of Power Under Vladimir Putin'. *Problems of Post-Communism*, 61 (2), 23–5.

Rivkin-Fish, Michele (2010). 'Pronatalism, Gender Politics, and the Renewal of Family in Russia: Toward a Feminist Anthropology of "Maternity Capital"'. *Slavic Review*, 3, 701–24.

Robinson, Neil. (2017). 'Russian Neo-patrimonialism and Putin's "Cultural Turn"'. *Europe-Asia Studies*, 69 (2). doi 10.1080/09668136.2016.1265916 (Published online 25 January 2017).

Rogov, Kirill (2015). 'Triumphs and Crises of Plebiscitary Presidentialism'. In Leon
    Aron (ed.). *Putin's Russia. How It Rose, How It Is Maintained, and How It Might End.*
    Washington, DC: American Enterprise Institute, pp. 83–106.
Rossiiskaia Gazeta (2011). F'ederalnyi zakon at 21 noyabrya 2011. N 323-FZ "Ab
    osnavakh okhranyı zdorovya grazhdan v Rossiiskoy Federatsiyi". 23 November 2011.
    [Online]. Available at: https://rg.ru/2011/11/23/zdorovie-dok.html [Accessed 27
    January 2017].
Rosstat (2015). 'Russia in Figures 2015 Statistical Handbook'. [Online]. Available at: http://
    www.gks.ru/free_doc/doc_2015/rusfig/rus-15e.pdf [Accessed 17 December 2018].
Rosstat (2016). 'Organizations Carrying Out Educational Activities on Preschool
    Programmes Supervision and Child Care'. [Online]. Available at: http://www.gks.ru/wps/
    wcm/connect/rosstat_main/rosstat/en/figures/education/[Accessed 17 December 2018].
Rotkirch, Anna, Temkina, Anna, and Zdravomyslova, Yelena (2007). 'Who Helps the
    Degraded Housewives?: Comments on Vladimir President Putin 's Demographic
    Speech'. *European Journal of Women's Studies*, 14 (4), 349–57.
RT (2017). *Orthodox Church Presses for Total Abortion Ban in Russia*, 18 May 2017.
    [Online]. Available at: https://www.rt.com/politics/388802-orthodox-church-presses-
    for-total/ [Accessed 2 September 2017].
Rutland, Peter. (2014). 'The Pussy Riot affair: gender and national identity in Putin's
    Russia'. *Nationalities Papers*, 42 (4), 575–82.
Sabah (2008). *Batı'nın ilmini değil ahlaksızlığını aldık*, 25 January 2008. [Online]. Available
    at: http://arsiv.sabah.com.tr/2008/01/25/haber,8B601321AE6D4C2287A5CBC5E77
    7E323.html [Accessed 12 December 2018].
Saktanber, Ayşe (1997). 'Women, Islamism and Politics in Turkey: A Critical Perspective'.
    Middle East Policy, 5 (3), September.
Sakwa, Richard (1997). 'The Regime System in Russia'. *Contemporary Politics*, 3 (1), 7–25.
Sakwa, Richard (2010). 'The Dual State in Russia'. *Post Soviet Affairs*, 26 (3), 185–206.
Schwartz, Janet S. (1979). 'Women under Socialism: Role Definitions of Soviet Women'.
    Social Forces, 58 (1), 67–88.
Scott, James W., and Henk Van Houtum (2009). 'Reflections on EU Territoriality and the
    "Bordering" of Europe'. *Political Geography* 28 (5), 271–73.
Selçuk, Orçun (2016). 'Strong Presidents and Weak Institutions: Populism in Turkey,
    Venezuela and Ecuador'. *Southeast European and Black Sea Studies*, 16 (4), 571–89.
Shadrina, Anna (2015). *What Is Threatening 'Traditional Family Values' in Russia Today?*
    [Online]. Available at: https://www.opendemocracy.net/anna-shadrina/what-is-
    threatening-%E2%80%98traditional-family-values%E2%80%99-in-russia-today
    [Accessed 2 September 2017].
Shlapentokh, Vladimir (2007). 'Perceptions of a Threat to the Regime as a Major Factor
    of Russian Foreign Policy: From Lenin to Putin'. *Johnson's Russia List*. [Online].
    Available at: http://www.russialist.org/archives/2007-199-28.php [Accessed 11
    December 2017].
Shnyrova, Olga (2007). 'Feminism and Suffrage in Russia: Women, War and Revolution
    1914-1917'. In A. Fell and I. Sharp (eds). *The Women's Movement in Wartime*. London:
    Palgrave Macmillan, pp.124–40.
Sirman, Nükhet (1989). 'Feminism in Turkey: A Short History'. *New Perspectives on
    Turkey*, 3 (1), 1–34.
Slater, Wendy (1995). '"Women of Russia" and Women's Representation in Russian
    Politics'. In David Lane (ed.). *Russia in Transition. Politics, Privatisation and Inequality*.
    London and New York: Longman Group, pp. 76–90.

Smolentceva, Natalia, Gribova, Darina, von Abo, Matthew, Zarif, Pourang, and Sinepol, Eugenia (2017). *You're a Woman, I'm a Man: Gender Equality in Russia*. [Online]. Available at: https://nataliasmolentceva.atavist.com/gender-equality-in-russia [Accessed 1 April 2017].

Smyth, Regina, and Soboleva, Irina (2014). 'Looking Beyond the Economy: Pussy Riot and the Kremlin's Voting Coalition'. *Post-Soviet Affairs*, 30 (4), 257–75.

Smyth, Regina, Sobolev, Anton, and Soboleva, Irina (2013). 'Patterns of Discontent: Identifying the Participant Core in Russian Post-Election Protest'. *Paper prepared for the conference Russia's Winter of Discontent: Taking Stock of Changing State-Society Relationships*. Uppsala University, Sweden, 6–7 September 2013.

Soyarık-Şentürk, Nalan (2012). 'The AKP and the Gender Issue: Shuttling between Neoliberalism and Patriarchy'. In *Silent Violence. Neliberalism, Islamist Politics and the AKP Years in Turkey*. Ottawa: Red Quill Books, pp. 153–78.

Sperling, Valerie (1999). *Organizing Women in Contemporary Russia*. Cambridge: Cambridge University Press.

Sperling, Valerie (2006). 'Women's Organisations. Institutionalised Interest Groups or Vulnerable Dissidents?'. In Alfred B. Evans Jr., Laura A. Henry, and Lisa McIntosh Sundstrom (eds). *Russian Civil Society. A Critical Assessment*. London and New York: M.E Sharpe, pp. 161–77.

Sperling, Valerie (2015). *Sex, Politics and Putin: Political Legitimacy in Russia*. Oxford: Oxford University Press.

Stites, Richard (1991). *The Women's Liberation Movement in Russia. Feminism, Nihilism, and Bolshevism. 1860–1930*. Princeton, NJ: Princeton University Press.

STOPWAV (2014). 'Violence Against Women in the Russian Federation'. [Online]. Available at: http://www.stopvaw.org/russian_federation#_edn25 [Accessed 2 September 2017].

Surkov, Vladislav (2007). Russkaya politicheskaya kultura. Vzglyad iz utopiyi. *Ruskiy Dcurnal*. [Online]. Available at: http://www.russ.ru/pole/Russkaya-politicheskaya-kul-tura.-Vzglyad-iz-utopii [Accessed 21 December 2018].

Taş, Hakkı (2015). 'Turkey – From Tutelary to Delegative Democracy'. *Third World Quarterly*, 36 (4), 776–91.

Taylor, Adam (2014). 'Birth Control as "Treason?" The Logic Behind the Turkish President's Latest Controversy'. *Washington Post*, 12 December 2014. [Online]. Available at: https://www.washingtonpost.com/news/worldviews/wp/2014/12/24/birth-control-as-treason-the-logic-behind-the-turkish-presidents-latest-controversy/(accessed April 6, 2016) [Accessed 21 January 2018].

Tekeli, Şirin (1981). 'Women in Turkish Politics'. In *Women in Turkish Society*. Leiden: Brill, pp. 1–22.

Tekeli, Şirin (1986). 'The Emergence of the Feminist Movement in Turkey'. In Drude Dahlerup (ed.). *The New Women's Movement*. London: Sage Publications, pp. 179–99.

Tekeli, Şirin (1990). 'Women in the Changing Political Associations of the 1980s'. In Nükhet Sirman and Andrew Finkel (eds). *Turkish State, Turkish Society*. New York: Routledge, pp. 259–88.

Temkina, Anna, and Zdravomyslova, Elena (2014). 'Gender's Crooked Path: Feminism Confronts Russian Patriarchy'. *Current Sociology*, 62 (2), 1–18.

TEPAV (2012). *Türkiye'de Kadınların İşgücüne Katılımı: İstanbul ve Ankara'da Katılım Bingol ve Tunceli ile Aynı*. [Online]. Available at: http://www.tepav.org.tr/tr/yayin/s/609 [Accessed 9 December 2013].

Tepe, Sultan (2005). 'Turkey's AKP: A Model "Muslim-Democratic" Party?'. *Journal of Democracy*, 16 (3), July, 69–82.

Teplova, Tatyana (2005). 'Balancing Work and Care in the Post-Soviet Russian Labour Market'. *Carleton Economic Papers*, 05-04, 2–30.

Teplova, Tatyana (2007). 'Welfare State Transformation, Childcare, and Women's Work in Russia'. *Social Politics*, 14 (3), 284–322.

Timisi, Nilüfer, and Ağduk-Gevrek, Meltem (2002). '1980'ler Türkiye'sinde Feminist Hareket'. In *90'larda Türkiye'de Feminizm*. İstanbul: İletişim, pp.13–40.

Tkachenko, Maxim (2011). 'Women of "Putin's Army" Support Russia's PM with Racy Video'. *CNN*, 19 July 2011. [Online]. Available at: http://edition.cnn.com/2011/WORLD/europe/07/19/russia.putin.support.video/[Accessed 21 March 2016].

Toksöz, Gülay (2012). 'The State of Female Labour in the Impasse of the Neo-liberal Market and Patriarchal Family'. In *Gender and Society in Turkey: The Impact of Neoliberal Policies, Political Islam and EU Accession*. London: I.B. Tauris, pp.47–64.

Toprak, Binnaz (1994). 'Women and Fundamentalism: The Case of Turkey'. In Valerie M. Moghadam (ed.). *Identity Politics and Women: Cultural Reassertions and Feminisms in International Perspective*. Oxford: Westview Press, pp. 293–306.

Toska, Zehra (1998). 'Cumhuriyet'in Kadın İdeali. Eşiği Aşanlar ve Aşamayanlar'. In *75 Yılda Kadınlar ve Erkekler*. Koç University Press, pp. 71–88.

Trenin, Dmitri (2007). 'Russia Redefines Itself and Its Relations with the West'. *Washington Quarterly*, 30 (2), 95–105.

Tsentr sotsial'no-trudovih prav. (n.d.-a). 'Problemıy Rabotayushih Zhenshin'. 5 March 2016. [Online]. Available at: http://trudprava.ru/expert/article/genderart/1601 [Accessed 21 August 2017].

Tsentr sotsial'no-trudovih prav (n.d.-b). 'Vashi Prava: Posobiya v Svyazi c Razhdeniyem I Vospitanniyem Detey'. [Online]. Available at: http://trudprava.ru/base/child/1106 [Accessed 21 August 2017].

Tsygankov, Andrei (2015). 'Vladimir Putin's Last Stand: The Sources of Russia's Ukraine Policy'. *Post-Soviet Affairs*, 31 (4), 279–303.

Tuğal, Cihan (2009). 'Transforming Everyday Life: Islamism and Social Movement Theory'. *Theory and Society*, 38 (5), 423–58.

TÜİK (2011). *Population and Housing Survey*. Ankara: Turkish Statistical Institute. [Online]. Available at: http://www.tuik.gov.tr/Kitap.do?metod=KitapDetay&KT_ID=11&KITAP_ID=276 [Accessed 18 December 2013].

TÜİK (2017). 'Nüfus ve Demografi'. [Online]. Available at: http://tuik.gov.tr/UstMenu. do?metod=temelist [Accessed 29 January 2018].

TÜİK (2018). 'İşgücü İstatistikleri'. [Online]. Available at: http://www.tuik.gov.tr/ PreHaberBultenleri.do?id=27697 http://www.tuik.gov.tr/jsp/arama/konu_arama_tem. jsp?araType=hb_x&metod=search&d-5442-p=2 [Accessed 17 December 2018].

T24 (2013). *Erdoğan: Böyle bir Avrupa Birliği Parlamentosu tanımıyorum*, 17 June 2013. [Online]. Available at: http://t24.com.tr/haber/erdogan-boyle-bir-avrupa-birligi-parlamentosunu-tanimiyorum,232170 [Accessed 18 December 2017].

UN (n.d.). [Online]. Available at: http://www.un.org/ru/publications/pdfs/national%20 human%20development%20report%20in%20the%20russian%20federation%202010. pdf [Accessed 12 November 2016].

UNDP (2005). *Human Development Report 2005 for the Russian Federation. Russia in 2015: Development Goals and Policy Priorities*, Moscow. [Online]. Available at: http://hdr. undp.org/sites/default/files/russian_federation_2005_en.pdf [Accessed 21 May 2014].

UNDP (2010). *National Human Development Report in the Russian Federation 2010. Millennium Development Goals in Russia: Looking into the Future*. Moscow. [Online]. Available at: http://www.un.org/ru/publications/pdfs/national%20human%20

development%20report%20in%20the%20russian%20federation%202010.pdf [Accessed 21 May 2014].

UNECE (n.d.). [Online]. Available at: http://www.unece.org/fileadmin/DAM/Gender/ documents/Beijing+15/Turkey.pdf [Accessed 12 December 2018].

United Nations in the Russian Federation (2016). *Russia's List of Banned Jobs for Women Violated Woman's Rights, Needs Amending – UN Experts*. [Online]. Available at: http://www.unrussia.ru/en/taxonomy/term/4/2016-03-15-0. [Accessed 17 December 2018].

Utrata, Jennifer (2015). *Single Mothers and Family Change in the New Russia*. Ithaca, NY: Cornell University Press.

Vasilyeva, Nataliya (2016). 'Church, State Seeing Eye to Eye in Putin's Orthodox Russia'. 16 December 2016. [Online]. Available at: http://bigstory.ap.org/article/3d62ef0a45eb4 ca8a51082d44201c80a/church-state-seeing-eye-eye-putins-orthodox-russia [Accessed 11 May 2017].

Verkhovsky, Aleksander (2002). 'The Role of the Russian Orthodox Church in Nationalist, Xenophobic and Anti-Western Tendencies in Russia Today: Not Nationalism but Fundamentalism'. *Religion, State and Society*, 30 (4), 333–45.

Vinokurova, Natalia (2007). 'Reprivatising Women's Lives: from Khrushchev to Brezhnev'. In Rebecca Kay (ed.). *Gender, Equality and Difference During and After State Socialism*. London: Palgrave Macmillan, pp. 63–84.

Voronina, Olga (1993). 'Soviet Patriarchy: Past and Present'. *Hypatia*, 18 (4), 97–112.

VTsIOM (2015). 'Russia in the 1990s: Time of Failures or Victories'. [Online]. Available at: www.wciom.com/index.php?id=61&uid=1210 [Accessed 20 October 2018].

VTsIOM (2016). 'Yeltsin's Time: What We Remember'. [Online]. Available at: www.wciom. com/index.php?id=61&uid=1225 [Accessed 20 October 2018].

Walker, Shaun (2017). 'Fury at Russian Move to Soften Domestic Violence'. *The Guardian*, 19 January 2017. [Online]. Available at: https://www.theguardian.com/world/2017/ jan/19/russian-soften-domestic-violence-law-decriminalise-womens-rights [Accessed 2 September 2017].

Waters, Elizabeth (1992). 'Cuckoo-mothers' and Apparatchiks': Glasnost and Children's Homes'. In Mary Buckley (ed.). *Perestroika and Soviet Women*. Cambridge: Cambridge University Press, pp. 123–41.

White, Jenny (2003). 'State Feminism, Modernization, and the Turkish Republican Women'. *NWSA Journal*, 15 (3), 145–59.

White, David, and Herzog, Marc (2016). 'Examining State Capacity in the Context of Electoral Authoritarianism, Regime Formation and Consolidation in Russia and Turkey'. *Southeast European and Black Sea Studies*, 16 (4), 551–69.

White, Stephen (2014). 'Did Russia (Nearly) Have a Facebook Revolution in 2011? Social Media's Challenge to Authoritarianism'. *Politics*, 34 (1), 72–84.

WHO (2007). 'World Health Statistics 2007'. [Online]. Available at: http://www.who.int/ whosis/whostat2007/en/index.html [Accessed 28 March 2017].

WHO (2008). 'World Health Statistics 2008'. [Online]. Available at: http://www.who.int/ whosis/whostat/2008/en/index.htm [Accessed 28 March 2017].

WHO (2018). *European Health Information Gateway*. [Online]. Available at: https:// gateway.euro.who.int/en/indicators/hfa_587-7011-number-of-abortions-all-ages/ visualizations/#id=19682 [Accessed 17 December 2018].

Wilkinson, Cai (2014). 'Putting "Traditional Values" into Practice: The Rise and Contestation of Anti-Homopropaganda Laws in Russia'. *Journal of Human Rights*, 13 (3), 363–79.

Willerton, John P. (2017). 'Searching for a Russian National Idea: Putin Team Efforts and Public Assessments'. *Demokratizatsiya: The Journal of Post-Soviet Democratization*, 25 (3), Summer, 209–34.

Wood, Elizabeth A. (1997). *The Baba and the Comrade. Gender and Politics in Revolutionary Russia*. Bloomington and Indianapolis: Indiana University Press.

Wood, Elizabeth A. (2016). 'Hypermasculinity as a Scenario of Power'. *International Feminist Journal of Politics*, 18 (3), 329–50.

The World Bank (2015). *Supply and Demand for Child Care Services in Turkey*, September.

The World Bank (2018). 'Labour Force Participation Rate, Female (% of female population ages 15+)'. [Online]. Available at: https://data.worldbank.org/indicator/SL.TLF.CACT. FE.ZS?name_desc=true. [Accessed 17 December 2018].

WWHR (2005). *Turkish Civil and Penal Code Reforms From a Gender Perspective: The Success of Two Nationwide Campaigns*. [Online]. Available at: http://www.wwhr.org/ category/booklets/30280/turkish-civil-and-penal-code-reforms-from-a-gender-perspective-the-success-of-two-nationwide-campaigns-2005-in-english [Accessed 31 August 2013].

Yablokov, Ilya (2014). 'Pussy Riot as Agent Provocateur: Conspiracy Theories and the Media Construction of Nation in Putin's Russia'. *Nationalities Papers*, 42 (4), 622–36.

Yaraman, Ayşegül (2001). *Resmi Tarihten Kadın Tarihine: Elinin Hamuruyla Özgürlük*. İstanbul: Bağlam.

Yavuz, M. Hakan (2009). *Secularism and Muslim Democracy in Turkey*. Cambridge and New York: Cambridge University Press.

Yazıcı, Berna (2012). '"The Return to the Family: Welfare, State, and Politics of the Family in Turkey'. *Anthropological Quarterly*, 85 (1), 103–40.

Yeğenoğlu, Metin, and Coşar, Simten (2012). 'The AKP and the Gender Issue: Shuttling between Neo-liberalism and Patriarchy'. In *Silent Violence. Neo-liberalism, Islamist Politics and the AKP Years in Turkey*. Ottawa: Red Quill Books, pp. 179–209.

Yeni Şafak (2016). *Erdoğan AB'ye çok sert eleştiriler yöneltti*, 10 May 2016. [Online]. Available at: http://www.yenisafak.com/video-galeri/haber/erdogan-abye-cok-sert-elestiriler-yoneltti-2093733 [Accessed 21 March 2016].

Yuval-Davis, Nira (1997). *Cinsiyet ve Millet*. İstanbul: İletişim.

Yılmaz, Zafer (2015). '"Strengthening the Family" Policies in Turkey: Managing the Social Question and Armoring Conservative–Neoliberal Populism'. *Turkish Studies*, 16 (3), 371–90.

Zetkin, Clara (2004). *Lenin on the Women's Question*. [Online]. Available at: https://www. marxists.org/archive/zetkin/1920/lenin/zetkin1.htm [Accessed 10 October 2018].

Zdravomyslova, Yelena, and Temkina, Anna (2005). 'Gendered Citizenship in Soviet and Post-Soviet Societies'. In Vera Tolz and Stephenie Booth (eds). *Nation and Gender in Contemporary Europe*. Manchester and New York: Manchester University Press.

Zihnioğlu, Yaprak (2003). *Kadınsız Inkilap [Revolution Without Woman]*. Istanbul: Metis Yayınları.

Zizek, Slavoj (2016). 'The Spectre of Putogan'. *New Statesman*, 3 February 2016. [Online]. Available at: http://www.newstatesman.com/2016/02/slavoj-i-ek-spectre-putogan [Accessed 25 July 2016].

Zimmerman, William (2014). *Ruling Russia. Authoritarianism from the Revolution to Putin*. Princeton, NJ, and Oxford: Princeton University Press.

Index